CAMBRIDGE

Grammar for
IELTS
with answers

**Self-study grammar
reference and practice**

DIANA HOPKINS with
PAULINE CULLEN

CAMBRIDGE UNIVERSITY PRESS
Cambridge, New York, Melbourne, Madrid, Cape Town, Singapore,
São Paulo, Delhi, Dubai, Tokyo

Cambridge University Press
The Edinburgh Building, Cambridge CB2 8RU, UK

www.cambridge.org
Information on this title: www.cambridge.org/9780521604628

First published 2007
7th printing 2010

Printed in Dubai by Oriental Press

A catalogue record for this publication is available from the British Library

ISBN 978-0-521-60462-8 Student's Book with answers and Audio CD
ISBN 978-0-521-60463-5 Student's Book without answers

Produced by Kamae Design, Oxford.

Acknowledgements

My thanks go firstly to my editor, Jessica Roberts, who has worked tirelessly and patiently with me and kept me going through her endless words of encouragement. Thanks also to my commissioning editor, Alison Sharpe, whose encouragement and gentle persuasion have led the project to completion, and to Anna Teevan, who saw me through the initial stages. Many thanks also to all at Cambridge University Press who have contributed along the way, and to the teachers and readers involved in commenting on the material. And of course I would like to thank Pauline Cullen, without whom this book may never have quite reached the final stages and whose contribution has been much appreciated.

Finally, a thank you to my children Laura and Alexander, my partner, Ned Garnett and my mother, for their support, encouragement and help at every stage.

Diana Hopkins

The authors and publishers would like to thank the following teachers and readers who commented on the material in its draft form:

Guy Brook-Hart, Valencia, Spain; Mike Gutteridge, Cambridge, England; Vanessa Jakeman, Hove, England; Barbara Thomas, Cambridge, England.

The authors and publishers are grateful to the following for permission to reproduce copyright material. It has not always been possible to identify the sources of all the material used and in such cases the publishers would welcome information from the copyright owners.

p.14: *New Scientist* for the adapted article 'Good vibrations help jumping spiders to hunt' by Peter Aldous, 24 February 1996 from www.newscientist.com; p.60: *The Economist* for the text adapted from the article 'Dressed to dazzle' by Barney Southin, and for p.71: listening text adapted from 'Back on the treadmill' by Konstantin Kakaes, *Economist Intelligent Life*, Summer 2004, © The Economist Newspaper Limited; p.64: ESA for adapted listening text 'World's Largest Switchboard for Climate Monitoring' from www.innovations-report.com; p.87: Wcities for the adapted text from www.wcities.com, Wcities © 2006; p.88: adapted from an article 'Great Guide – Buying a Backpack' in the *Rambler*, former members' magazine of the Ramblers' Association, www.ramblers.org.uk; p.103: Professor Rajendra Persaud for the text 'Practical Intelligence Lends a Hand' taken from www.caribvoice.org; p.113: Roger Hedge for the adapted text 'Discovery and Prehistory of Soap' from www.butser.org.uk; p.140: Professor John Maule for the adapted article 'How Consumers Decide' from www.faradaypackaging.com; p.160: Bristol Magazines Ltd for the adapted article 'We are family' by Philip Dalton from *BBC Wildlife Magazine*, November 2004; p.180: Auspac Media for the adapted text from 'Robotic Approach to Crop Breeding' by Jennifer Manyweathers, *Australasian Science Magazine*, March 2006; p.206: Scientific American Inc., for article adapted from 'Experience Versus Speed' by Marion Sonnenmoser, *Scientific American Mind*, Volume 16, Number 2, 2005, Copyright © 2005 by Scientific American Inc, All rights reserved.

Photographs: Alamy Images/©Stockdisc for p8 (crt), /©Mark Sykes for p8 (crb), /©D Hurst for p11 (r), /©Lebrecht Music & Arts PL for p27, /©Rena Pearl for p80 (l), /©B.Mete Uz for p80 (m), /©Sciencephotos for p140, /©Motoring Picture Library for p144 (l), /©Epictura for p144 (ml), /©Image Broker for p169; Corbis Images/©Bettmann for p11 (l), /©David Ball for p38 (c), /©Gideon Mendel for p41, /©Charles Jean Marc/Sygma for p42, /©Viviane Moos for p80 (r), /©Richard Klune for p98 (l), /©Stephen Frink for p 98 (r), /©Royalty Free for p144 (cr), /©Chris Collins for p144 (br), /©Keith Dannemiller for p150, /©Guenter Rossenbach/Zefa for p188, /©Photocuisine for p198; Dell for p8 (cl); Empics/©AP/Vincent Thian for p69; FLPA/©Mark Moffett/Minden Pictures for p14; Getty Images for pp8 (r), 38 (r), 90; Photolibrary.com/©Thom DeSanto for p8 (c), /©Royalty Free for p38 (l); Punchstock/©Image Source for p144 (tr), /©Digital Vision for p160, /©Image Source for p154, /©Bananastock for p210 (l); Rex Features for pp8 (l), 32, 64, 210 (r); Royal Ontario Museum ©ROM for p112 (reproduced with permission); Topfoto/©UPP for p158.

Key: l = left, c = centre, r = right, t = top, b = bottom

Picture Research by Hilary Luckcock

Contents

11 Comparing things:

12 The noun phrase

13 Modals 1

14 Modals 2

15 Reported speech

16 Verb + verb patterns

17 Likelihood based on conditions 1

18 Likelihood based on conditions 2

19 Prepositions

20 Relative clauses

21 Ways of organising texts

22 The passive

23 Linking ideas

24 Showing your position in a text

25 Nominalisation in written English

To the student

Who is this book for?

This book is for anyone preparing for IELTS. Although the IELTS test does not include a specific grammar module, it is important to be able to recognize and use grammar appropriately. This book covers the grammar you will need to be successful in the test. You can use it to support an IELTS coursebook, with a general English language course for extra grammar practice, or with practice tests as part of a revision programme. You can use it in class or for self-study.

How do I use this book?

There are two ways to use this book. You can either start at Unit 1 and work through to the end of the book, or you can do the Entry test on page ix to find out which units you need most practice in and begin with those.

What is in this book?

This book contains 25 units. Each unit is in four parts:

A: Context listening This introduces the grammar of the unit in a context that is relevant to the IELTS test. This will help you to understand the grammar more easily when you study section B. It also gives you useful listening practice. Listen to the recording and answer the questions. Then check your answers in the Key before you read the Grammar section.

B: Grammar Read through this section before you do the grammar exercises. For each grammar point there are explanations with examples. You can refer back to this section when you are doing the exercises.

C: Grammar exercises Write your answers to each exercise and then check them in the Key.

D: Test practice Each unit has a test task. These help you practise the different parts of the test. The test task is followed by a grammar focus task, which gives you extra practice in the grammar from the unit.

The Key

The Key contains:

- answers for all the exercises. Check your answers at the end of each exercise. The Key tells you which part of the Grammar section you need to look at again if you have any problems.
- sample answers for exercises where you use your own ideas to help you check your work.
- test tips for each exercise type in the Test practice section.
- sample answers for all the writing tasks in the Test practice section. Read these after you have written your own answer. Study the language used and the way the ideas are organised.

Recording scripts

There are recording scripts for the Context listenings in each unit and for the Test practice listening tasks. Do not look at the script until after you have answered the questions. It is a good idea to listen to the recording again while you read the script.

The Entry test

You can do this test before using the book to help you choose what to study. Answer the questions and then check your answers in the Key. The Key tells you which units are most important for you.

To the teacher

This book offers concise yet comprehensive coverage of the grammar necessary in order to be successful in the IELTS test. It can be used for self-study or with a class. It will be particularly useful for a class where all the students are preparing for IELTS. It will also be useful for revision, and for candidates in classes where some students are not entered for the test, as sections A, B and C are designed to be useful for all students.

The Entry test

The Entry test can be used diagnostically as a means of prioritising the language areas to be covered, either for a class, or for individual students.

A: Context listening This section is suitable for classroom use. Many of the tasks can be done in pairs or small groups if appropriate.

B: Grammar This section is designed for private study, but you may wish to discuss those parts which are particularly relevant to your students' needs.

C: Grammar exercises This section can be done in class or set as homework. Students can be encouraged to check their own work and discuss any difficulties they encounter.

D: Test practice This section can be used to familiarize students with the test task types while offering further practice in the grammar for each unit. Each task is followed by a Grammar focus task, designed to raise students' awareness of a particular language point covered in that unit. The book contains at least one task from each part of the Listening, Academic Reading, General Training Reading, Academic Writing and General Training Writing modules.

In classes where there are students who are not entered for the test, you may prefer to set Section D tasks as extra work for IELTS candidates only. However, they offer all students valuable opportunities to practise the grammar of the unit and provide an effective teaching resource for EAP classes.

You can do this test before using the book to help you choose what to study. Choose the correct answer, A, B or C, for each question. When you have finished, check your answers on page 223. The key tells you which units are most important for you.

1 Most university students ...Live... on campus in their first year.
   A lives
   B live
   C are living

2 From this graph we can see that the economy .... at the moment.
   A improves
   B improve
   C is improving

3 They .... personal computers when my father was a student.
   A hadn't
   B didn't have
   C weren't having

4 I .... want to be a practising doctor but now I'm more interested in research.
   A was used to
   B used to
   C would

5 The teacher .... us how to do the experiment when the fire bell rang.
   A showed
   B shown
   C was showing

6 I finished my essay yesterday but .... it in to the tutor yet.
   A I've given
   B I haven't given
   C I didn't give

7 .... the experiment three times now with different results each time!
   A We've done
   B We did
   C We've been doing

8 When I arrived the lecture .... so I didn't find it easy to follow.
   A started
   B had started
   C had been starting

9 She .... well at school but that changed when she became friends with a different group of girls.
   A did
   B had done
   C had been doing

10 .... the doctor at 2.00 this afternoon so I can't go to the lecture.
   A I'm seeing
   B I see
   C I will see

11 My sister .... economics and politics when she goes to university.
   A is going to study
   B studies
   C will study

12 While we're working on the project our boss .... on a beach in Greece!
   A will sit
   B will have sat
   C will be sitting

13 If the trend continues, the average
income .... by 107% by 2020.
  (A) will increase
  B will have increased
  C will be increasing

14 You can base your geography
assignment on .... country – it
doesn't matter which.
  A a
  B some
  (C) any

15 There aren't .... places left on
the course so you'd better apply soon.
  A much
  (B) many
  C lots of

16 I don't know whether to accept the job
offer. It's ....
  (A) a difficult decision
  B the difficult decision
  C difficult decision

17 For those of you new to the company,
this leaflet is full of ....
  A a valuable information
  B the valuable information
  (C) valuable information

18 The manager interviewed ....
candidates in turn.
  A each of the
  B each
  (C) every

19 I know it's not much of a present but I
made it ....
  A me
  B myself
  (C) by myself

20 You should visit Bath. It's ....
city.
  A a historical and interesting
  B a historical interesting
  (C) an interesting historical

21 The government has released some
.... data showing how schools are
not providing an adequate education to
our children.
  A shocking
  (B) shock
  (C) shocked

22 You really should go to Namibia. The
scenery is .... stunning and the
people are very friendly.
  A very
  B fairly
  (C) absolutely

23 This factory produces some of
.... cameras in the world.
  A best
  (B) the best
  C the most best

24 .... people live in the countryside
than 100 years ago.
  A Less
  B Few
  (C) Fewer

25 The bookshop .... the end of the
road is excellent.
  A at
  B on
  C in

26 There were millions of people around
   the world .... the football match
   live on television.
   A watched
   B watching
   C were watching

27 Scientists finally .... find a cure
   for the disease after years of research.
   A managed to
   B can
   C could

28 She got a terrible mark in the exam so
   she .... very hard at all.
   A mustn't have worked
   B can't have worked
   C didn't work

29 What .... in order to get a permit
   to work in your country?
   A do I need to do
   B must I do
   C ought I do

30 When you write your essays you
   .... copy ideas from books
   without referencing them properly.
   A mustn't
   B don't have to
   C have to

31 Doctors have .... us to cut down
   on salt in our diets if we want to reduce
   the risk of getting heart disease.
   A insisted
   B suggested
   C advised

32 .... this newspaper report, more
   women smoke than men nowadays.
   A Apparently
   B According to
   C Supposedly

33 My parents encouraged .... this
   course.
   A me to do
   B me doing
   C me do

34 What will you do if ....
   A you don't get a good IELTS score?
   B you didn't get a good IELTS score?
   C you won't get a good IELTS score?

35 A recent government report has warned
   that .... we act immediately to
   reduce pollution, there will be serious
   consequences for the planet.
   A provided that
   B in case
   C unless

36 If I didn't have to work tonight, ...
   A I'd be able to relax now.
   B I'm able to relax now.
   C I'll be able to relax now.

37 I wish that man .... tapping his
   fingers on the table. It's really
   annoying me.
   A stopped
   B had stopped
   C would stop

38 I'm aiming .... a band 7 in IELTS.
   A on
   B for
   C to

66%

17 – X
50 ~100

39 Do you have any knowledge .... how our education system works?
 A of
 B on
 C for

40 The minister .... is responsible for education has just resigned.
 A which
 B who
 C what

41 The University of St Andrews .... is the oldest university in Scotland.
 A which was founded in 1413
 B , which was founded in 1413,
 C , that was founded in 1413,

42 Many children these days do not have a healthy diet. .... is possible that this is because less healthy foods are cheaper than healthy ones.
 A What
 B That
 C It

43 The charity is trying to find ways to save and .... the world's endangered animal species.
 A the charity is trying to find ways to protect
 B to find ways to protect
 C protect

44 In the past we threw a lot of our kitchen waste away, but today many items such as plastic bottles and newspapers ....
 A are recycled
 B recycle
 C need recycling

45 I can't pick you up from the station on Wednesday because .... on that day.
 A I'm fixing my car
 B I'm having my car fixed
 C I need my car fixed

46 These drugs are the best medicine available as a treatment at the moment, ... they are expensive, unfortunately.
 A although
 B because
 C so

47 Learning a foreign language is important because it helps you to understand other cultures better. .... it can be a useful skill in many areas of work.
 A However,
 B Despite this,
 C In addition,

48 .... I can't go to the conference as I've got to go to Sydney on business.
 A Frankly
 B Unfortunately
 C Personally

49 .... I think it's useful to write an outline of your essay before you start to write the first draft.
 A Interestingly,
 B Definitely,
 C Personally,

50 The .... of dark red spots is one of the first signs of the disease.
 A appearance
 B appearing
 C appear

A Context listening

1 You are going to hear a woman interviewing a student for a survey about what people do in their free time. Before you listen, look at the pictures. Which activities do you think the student does in his free time?

2 🎧 **1** Listen and check if you were right.

3 ⏮ **1** Listen again and decide if the following statements are true or false. If a statement is false, write the correction.

1 Peter is waiting for his friends. ....

2 He isn't studying much this month. ....

3 His parents own a shop. ....

4 He practises the guitar most mornings. ....

5 He frequently uses the Internet. ....

6 His cousin is living in America at the moment. ....

7 Peter doesn't support any football teams. ....

4 Look at your answers to Exercise 3 and answer these questions.

1 Which sentences are about a situation that is permanent or a fact? ....

2 Which sentences are about everyday habits? ....

3 Which sentence is about an action happening at the moment of speaking? ....

4 Which sentences are about a temporary situation? ....

B Grammar

1 Present simple

+	verb/verb + (e)s	He **plays** tennis.
–	do/does not + verb	She **doesn't play** tennis.
?	do/does ... + verb?	**Do** you **play** tennis?

We use the present simple
- to talk about regular habits or repeated actions:
  *I **get up** really early and **practise** for an hour or so **most days**.*
  *I **use** the Internet **just about every day**.*
  Words that describe how often or when are often used (e.g. *always, generally, normally, usually, often, sometimes, rarely, never, every day, every evening*).
- to talk about permanent situations:
  *My parents **own** a restaurant.*
  ⚠ We use the present perfect, not the present simple, to say how long something has continued:
  *I **have worked** there since I was 15.* (**not** ~~I work there since I was 15~~ : see Unit 3)
- to talk about facts or generally accepted truths:
  *Students **don't generally have** much money.*
  *If you heat water to 100°C, it **boils**.* (see Unit 17)
  The following words are often used: *generally, mainly, normally, usually, traditionally*.
- to give instructions and directions:
  *You **go** down to the traffic lights, then you **turn** left.*
  *To start the programme, first you **click** on the icon on the desktop.*
- to tell stories and talk about films, books and plays:
  *In the film, the tea lady **falls** in love with the Prime Minister.*

2 Present continuous

+	am/is/are + verb + -ing	He's **living** in Thailand.
–	am/is/are not + verb + -ing	I'm **not living** in Thailand.
?	am/is/are ... + verb + -ing?	Are they **living** in Thailand?

We use the present continuous
- to talk about temporary situations:
  *I'm **studying** really hard for my exams.*
  *My cousin **is living** in Thailand **at the moment**.* (= he doesn't normally live there)
  Words like *at the moment, currently, now, this week/month/year* are often used.
- to talk about actions happening at the moment of speaking:
  *I'm **waiting** for my friends.*

◆ to talk about trends or changing situations:
*The Internet **is making** it easier for people to stay in touch with each other.*
*The price of petrol **is rising** dramatically.*

◆ to talk about things that happen more often than expected, often to show envy or to criticise
with words like *always, constantly, continually, forever*:
*My mum's **always saying** I don't help enough!* (complaint)
*He's **always visiting** exciting places!* (envy)

3 State verbs

The present continuous is not normally used with state verbs because the meaning of the verb
itself is a general truth rather than something temporary. These verbs describe thoughts,
feelings, senses, possession and description.

Here are some examples of state verbs.

◆ thoughts: *agree, assume, believe, disagree, forget, hope, know, regret, remember, suppose, think,
understand*
*I **assume** you're too busy to play computer games.*

◆ feelings: *adore, despise, dislike, enjoy, feel, hate, like, love, mind, prefer, want*
***Do you mind** if I ask you a few questions?*
*I **love** music.*

◆ senses: *feel, hear, see, smell, taste*
*This pudding **smells** delicious.*

⚠ To talk about something happening now we use *can*:
*I **can smell** something burning.*

◆ possession: *have, own, belong*
*My parents **own** a restaurant.*

◆ description: *appear, contain, look, look like, mean, resemble, seem, smell, sound, taste, weigh*
*You **look like** your mother.* (= a permanent situation, not a temporary one)

⚠ Some state verbs can be used in the continuous form when the meaning is temporary.
Compare:
*What **are** you **thinking** about?* (now)
*I **think** you should tell her exactly what happened.* (my opinion, so not temporary)

*I'**m tasting** the sauce to see if it needs any more salt.*
*The sauce **tastes** delicious.*

*She's **having** a great time.* (*is having* = is experiencing, not possession)
*Students **don't** generally **have** much money.* (*have* = possession)

C Grammar exercises

1 Choose the best endings for sentences 1–8.

1 Fiona is watching television
    (a) because her favourite film star is on.
    b when she has time.

2 I'm having my lunch
    a at one o'clock every day.
    b early today as I have an appointment.

3 I do the shopping
    a at the same time every week.
    b today for a friend who's ill.

4 What are you doing
    a to your sister when she behaves badly?
    b to your sister? Leave her alone!

5 I wear casual clothes
    a at the weekend.
    b because we're having a party at lunchtime.

6 Teachers work hard
    a to get the concert ready for next week.
    b but they get long holidays.

7 The company's financial
   situation is improving
    a now that it has a new Chief Executive.
    b when there is greater demand for its products.

8 Serge is thinking of retiring early
    a every time something bad happens at work.
    b because he isn't happy at work any more.

2 Fill in the gaps with the correct form of the verbs in brackets.

1 I'm busy right now. I 'm filling in .... (*fill in*) an application form for a new job.

2 My tutor .... (*see*) me for a tutorial every Monday at two o'clock.

3 John .... (*not/study*) very hard at the moment. I ....
(*not/think*) he'll pass his exams.

4 'What .... (*he/do*)?' 'He .... (*try*) to fix the television
aerial.'

5 Animals .... (*breathe in*) oxygen and .... (*give out*)
carbon dioxide.

6 Be quiet! I .... (*want*) to hear the news.

7 In my country we .... (*drive*) on the right-hand side of the road.

8 My friend Joe's parents .... (*travel*) round the world this summer, and
probably won't be back for a couple of months.

9 The college .... (*run*) the same course every year.

10 Numbers of wild butterflies .... (*fall*) as a result of changes in
farming methods.

3   Fill in the gaps with the verbs in the box in the correct present tense.

> agree   catch up   cause   have   go up   know   think   use

We 1 ....*use*........ energy for three main things: electricity production, heating and transport. For the first two, we 2 .... options such as solar and wind power, or natural gas. But oil is still the world's number one source of energy, and for transport at least, there is currently no alternative. In China, domestic energy consumption 3 .... year by year and demand in similar regions 4 .... fast. We 5 .... how to use energy more efficiently now than in the past but the worldwide rise in demand 6 .... concern amongst experts. Some experts 7 .... that oil supplies will start to fall within the next twenty years. Most experts 8 .... that we need to find a new source of energy soon.

4   Look at the following extracts. There are six incorrect verbs. Find and correct them.

Extract A

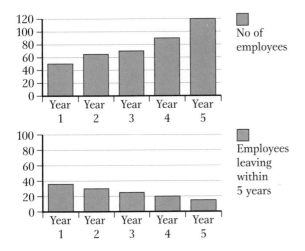

From the graphs, we <u>are seeing</u> that the number of employees employed by this firm increases each year and the number of employees leaving after less than five years decreases.

Extract B

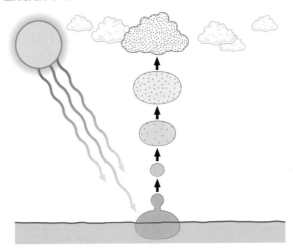

The sun heats the ground. This is warming the air nearby and the warm air rises into the sky. As the air is rising, it becomes cooler and the water vapour inside it change into droplets of water. These join together to form a cloud.

1   *can see*

2   ....

3   ....

4   ....

5   ....

6   ....

D Test practice

Listening Section 1

Questions 1–3

*Choose the correct letter, **A**, **B** or **C**.*

> *Example*
> Which sport is the woman interested in?
> **A** gymnastics
> **(B)** swimming
> **C** tennis

1 How long is the heated pool?

  A 15 metres
  B 25 metres
  C 50 metres

2 Which of these is free for all members?

  A the beginners swimming class
  B the training session
  C the keep-fit class

3 Which of these does the woman need to book?

  A swimming lanes
  B gym equipment
  C sauna

Questions 4–10

Complete the notes below.

Write **NO MORE THAN THREE WORDS AND/OR A NUMBER** *for each answer.*

Yoga classes

- held on Monday, **4** .... and .... mornings
- weekend evenings from **5** .... to ....
- attend **6** .... per week
- see instructor to change **7** ....
- cost £1.50

Meet John **8** ....

Office located on first floor

Meet at **9** .... tomorrow

Tel: **10** ....

Grammar focus task

Look at the following extracts from the conversation and <u>underline</u> the tenses that the speakers used.

1 I*'m wanting / want* to do some sports activities.

2 Our tennis team *are always looking / always look* for new people.

3 *Are members having to / Do members have to* pay to use the pools?

4 We*'re not actually allowing / don't actually allow* anyone to book the swimming lanes or the gym equipment.

5 What time *is suiting / suits* you?

6 Great, well, I*'m thinking / think* that's everything.

A Context listening

1 You will hear a man giving a talk on the radio about protecting your home from burglaries. Before you listen look at the pictures below. Make a list of all of the items.

2 🎧 2 Listen and answer the following questions.

1 Which three items from your list were stolen?

2 Why did the man tell this story?

A to show that crime has increased

B to show that crime can happen at any time

C to show that burglars can open any lock

3 2 ◀◀ Listen again and complete these sentences.

1 A few weeks ago a woman .... to report a burglary.

2 It .... at five in the afternoon when she .... the news on TV.

3 This woman .... the front door locked.

4 When her son got older she .... the door unlocked whenever she was at home.

5 The burglar simply .... in through the front door.

6 The son .... anything because he .... to music.

7 Then the burglar .... into the front room, ... all the cupboards and .... a valuable collection of CDs.

4 Look at sentences 1–7 above and answer the following questions.

1 Which two sentences provide a background scene and an action? ....

2 Which two sentences talk about a single completed action in the past? ....

3 Which sentence describes a series of completed actions in the past? ....

4 Which two sentences talk about a repeated action in the past? ....

5 Which four tenses or structures are used in sentences 1–7? ....

B Grammar

1 Past simple

+	verb + -ed (or -d)	He **worked** for the police.
–	did not + verb	She **didn't work** for the police.
?	did ... + verb?	**Did** they **work** for the police?

⚠ **Irregular verbs**

Many verbs are irregular: **went** (go), **came** (come), **wrote** (write) (see Appendix 1)
Note the verb be is irregular: I/he/she/it **was**; you/we/they **were**

We use the past simple

◆ to talk about single past completed actions. Often the time is mentioned:
*A few weeks ago a woman **called** to report a robbery at her house.*
But no time reference is necessary if it is already known:
*How **did** the burglar **break** in without anybody hearing him?* (in the story I just told you about)

◆ to give a series of actions in the order that they happened:
*The burglar **came in** through the front door, **picked up** the woman's handbag, **emptied** it out and **stole** her purse.*

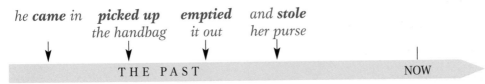

he **came** in   **picked up**   **emptied**   and **stole**
　　　　　　the handbag   it out   her purse

THE PAST　　　　　　　　　　　　NOW

We often use words like *next* or *then* to indicate the sequence of events:
***Then**, the burglar **went** into the front room, **opened** all the cupboards and **took** a valuable collection of CDs.*

◆ to talk about past repeated actions:
*When her son got older he often **went out** to visit his friends after school.*
Notice that *used to* and *would* can also be used (see B3).

◆ to talk about long-term situations in the past which are no longer true:
*Bill Murphy **worked** for the police force for over 17 years.*

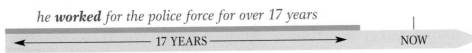

he **worked** for the police force for over 17 years

————— 17 YEARS —————　　　NOW

*Explorers at that time **believed** that the world was flat.*
Notice that *used to* can also be used (see B3).

2 Past continuous

+	was/were + verb + -ing	She **was watching** the news.
−	was/were not + verb + -ing	They **weren't watching** the news.
?	was/were ... + verb + -ing?	**Were** you **watching** the news?

We use the past continuous

◆ to provide the background scene to an action or event (usually in the past simple). We often use words like *when*, *while* and *as*:
*It happened at five in the afternoon **while** she **was watching** the news on TV.*
*He **was doing** his homework in his bedroom **when** the burglar came into the house.*

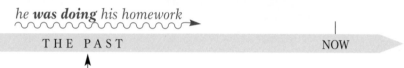

It is possible to have more than one background scene happening at the same time:
*He **was listening** to music and **working** on his computer.*

◆ when we want to emphasize the activity without focusing on its completion. Compare:
*For a while last year I **was working** at the cinema, **studying** for my degree and **writing** a column for the local newspaper.* (we don't know if the actions were completed or not, or whether they happened at the same time)
*Last year I **worked** at the cinema, **studied** for my degree and **wrote** a column for the local newspaper.* (suggests all of the jobs are now complete, and probably happened in that order)
⚠ State verbs (see Unit 1) do not generally have a continuous form.

3 *Used to* and *would*

+	used to / would + infinitive	She **used to / would lock** the door.
−	did not + use to + infinitive	I **didn't use to lock** the door.
?	did ... use to + infinitive?	**Did** they **use to lock** the door?

We use *used to* + infinitive or *would* + infinitive (contracted to *'d* in spoken English) to talk about past repeated actions:
*She **used to keep** the front door locked.* (but she stopped doing this)
*She **would leave** the door unlocked whenever she was at home.*
⚠ *Would* is unusual in the negative form and in *Yes/No* questions.

We use *used to* + infinitive to talk about permanent situations that are usually no longer true:
*Bill Murphy **used to work** for the police force.* (but he doesn't now: **not** ~~Bill Murphy would work for the police force.~~)

We do not use *used to* if we want to talk about how long the situation lasted:
*Bill Murphy **worked** for the police force for over 17 years.* (**not** ~~Bill Murphy used to work for the police force for over 17 years.~~)
⚠ We do not use *would* with state verbs.

C Grammar exercises

1 Fill in the gaps in this model answer with verbs from the box in the past simple.

Thanks to modern technology, there have been enormous changes in the workplace over the past 100 years.

What are the most significant changes that have occurred and what changes do you foresee in the next 100 years?

allow	~~be~~	be	be	invent	increase	lay
mean	own	receive	replace	ride	take	walk

The pace of change in the world of technology is amazing. It **1** ...wasn't... (not) long ago that the postal service **2** .... our only way to communicate over any distance. It **3** .... days and sometimes weeks to receive letters from within the same country. As a result, the news in the letters **4** .... already out of date when people **5** .... them. In the workplace, this **6** .... that business was mostly conducted locally, over relatively short distances.

When Alexander Graham Bell **7** .... the telephone in 1876 it **8** .... the foundation for the communication systems we have today. The telephone **9** .... two people to communicate instantly across a great distance. Eventually computers **10** .... typewriters and dramatically **11** .... the speed of our daily work life. Nowadays the Internet is an essential part of every business.

However, it is not just communications that have changed. Only 50 years ago most people **12** .... (not) a car. People **13** .... to work or **14** .... bicycles. Changes in travel as well as the increased speed of communications have led to the global business world that we have today.

2 Fill in the gaps with the past simple or past continuous form of the verbs in brackets. In which gaps could you use *used to*?

I **1** .... had .... (*have*) a wonderful biology teacher, Mrs Hughes. She **2** .... (*make*) us excited about the subject because she was so interested herself. I remember one lesson in particular; we **3** .... (*study*) different types of plants, and Mrs Hughes **4** .... (*describe*) the different parts of the flower. She **5** .... (*pick up*) a purple flower, I can't remember exactly what it was, and then suddenly we **6** .... (*notice*) that she **7** .... (*cry*)! She **8** .... (*apologise*) and **9** .... (*say*) that sometimes nature was so beautiful it just made her cry! We **10** .... (*not/know*) what to do at first, but it certainly **11** .... (*make*) us think. Something similar **12** .... (*happen*) while she **13** .... (*show*) us how to work the microscope. She **14** .... (*examine*) a slide of some plant tissue and she **15** .... (*smile*) all over her face. She suddenly **16** .... (*get*) all excited and **17** .... (*say*), 'Isn't it wonderful?' Some students **18** .... (*laugh*) at her when she **19** .... (*not/look*) but I didn't. Somehow her enthusiasm **20** .... (*inspire*) me, and I **21** .... (*start*) to like biology.

3 A teacher and student are talking about local customs. Fill in the gaps with the verbs in brackets in the correct form. Use *would* or *used to* where possible.

Teacher: What sort of things **1** ...did you use to do... (*you/do*) as a child?

Yoko: Oh, when I was a child growing up in Japan there were many customs that we **2** .... (*follow*). For example, I remember we **3** .... (*move*) house when I was seven and we **4** .... (*visit*) our new neighbours with gifts. At that time the tradition was that people **5** .... (*give*) gifts of Japanese noodles, but it is different now and people tend to give things like soap or towels or nothing at all.

Teacher: **6** .... (*have*) one tradition that you particularly remember?

Yoko: Yes, one tradition that I **7** .... (*really/like*) was in the spring when the cherry blossoms were out. As a family we **8** .... (*go*) into the countryside and we **9** .... (*spend*) the day eating, drinking and singing. One year my father **10** .... (*take*) a lovely photo of me and my sisters and I still keep that picture on my wall today.

Teacher: And **11** .... (*you/have to*) do anything you didn't like?

Yoko: Yes. I remember how we **12** .... (*have to*) clean the house thoroughly. This ceremony is called Osoji and my sisters and I **13** .... (*not/look forward to*) it very much!

4 Read the test task and a student's response. Tick (✓) the <u>underlined</u> verbs if they are right, and correct them if they are wrong.

> **Describe an unforgettable trip you once made.**
> **You should say:**
> **where you went**
> **why you went there**
> **what happened**
> **and explain why you remember it so well.**

I remember a trip I once **1** <u>made</u> to my grandmother's house. She **2** <u>would live</u> about 30 kilometres away from us and we **3** <u>used to going</u> there quite often with our mother. On this occasion we **4** <u>set off</u> to my grandmother's after school on a cold winter's day. When we were about to leave we **5** <u>were noticing</u> that some snow was beginning to fall, and as we **6** <u>were driving</u> along we **7** <u>were realising</u> that it **8** <u>snowed</u> more and more heavily. Suddenly we had to brake hard as the car in front stopped suddenly. We **9** <u>were skidding</u> and **10** <u>went off</u> the road into a ditch! It was pretty scary, but we were lucky and none of us were hurt. We got out of the car, and my mother **11** <u>was phoning</u> for help on her mobile phone. While we **12** <u>were waiting</u> for help it **13** <u>was stopping</u> snowing and we **14** <u>sang</u> lots of songs to keep ourselves cheerful. Eventually the truck **15** <u>was coming</u> and pulled our car out of the ditch. The car wasn't badly damaged, but we **16** <u>decided</u> to turn round and go home. We didn't manage to see our grandmother that day, but it was so frightening that I will never forget it.

1 ....✓............................
2 .....used to live / lived.....
3 ....
4 ....

5 ....
6 ....
7 ....
8 ....
9 ....
10 ....

11 ....
12 ....
13 ....
14 ....
15 ....
16 ....

Academic Reading

*You should spend about 20 minutes on **Questions 1–13** which are based on the Reading Passage below.*

Jumping spiders

Peter Aldhons examines how Portia spiders catch their prey

A

For a stalking predator, the element of surprise is crucial. And for jumping spiders that sneak onto other spiders' webs to prey on their owners, it can be the difference between having lunch and becoming it. Now zoologists have discovered the secret of these spiders' tactics: creeping forward when their prey's web is vibrating.

B

The fifteen known species of Portia jumping spiders are relatively small, with adults being about two centimetres long (that's smaller than the cap on most pens). They habitually stay in the webs of other spiders, and in an area of these webs that is as out-of-the-way as possible. Portia spiders live mostly in tropical forests, where the climate is hot and humid. They hunt a range of other spiders, some of which could easily turn the tables on them. 'They will attack something about twice their own size if they are really hungry,' says Stimson Wilcox of Binghamton University in New York State. Wilcox and his colleague, Kristen Gentile of the University of Canterbury in Christchurch, New Zealand, wanted to find out how Portia spiders keep the upper hand.

C

All jumping spiders have large eyes that look like binocular lenses, and they function pretty much the same way. Most jumping spiders locate their prey visually, and then jump and capture from one centimetre to over ten centimetres away. Only a few species of jumping spiders invade the webs of other spiders, and the Portia spider is among them. Jumping spiders, including Portia spiders, prey on insects and other arthropods by stalking. Sometimes the spiders lure their victims by vibrating the web to mimic the struggles of a trapped insect. But many web-weaving spiders appear to be wise to these tricks, so stalking is often a better strategy. Sometimes, the researchers found, Portia spiders take advantage of the vibrations created in the web by a gentle breeze. But, if necessary, they will make their own vibrations.

D
The researchers allowed various prey spiders to spin webs in the laboratory and then introduced Portia spiders. To simulate the shaking effect of a breeze the zoologists used either a model aircraft propeller or attached a tiny magnet to the centre of the web which could be vibrated by applying a varying electrical field. The researchers noticed that the stalking Portia spiders moved more when the webs were shaking than when they were still, and they were more likely to capture their prey during tests in which the webs were periodically shaken than in those where the webs were undisturbed. If the spiders were placed onto unoccupied webs, they would make no attempt to change their movements.

E
It is the Portia spider's tactic of making its victims' webs shake that has most intrigued the researchers. They noticed that the spiders would sometimes shake their quarry's web violently, then creep forwards up to five millimetres before the vibrations died down. 'They'd make a big pluck with one of their hind legs,' says Wilcox. These twangs were much more powerful than the gentler vibrations Portia spiders use to mimic a trapped insect, and the researchers were initially surprised that the prey spiders did not respond to them in any way. But they have since discovered that the violent twanging produces a pattern of vibrations that match those caused by a twig falling onto the web.

F
Other predators make use of natural 'smokescreens' or disguises to hide from their prey: lions hunting at night, for example, move in on their prey when clouds obscure the moon. 'But this is the first example of an animal making its own smokescreen that we know of,' says Wilcox. 'Portia spiders are clearly intelligent and they often learn from their prey as they are trying to capture it. They do this by making different signals on the web of their prey until the prey spider makes a movement. In general, Portia spiders adjust their stalking strategy according to their prey and what the prey is doing. Thus, Portia spiders use trial-and-error learning in stalking. Sometimes they will even take an indirect route to reach a prey spider they can see from a distance. This can sometimes take one to two hours following a predetermined route. When it does this, the Portia spider is actually solving problems and thinking ahead about its actions.'

Questions 1–9

The Reading Passage has six paragraphs labelled **A–F**.

Which paragraph contains the following information?

*Write the correct letter **A–F** next to Questions 1–9.*

NB *You may use any letter more than once.*

1 the reaction of the Portia spider's prey to strong web vibrations

2 a description of how the researchers set up their experiment

3 a comparison between Portia spiders and another animal species

4 an explanation of how the researchers mimicked natural conditions

5 a comparison between Portia spiders and their prey

6 the reason why concealment is important to Portia spiders

7 a description of the Portia spider's habitat

8 the number of species of Portia spiders

9 an example of the Portia spider's cleverness

Questions 10–13

*Choose the correct letter, **A, B, C** or **D**.*

10 In their laboratory experiments, the researchers found that the Portia spiders moved most when the web was

    A vibrating.
    B motionless.
    C undisturbed.
    D unoccupied.

11 What discovery did the researchers make about Portia spiders?

    A They make very strong vibrations with one leg.
    B They move 5 mm at a time on a still web.
    C They move slowly when vibrations stop.
    D They use energetic vibrations to mimic a trapped insect.

12 Portia spiders are the only known animal to

    A use the weather to disguise themselves.
    B mimic other prey-eating animals.
    C create their own smokescreen.
    D stalk using 'trial and error'.

13 The Portia spider demonstrates 'thinking ahead' when it

    A chooses prey that is a short distance away.
    B takes a longer route to reach its prey.
    C reaches its prey in a short time.
    D solves the problem of locating its prey.

Grammar focus task

Look at the underlined verbs in these sentences from the text. Match the sentences (1–3) to the explanations (a–c).

1 The researchers allowed various prey spiders to spin webs in the laboratory and then introduced Portia spiders.

2 Portia spiders moved more when the webs were shaking than when they were still.

3 They noticed that the spiders would sometimes shake their quarry's web violently.

a a series of single past completed actions

b a repeated action in the past

c a background scene and an action

A Context listening

1 You are going to hear two university students, Carl and Sue, talking about an assignment. Before you listen, look at the list of activities (A–F). Put the activities in the order which you think is best when writing an assignment.

> A make notes
> B start to write
> C do research
> D make a plan
> E re-read books
> F get a book list

2 🎧 3 Listen to the first part of the conversation. Which five activities does Sue mention? Write the letters A–F in the correct order in boxes 1–5 on the flowchart.

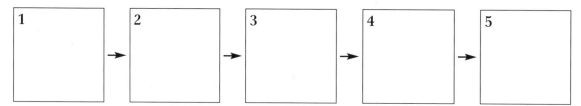

| 1 | 2 | 3 | 4 | 5 |

3 🎧 3 Listen to the second part of the conversation and fill in the gaps.

1 Sue: I .... plenty of information for the assignment.

2 Sue: When I was in the library last week, I .... those leaflets.

3 Carl: I .... tired since I started this course!

4 Carl: I .... and I'm already tired.

4 Look at your answers to Exercise 3 and find examples of each of the following:

a something that only happened recently ....

b something that happened at some time before now, but we do not know when ....

c an action + the length of time it has been going on ....

d something that happened at a stated time in the past ....

Which tense is used in each of the examples a–d above?

B Grammar

We use the present perfect when we want to show a link between the present and the past.

1 Present perfect simple

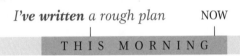

+	have/has + past participle	She's **started** the assignment.
−	have/has not + past participle	I **haven't started** the assignment.
?	have/has ... + past participle?	**Have** you **started** the assignment?

We use the present perfect simple
- to talk about a time period that is not finished (e.g. *today*, *this week*):
  *I've **written** a rough plan this morning.* (it is still morning)

*I've **written** a rough plan*   NOW

T H I S   M O R N I N G

- to show that something happened at some point in the past before now. We don't state when it happened:
  *I've **collected** plenty of information.* (at some point before now and I will use it to write my essay)

  The following time expressions are often used: *ever, never, before, up to now, still, so far.*
  *It's the longest I've **ever had** to write.* (at any point before now)

  ⚠ If we state when something happened we must use the simple past:
  *I **wasted** a lot of time last week.* (**not** ~~I have wasted a lot of time last week~~)

- to talk about a present situation which started in the past, usually with *for/since*:

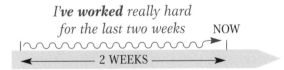

*I've **worked** really hard*
for the last two weeks   NOW

2 WEEKS

*I've **worked** really hard for the last two weeks.* (I've worked hard till now)
We use *for* with a length of time (e.g. *for two hours, for three days, for six months*) and *since* with a point in time (e.g. *since 2001, since Monday, since ten o'clock, since I was four, since I started the course*).

- to talk about something that happened at an unstated time in the past but is connected to the present:
  *I've **read** all the books on the reading list.* (I have the notes now)

  The following time expressions are often used: *recently, just, already,* and *yet* with negatives or questions.
  *I've **just got** up.*
  ***Have** you **written** your assignment **yet**?*

Compare the use of the present perfect with the past simple:

Present perfect

♦ links the past with the present:
I've made quite a lot of notes. (at some point before now and I may make more notes)

♦ does not talk about a specific time in the past:
Have you read the leaflet? (at some time before now)

♦ uses time expressions that show the time period is unfinished:
I've read six articles this week. (the week isn't finished)

Past simple

♦ only talks about the past:
I made notes on the most important things. (when I did the reading and I've finished making notes)

♦ states a specific past time, or the time is understood:
I read the leaflets when I was in the library. (I'm not in the library now and the reading is finished)

♦ uses time expressions that show the time is finished:
I read five books last week. (last week has finished)

Note the position of the following time expressions that occur with the present perfect:
♦ between the auxiliary and main verb (e.g. *recently, already, always, ever, just, never*)
*I've **already** written the notes.*
*I've **just** finished my essay.*

Ever is generally used with questions or negatives:
*Have you **ever** been to Buenos Aires?*

♦ after the main verb (e.g. *all my life, every day, yet, before, for ages, for two weeks, since 2003, since I was a child* etc.)
*I've felt tired **for weeks**.*
*I haven't flown **before**.*

If there is an object clause, the time expression comes at the end:
*I've gone to bed early **every night since then**.*
*I've written more than ten assignments **since I started this course**.*

2 Present perfect continuous

+	*have/has been + verb + -ing*	*I've **been studying** really hard.*
−	*have/has not been + verb + -ing*	*He **hasn't been studying** really hard.*
?	*have/has ... been + verb + -ing?*	***Have** you **been studying** really hard?*

We can use either the present perfect simple or the present perfect continuous to say how long a situation or activity has been going on (often with *for* or *since*):
*I've **felt** tired **for** weeks.*
*I've **been feeling** tired **since** I started this course.*
*I've **worked** at the restaurant **since** I moved here.*
*I've **been working** at the restaurant **for** three years.*

Compare the different uses of the present perfect simple and the present perfect continuous:

<table>
<tr><td>

Present perfect continuous

◆ emphasises how long:
I've been reading for the past two weeks.

◆ focuses on the activity itself (it does not show whether the activity is completed or not):
I've been writing my essay. (we don't know if the essay is finished or not)

</td><td>

Present perfect simple

◆ says how many times:
I've read three articles.

◆ focuses on the result or completion of the activity:
I've written my essay. (the essay is finished but we don't know when)

</td></tr>
</table>

What have you been doing? (the boy's mother is interested in the activity that made him so dirty now)

What have you done? (the boy's mother is interested in the result of the action: the broken window)

⚠ State verbs (see Unit 1) do not generally have a continuous form:
*I've **known** them since I was a child.* (**not** ~~I've been knowing them since I was a child~~)

Grammar extra: *This is the first time* etc.
We use the present perfect tense with the following structures: *it/this/that is the first / the second / the best / the only / the worst ...*
***It's the first time** I've ever had to write such a long assignment.*
***Is this the only time** you've travelled abroad?*
***That's the sixth cup of coffee** you've had today.*

C Grammar exercises

1 Tick (✓) the correct <u>underlined</u> verbs, and correct the verbs that are wrong.

I would like to be considered for your degree course in Zoology, starting in October next year. I feel I am a good candidate for this course as I **1** <u>have always been</u> interested in natural history and even as a child I **2** <u>have enjoyed</u> studying animals and insects in my garden. Your science faculty has a good reputation and I would very much like to be part of it.

As you **3** <u>already saw</u> in Section A of this application, I have a good academic record and I **4** <u>just received</u> the results of my recent exams, all of which **5** <u>have been</u> excellent.

In addition, your university attracts me because I enjoy sports and I **6** <u>have read</u> in your prospectus about the large number of sports on offer. Last year I **7** <u>have represented</u> my school at badminton and I **8** <u>played</u> in football teams since I was eleven. I **9** <u>have recently joined</u> a basketball team which competes at a national level.

I **10** <u>did not travel</u> abroad much yet, although as a young child I **11** <u>have been</u> to Singapore and Hong Kong with my family. I realize that I **12** <u>have not spent</u> much time away from home up to now, but am keen to become more independent.

1 .... ✓ ....
2 ... enjoyed ...
3 ....
4 ....
5 ....
6 ....
7 ....
8 ....
9 ....
10 ....
11 ....
12 ....

2 Look at the chart and fill in the gaps with the past simple or present perfect simple of the verbs in brackets to make true sentences.

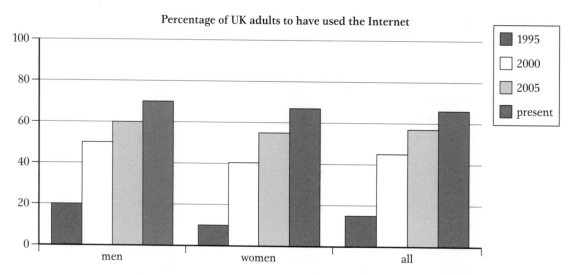

Percentage of UK adults to have used the Internet

1 The chart shows the percentage of British adults who ......*have used*...... (*use*) the Internet since 1995.

2 The number of women who have ever used the Internet .... (*increase*) by more than 60% since 1995.

3 The percentage of men who have accessed the Internet .... (*rise*) to 60% in 2005.

4 The number of women to have accessed the Internet .... (*rise*) each year.

5 The percentage of men who used the Internet .... (*be*) greater than the percentage of women from 1995 to 2005.

6 However, British women .... (*overtake*) British men in Internet usage since 2005.

7 The total number of people accessing the Internet .... (*grow*) each year although the most significant rise .... (*occur*) between 1995 and 2000.

3 Underline the correct form of the verbs.

To:	**Paul Johnson**
From:	**Sunita Soh**
Subject:	**Seminar presentation on Friday**

Dear Paul

1 *I've just received / I've just been receiving* your message to us all about the seminar on Friday. 2 *I've worked / I've been working* on my presentation for the last week, and 3 *have now finished / now finished* it, so I am happy to be one of the first to present it. However, 4 *I've made / I made* an appointment to see the university careers advisor immediately after the seminar, so I will need to leave on time.

I'd like some advice about my presentation. At last week's lecture 5 *you've said / you said* that we should use visual aids as much as possible. 6 *I haven't found / I didn't find* anything to use. Is it essential? 7 *I've done / I did* lots of presentations before, and I feel OK about this one. In my last presentation 8 *I used / I have been using* the overhead projector, and I want to do this again – does this count as a visual aid?

One last question: 9 *I've been / I went* to Professor Russell's lecture yesterday, and 10 *have been learning / learnt* quite a lot that is relevant to this course. Is it okay to refer to another course in my presentation? 11 *I've been wondering / I wondered* about this – maybe it is better to stick to the materials and references 12 *you've given / you've been giving* us. I hope you can let me know.

Thanks for your help.

Sunita

4 Fill in the gaps with a verb from the box in the present perfect simple or present perfect continuous. You will need to use some verbs more than once.

be	do	feel	have	live	pass	study	start	take	travel	want	work

Interviewer: How long ..*have you been living*.. (**1** *you*) here?

Student: I .... (**2**) in London for the past three years. I come from Japan originally. I .... (**3**) at a college here since I arrived.

Interviewer: .... (**4** *you*) any travelling over the past three years?

Student: Yes, I .... (**5**) really lucky. I have long holidays so I .... (**6**) all over Europe. I especially liked Spain.

Interviewer: What is the most interesting thing you .... (**7**) recently?

Student: Well, I .... (**8**) to play tennis, and I .... (**9**) singing lessons for a few months now too. But the thing that I am most proud of is that I .... (**10** *just*) my driving test. It's the first time I .... (**11**) it so I'm really pleased but I .... (**12** *never*) so nervous in all my life!

Interviewer: How do you think English will be useful in your life?

Student: I .... (**13**) a Hospitality and Tourism course over here, so I need English for my studies and my job. I .... (**14** *always*) to work in the tourist industry because I .... (**15** *always*) interested in history and cultural sites, and I .... (**16** *already*) as a tour guide in my home town.

Now answer these questions about yourself.

17 How long have you been studying English?

....

18 Have you studied any other languages? (Which ones? For how long?)

....

19 Have you travelled very much? (Where have you been to?)

....

20 What have you been doing to prepare for this exam?

....

21 How has your life changed over the past ten years?

....

D Test practice

General Training Writing Task 1

You should spend about 20 minutes on this task.

> *You have seen an advertisement for a weekend job as a local tour guide showing visitors around your city.*
>
> *Write a letter of application to the tourism office. In the letter*
>
> - *give your reasons for wanting the job*
> - *explain why you think you can do the job*
> - *describe any relevant experience you have*

Write at least 150 words.

You do **NOT** need to write any addresses.

Begin your letter as follows:

Dear Sir or Madam,

Look at the model answer. Find one example each of:

1 a sentence which uses the present perfect simple to show something which started in the past and is still going on

2 a sentence which uses the present perfect continuous to show something which started in the past and is still going on

3 a sentence which uses the present perfect simple to show something happened at an unstated time in the past but has a present result

---

Dear Sir or Madam,

I am writing to apply for the post of tour guide advertised on your website. I believe I fulfil all the necessary criteria, and very much hope that you will consider my application.

I have lived in this town all my life, and therefore know all about the places of interest and their history. I have visited the castle and the cathedral many times and I have read many guide books full of interesting historical facts. I therefore feel that I am in a good position to lead visitors around these sites. I have always been interested in history and over the past few years I have regularly participated in activities at the castle and at other sites.

Recently I have been working as a receptionist at a local hotel in the evenings, so I have experience of dealing with overseas visitors, and I enjoy talking to them.

I do hope you will consider me for this post, and I look forward to hearing from you.

Yours sincerely,

A Context listening

1 You will hear a woman giving a talk on the famous composer, Mozart. Before you listen match the words (1–10) with the correct meanings (a–j).

1	extraordinary	a	brother or sister
2	sibling	b	reach a high level in something
3	achievement	c	part of a piano or computer
4	keyboard	d	amazing
5	demand	e	status
6	master (*verb*)	f	success
7	gifted	g	very talented
8	in rapid succession	h	ask in a forceful way
9	reputation	i	fast development at a very early age
10	precocious	j	quickly one after another

2 🎧 4 Now listen and complete the notes below.

Name:

.... Wolfgang Amadeus Mozart ....

Date of birth:

1 ....

Number of surviving brothers and sisters:

2 ....

Profession of father:

3 ....

Wrote first composition before the age of:

4 ....

Taught self to play:

5 ....

4

3 **4 ◄◄** Listen to the text again and fill in the gaps.

1 However, when Mozart .... five of his siblings .... in infancy or early childhood.

2 Mozart's father, Leopold, ... a composer, and his grandfather .... a musician.

3 In just 30 minutes Mozart .... the piece of music, which his father .... into Nannerl's notebook.

4 By the time he .... six, the little boy .... a composition of his own.

5 They .... to Vienna and .... sensational reports of Mozart's talent.

6 His family .... richer than they .... before.

For each sentence <u>underline</u> which event happened first.

4 Look at your answers to Exercise 3 and answer these questions.

1 Which tense is used in sentence 5 to show that the events took place in chronological order? ....

2 Which tense is used in the other sentences to show that the second event the speaker mentioned actually happened first? ....

B Grammar

1 Past perfect simple

+	*had* + past participle	*They **had listened** to his music.*
–	*had not* + past participle	*They **hadn't listened** to his music.*
?	*had ...* + past participle?	***Had** they **listened** to his music?*

We use the past perfect simple

♦ when we are talking about the past and want to mention something that happened earlier:
*His father was a composer and his grandfather **had** also **been** a musician.* (Mozart's grandfather was a musician and then later his father became a composer)
Sometimes we use words like *just* or *already*. Notice that these adverbs go between the auxiliary and the main verb:
*By the time he was 17, Mozart's reputation **had already begun** to spread through Europe.*
⚠ We use the past simple tense if the events are mentioned in chronological order:
*His grandfather **was** a musician and his father **was** also a composer.*

♦ with words like *when, as soon as, by the time, after* to show the order of events:
***When** Mozart was born, five of his siblings **had** already **died**.* (Mozart's siblings died first, then Mozart was born)
⚠ Notice the difference in meaning between these two sentences:
*When I got home, my husband **cooked** dinner.* (= I got home and then my husband cooked dinner)

*I **got** home   my husband **cooked** dinner*

THE PAST

*When I got home, my husband **had cooked** dinner.* (= my husband cooked dinner before I got home)

*my husband **had cooked** dinner   I **got** home*

THE PAST

♦ to talk about an indefinite time before a particular point in the past, often with words like *always, sometimes, never, before, by* + fixed time:
*His family were richer than they **had ever been before**.* (= they were not as rich at any time before this point in the past)
***By the time** he was six, the little boy **had written** a composition of his own.*

♦ to report past events using reporting verbs (see Unit 15):
*The man told me he **had met** my father a long time before.*

2 Past perfect continuous

+	had been + verb + -ing	She**'d been studying** for ages.
−	had not been + verb + -ing	He **hadn't been studying** for long.
?	had ... been + verb + -ing?	**Had** you **been studying** for long?

We use the past perfect continuous to focus on how long an activity continued or to focus on the activity itself:

*Times were hard and the family **had been struggling for some time**.* (to show how long)
*Mozart's sister was extremely gifted at the keyboard and she **had been making excellent progress**.* (focus on the activity)

⚠ We cannot use the past perfect continuous to say how many times something happened:
*I knew the way as I **had visited** her several times before.* (**not** *I knew the way as I had been visiting her several times before.*)

⚠ State verbs (see Unit 1) do not generally have a continuous form.

Grammar extra: Unfulfilled hopes
We use the past perfect to talk about past disappointments or things that did not happen as expected:
*The politician **had expected** to be re-elected, but in the end she only got ten per cent of the vote.*
*I **had been hoping** to go with my brother on his trip but I was too sick to go.*

C Grammar exercises

1 Fill in the gaps with the past perfect simple of the verbs in brackets in the positive or negative.

According to Dr Ken Winkle, Australia's Red-back spider is colonising the world. Dr Winkle, a venom expert from the University of Melbourne, said that authorities **1** ....had found.... (*find*) Red-back spiders in Japan and Belgium. They suspected that spiders or their eggs **2** .... (*enter*) these countries along with Australian trading goods. Furthermore, it was extremely likely that the spiders **3** .... (*make*) their way into other nations around the world but that people **4** .... (*discover*) them yet. Dr Winkle said the spiders **5** .... (*also/turn up*) in the port city of Osaka (which receives a variety of Australian trade goods) in the late 1990s and **6** .... (*multiply*) quickly. He said Australian spider experts were collaborating with Japanese officials to find a way to stop the venomous invader.

2 Complete the report with the past simple or past perfect simple of the verbs in brackets.

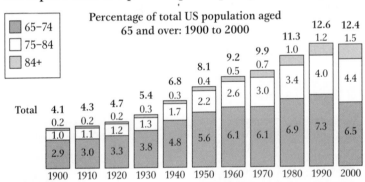

The chart shows the percentage of people aged 65 and over in the United States between 1900 and 2000. In the year 1900 just over 4% of the population **1** ....was.......... (be) aged over 65. However, by 1960 this figure **2** .... (double).

The number of people aged between 75 and 84 **3** .... (remain) fairly steady between 1900 and 1930, making up only 1–1.3% of the population. The figure **4** .... (begin) to rise more significantly in 1940 and by 1970 it **5** .... (triple) to reach 3% of the population.

Although there **6** .... (be) no change in the number of people aged 65–74 between 1960 and 1970, the number of people aged 75 and over **7** .... (increase) during this time. By the year 2000, 12.4% of the US population **8** .... (reach) the age of 65 or more, although this was slightly lower than in 1990 when it **9** .... (peak) at 12.6%.

The chart shows that today people in the United States can expect to live longer than in 1900. By the year 2000 more than 12% of the population **10** .... (manage) to live to the age of 65 and over compared to only 4.1% in 1900.

3 Fill in the gaps with the past simple, past perfect simple or past perfect continuous of the verbs in brackets.

Last year my friends ....arranged........ (**1** *arrange*) for us to try fire-walking, which is when you walk on hot coals. I .... (**2** *always/be*) fascinated by it and I .... (**3** *hear*) people say it was an unforgettable experience. I was very excited when I .... (**4** *arrive*) on the day, although beforehand I .... (**5** *feel*) a little frightened! My friends and I .... (**6** *come*) in the hope that by the end of the day we would be able to say we .... (**7** *walk*) across hot, burning coals.

Our teacher was very good, and by teatime we .... (**8** *learnt*) a great deal and .... (**9** *prepare*) the fires. I .... (**10** *expect*) to be terrified when the time came to walk, but as I .... (**11** *take off*) my shoes and socks I .... (**12** *not/feel*) afraid. I .... (**13** *approach*) the coals as all my friends before me .... (**14** *do*), and started walking! I could feel the heat, but as I .... (**15** *step*) back onto the grass at the other end I knew the coals .... (**16** *not/burn*) my feet at all. As I .... (**17** *hope*), all my friends .... (**18** *manage*) the walk and none of us were burnt. The whole experience was amazing, and I just wished I .... (**19** *do*) it sooner.

4 Fill in the gaps with a verb from the box in the past simple, past perfect simple or past perfect continuous tense. Use each verb once.

be buy decide develop discuss feel like make
phone run start stay take visit wait work

1 She 'd been working as a waitress for five years when he met her.

2 The lecture .... by the time they got there.

3 In the supermarket he .... all the ingredients he needed and then went home to make her birthday cake.

4 Holly did very well in her exam, which was a shock because she .... (never) an exam before.

5 They went on a big tour of Britain. First they .... in London for a few days. Then they .... Cambridge, York, and Edinburgh, and then Bath. They .... to Bath before, but they .... it so much that they .... to go back again.

6 Scientists announced the launch of the new drug last week. They .... it for five years.

7 By the time I got to the meeting they .... (already) the important issues and they .... the big decisions without me. I .... from my mobile to tell them the train was late and I .... annoyed that they .... (not) for me.

8 I looked terrible when I saw Joe last night because I .... for over an hour and I was exhausted.

Academic Reading

Questions 1–12

Read the passage below and answer Questions 1–12.

The history of the biro

A

One chilly autumn morning in 1945, five thousand shoppers crowded the pavements outside Gimbels Department Store in New York City. The day before, Gimbels had taken out a full-page newspaper advertisement in the *New York Times*, announcing the sale of the first ballpoint pens in the United States. The new writing instrument was heralded as "fantastic... miraculous... guaranteed to write for two years without refilling!" Within six hours, Gimbels had sold its entire stock of ten thousand ballpoints at $12.50 each – approximately $130 at today's prices.

B

In fact this 'new' pen was not new after all, and was just the latest development in a long search for the best way to deliver ink to paper. In 1884 Lewis Waterman had patented the fountain pen, giving him the sole rights to manufacture it. This marked a significant leap forward in writing technology, but fountain pens soon became notorious for leaking. In 1888, a leather tanner named John Loud devised and patented the first "rolling-pointed marker pen" for marking leather. Loud's design contained a reservoir of ink in a cartridge and a rotating ball point that was constantly bathed on one side with ink.

Loud's pen was never manufactured, however, and over the next five decades, 350 additional patents were issued for similar ball-type pens, though none advanced beyond the design stage. Each had their own faults, but the major difficulty was the ink: if the ink was thin, the pens leaked, and if it was too thick, they clogged. Depending on the climate or air temperature, sometimes the pens would do both.

C

Almost fifty years later, Ladislas and Georg Biro, two Hungarian brothers, came up with a solution to this problem. In 1935 Ladislas Biro was working as a journalist, editing a small newspaper. He found himself becoming more and more frustrated by the amount of time he wasted filling fountain pens with ink and cleaning up ink smudges. What's more, the sharp tip of his fountain pen often scratched or tore through the thin newsprint paper. Ladislas and Georg (a chemist) set about making models of new pen designs and creating better inks to use in them. Ladislas had observed that the type of ink used in newspaper printing dried rapidly, leaving the paper dry and smudge-free. He was determined to construct a pen using the same type of ink. However, the thicker ink would not flow from a regular pen nib so he had to develop a new type of point. Biro came up with the idea of fitting his pen with a tiny ball bearing in its tip. As the pen moved along the paper, the ball bearing rotated and picked up ink from the ink cartridge which it delivered to the paper.

D

The first Biro pen, like the designs that had gone before it, relied on gravity for the ink to flow to the ball bearing at the tip. This meant that the pens only worked when they were held straight up, and even then the ink flow was sometimes too heavy, leaving big smudges of ink on the paper. The Biro brothers had a rethink and eventually devised a new design, which relied on capillary action rather than gravity to feed the ink. This meant that the ink could flow more smoothly to the tip and the pen could be held at an angle rather than straight up. In 1938, as World War II broke out, the Biro brothers fled to Argentina, where they applied for a patent for their pen and established their first factory.

E

The Biros' pen soon came to the attention of American fighter pilots, who needed a new kind of pen to use at high altitudes. Apparently, it was ideal for pilots as it did not leak like the fountain pen and did not have to be refilled frequently. The United States Department of War contacted several American companies, asking them to manufacture a similar writing instrument in the U.S. Thus fortune smiled on the Biro brothers in May 1945, when the American company 'Eversharp' paid them $500,000 for the exclusive manufacturing and marketing rights of the Biro ballpoint for the North American market. Eversharp were slow to put their pen into production, however, and this delay ultimately cost them their competitive advantage.

F

Meanwhile, in June 1945 an American named Milton Reynolds stumbled upon the Biro pen while on vacation in Buenos Aires. Immediately seeing its commercial potential, he bought several pens and returned to Chicago, where he discovered that Loud's original 1888 patent had long since expired. This meant that the ballpoint was now in the public domain, and he therefore wasted no time making a copy based on the Biro design. Establishing his pen company with just $26,000, Reynolds quickly set up a factory with 300 workers who began production on 6th October 1945, stamping out pens from precious scraps of aluminum that hadn't been used during the war for military equipment or weapons. Just 23 days later, it was Reynolds' ballpoint pen that caused the stampede at Gimbels Department Store. Following the ballpoint's debut in New York City, Eversharp challenged Reynolds in the law courts, but lost the case because the Biro brothers had failed to secure a U.S. patent on their invention.

4

Questions 1–6

The reading passage has six paragraphs **A–F**.

Choose the most suitable heading for each paragraph from the list of headings below.

Write the correct number **i–ix** in the space provided.

List of Headings

i   Fountain pens are history

ii   Fame at last for the Biro brothers

iii   A holiday helps bring the biro to America

iv   A second design and a new country

v   War halts progress

vi   Dissatisfaction leads to a new invention

vii   Big claims bring big crowds

viii   A government request brings a change of ownership

ix   Many patents and many problems

---

1   Paragraph A ....

2   Paragraph B ....

3   Paragraph C ....

4   Paragraph D ....

5   Paragraph E ....

6   Paragraph F ....

Questions 7–9

Choose the correct answer, **A, B, C** or **D**.

7 The problem with the ballpoint pens invented between 1888 and 1935 was that
   A they cost a great deal of money to manufacture.
   B the technology to manufacture them did not exist.
   C they could not write on ordinary paper.
   D they were affected by weather conditions.

8 The design of the Biro brothers' first pen
   A was similar to previous pens.
   B was based on capillary action.
   C worked with heavy or light inks.
   D worked when slanted slightly.

9 Milton Reynolds was able to copy the Biro brothers' design because
   A the Biro brothers' original patent was out of date.
   B it was legal to copy other designs at the time.
   C they did not have a patent for North America.
   D the Biro brothers gave him permission.

Questions 10–12

Answer the questions below using **NO MORE THAN TWO WORDS AND/OR A NUMBER** *for each answer.*

Write your answers in the spaces provided.

10 What material was the first ballpoint pen designed to write on? ....

11 Where did the Biro brothers open their first factory? ....

12 In what year did the first American biro factory begin production? ....

Grammar focus task

Look at the extracts from the text. Without looking back at the text, fill in the gaps with the correct form of the verbs in brackets.

1 The day before, Gimbels .... (*take out*) a full-page newspaper advertisement in the *New York Times*, announcing the sale of the first ballpoint pens in the United States... Within six hours, Gimbels .... (*sell*) its entire stock of ten thousand ballpoints at $12.50 each – approximately $130 at today's prices.

2 In 1884 Lewis Waterman .... (*patent*) the fountain pen, giving him the sole rights to manufacture it. This marked a significant leap forward in writing technology, but fountain pens .... (*soon/become*) notorious for leaking.

3 Ladislas .... (*observe*) that the type of ink used in newspaper printing dried rapidly, leaving the paper dry and smudge-free.

4 Immediately seeing its commercial potential, he .... (*buy*) several pens and .... (*return*) to Chicago, where he .... (*discover*) that Loud's original 1888 patent .... (*long since/expire*).

5 Following the ballpoint's debut in New York City, Eversharp .... (*challenge*) Reynolds in the law courts, but .... (*lose*) the case because the Biro brothers .... (*fail*) to secure a U.S. patent on their invention.

Future 1

plans, intentions and predictions:
present continuous; *going to*; *will*

A   Context listening

1 You are going to hear Tim, a sports team
coach, talking to Amanda, a player in the
team, about a trip they are going to make.
Before you listen look at the pictures.
Which sport does the team play? Which
two countries will they visit?

2 ⌂ **5** Listen and complete the table below. Write no more than two words or a number
for each answer.

Country	Number of matches	Number of free days	Accommodation	Other plans
1	2	3	stay in a 4	do lots of walking
5	6	7	8	visit some 9 ....

3 **5◄◄** Now listen again and write

    A if Tim makes this statement
    B if Amanda makes this statement
    C if both Tim and Amanda make this statement

1 We're travelling to Scotland by plane. ....
2 We'll have fun even if the weather is bad. ....
3 The team will be pleased with the accommodation in Athens. ....
4 The two countries are going to provide very different experiences. ....
5 The team manager is holding a party on our return. ....

4 Look at the statements in Exercise 3 and answer these questions.

    1 Which tense is used in statements 1 and 5? ....
    2 Which structure is used in statements 2 and 3 to refer to the future? ....
    3 Which structure is used in statement 4 to refer to the future? ....
    4 Which statements talk about a fixed arrangement? ....
    5 Which statements are predictions? ....

B Grammar

1 Present continuous

We use the present continuous to talk about plans or definite arrangements for the future:
We're staying in a small hotel. (we have made the arrangements)
Notice that time expressions are used or understood from the context in order to show that we are talking about the future (and not the present):
The manager is having a party just after we get back. (time expression given)
We're playing four matches there. (future time expression understood)

2 Will

+	will + verb	We'll enjoy it.
−	will not (won't) + verb	He won't enjoy it.
?	will ... + verb?	Will they enjoy it?

We use *will*
- to make predictions, usually based on our opinions or our past experience:
  I think it'll be extremely hot there.

- to talk about future events we haven't arranged yet:
  We'll probably stay in some sort of mountain lodge there.

- to talk about future events or facts that are not personal:
  The best player on the tour will get a special trophy.
  The prime minister will open the debate in parliament tomorrow.

- to talk about something we decide to do at the time of speaking:
  Tell me all about it and I'll pass on the information to the rest of the team.
  We often use *will* to make offers, promises or suggestions:
  Don't worry, I'll let everyone know. (a promise)

3 Going to

+	am/is/are + going to + verb	We're going to hire a bus.
−	am/is/are not + going to + verb	He's not going to hire a bus.
?	am/is/are ... + going to + verb?	Are they going to hire a bus?

Going to often means the same as the present continuous and *will*.

We use *going to*
- to talk about events in the future we have already thought about and intend to do:
  We're going to hire a bus. (we intend to go, but we haven't made the arrangements yet)
  We're going to get a boat to a couple of the islands.

- to make predictions when there is present evidence:
  Well, we're certainly going to have a varied trip. (I am judging this from what I know about the plans)

Going to and *will* can follow words like *think, doubt, expect, believe, probably, certainly, definitely, be sure* to show that it is an opinion about the future:
I **think** it's **going to be** a great trip.
I'**m sure** we'**ll enjoy** it whatever the weather.
It'**ll probably rain** every day.

We can often choose different future forms to talk about the same future situation. It depends on the speaker's ideas about the situation:

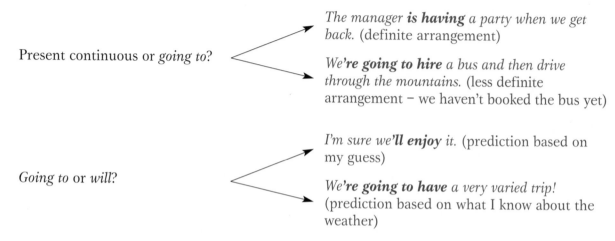

Present continuous or *going to*?

The manager **is having** a party when we get back. (definite arrangement)

We'**re going to hire** a bus and then drive through the mountains. (less definite arrangement – we haven't booked the bus yet)

Going to or *will*?

I'm sure we'**ll enjoy** it. (prediction based on my guess)

We'**re going to have** a very varied trip! (prediction based on what I know about the weather)

Often there is very little difference between *going to* and *will* for predictions.

Grammar extra: Making predictions using words other than *will*
In formal writing we often use expressions other than *will* to predict the future (e.g. *be likely to, be predicted to, be estimated to, be certain to*):
The population **is likely to** increase to 22 million in 2011.
The average annual rainfall **is predicted to** be ten per cent lower than today's figures.

C Grammar exercises

1 Fill in the gaps in the second half of this model answer with phrases from the box.

Thanks to modern technology, there have been enormous changes in the workplace over the past 100 years.

What are the most significant changes that have occurred and what changes do you foresee in the next 100 years?

are going to feel	are going to happen	are likely to lead to
~~are likely to occur~~	are predicted to work	is likely to become
will be	will continue	will develop
will find	will have	will result

… So, now let us consider the changes that **1** .are..likely..to..occur. in the next 100 years. Unfortunately, I believe that not all changes **2** .... for the better. For example, in the future more and more people **3** .... from home and so they **4** .... more isolated from their colleagues. On the other hand, they **5** .... (certainly) greater freedom to choose their working hours.

A further possible change is that handwriting **6** .... obsolete. We are already so used to using a keyboard that today's children are losing the ability to spell without the aid of a word processor.

Without a doubt, even greater changes **7** .... in technology used in the workplace. Computers **8** .... (undoubtedly) to grow even more powerful and this **9** .... (probably) in an even faster pace of life than we have now. Let us hope that our employers **10** .... a way to reduce the stress on workers this fast pace can bring.

I also think these improvements in technology **11** .... even more globalisation than now and companies **12** .... very strong international links.

2 Underline the most suitable form of the verbs.

Dear Paul and Claire

We're having a wonderful time here in France. The weather is beautiful and we've got lots of plans for how to spend the next couple of weeks. Tomorrow 1 *we're going out* / *we will go out* on a glass-bottomed boat to look at the wonderful sea life, and then on Wednesday we think 2 *we're taking* / *we'll take* a tour of the old town. Ollie's aunt lives quite close, so 3 *we're visiting* / *we're going to visit* her too if we have time.

The hotel is lovely and lively and has lots of good night life. Tonight 4 *they're holding* / *they'll hold* an international evening, with lots of food from different countries.

As you know, we're here with our friends, John and Wendy, but 5 *they aren't staying* / *they won't stay* as long as us, so 6 *we're probably doing* / *we'll probably do* the really 'touristy' things with them, and be lazy in our second week. You can hire small sailing boats for the day, so we think 7 *we're doing* / *we're going to do* that next week, and 8 *we're also going to try* / *we're also trying* to have time to do some shopping!

I hope you are ready for your big trip. 9 *You're loving* / *You'll love* Australia. In fact 10 *you're going to probably end up* / *you'll probably end up* staying there much longer than you've planned.

Have a great time, and 11 *we're going to see* / *we'll see* you when you get back.

Love Kath and Ollie

3 Fill in the gaps with the present continuous or *will*-future form of the verbs in brackets.

Kirsty: Hi Elaine. It's Kirsty, here.

Elaine: Hello, how are you?

Kirsty: Fine. Listen, I know this is very short notice but ..*are you doing*.. (**1** *do*) anything tonight?

Elaine: Nothing why?

Kirsty: Well I .... (**2** *take*) my class to the theatre, but one of them can't go. Would you like to come?

Elaine: I'd love to. What's the play about?

Kirsty: Oh, I .... (**3** *tell*) you all about that a little later. I .... (**4** *pick*) you up at 6.30 – is that okay?

Elaine: Yes, OK. Or how about meeting a bit earlier? We could have a coffee beforehand.

Kirsty: Well, I .... (**5** *see*) the school principal at four, but I suppose I could come after that. My meeting .... (**6** *probably/finish*) at about 5.30. Is that okay?

Elaine: Yes, of course. What time does the play actually start?

Kirsty: At 7.30, although we .... (**7** *need*) to be there before as I .... (**8** *meet*) my students at the theatre at seven. Afterwards they .... (**9** *probably/want*) to talk about the play for a little while. But I hope that .... (**10** *not/go on*) for too long. There .... (**11** *be*) plenty of time for us to discuss it at tomorrow's lesson.

Elaine: That's fine. I .... (**12** *see*) you at 5.30!

4 Write sentences about yourself.

1 Write two **intentions** about your future.

....

....

2 Write three **plans** or **arrangements** for your future.

....

....

....

3 **Predict** three things that you think will happen to the workplace in the future.

....

....

....

General Training Reading

Questions 1–9

Read the passage below and answer Questions 1–9.

How to choose a university course

How do I choose a course?

You've decided you want to do a course. Whether you would like a career change, a better job or simply to learn something new, it's a good idea to think carefully first. Here's a guide to help you.

Qualifications – why do I need them?

Qualifications prove you've acquired knowledge or developed skills. For some careers like medicine and law, it's essential you have specific qualifications. For others, such as journalism, it helps to have a particular qualification.

Most universities set entry requirements for degree courses. Mature entrants don't always need formal qualifications, but need evidence of recent study, relevant work experience or professional qualifications. Professional bodies may grant you membership if you have certain qualifications. It's not always essential to have a qualification. Working knowledge, such as being able to use computer software, can be just as important.

What type of course should I do?

Your motives will help you choose the best course for your aims and goals. If you are career-driven, you'll need a course relevant to your profession. If you are interested in self-development and meeting people, you should find out who else will be on the course.

There are work-related (vocational) and academic courses. Further education colleges offer academic courses and work-related courses. Universities offer higher education qualifications, such as academic first degrees and higher degrees and the more vocational diplomas.

For a career in plumbing, a vocational course is essential. For teaching, you need a degree. However, for many jobs, you have a choice between academic and vocational courses. A vocational course is better if you like doing things with your hands and working manually. You might prefer an academic course if you like researching, analysing and presenting arguments.

Which type of study would suit me best?

Do you prefer on-the-job training, or do you prefer to research and gather facts? Do you like working in a group covering the same topics and working towards the same goal? If you prefer to work on your own, at your own pace, an open or distance learning course might suit you. You study from home, with the help of tuition packs, computers and tutor support via telephone or email. You can speed through the course or take your time. But you do need self-discipline and motivation.

What about my personal circumstances?

You might prefer an open or distance learning course if:
• you're working and you don't know how much time a week you can commit to
• you work irregular hours
• you're at home looking after pre-school children.
Many colleges and training centres now offer flexible open-learning courses, where you can study at your own pace.

How do I know if it's a good course?

You've decided which subject and type of course you want, and how to study it. You now need to choose between different course titles and providers. There are many courses and they aren't of equal value. The only way to assess the quality and value of a course is by research. Read prospectuses (course guides) carefully and note if a course is accredited or validated by a recognised body (this might be an awarding body or a professional body). This can add extra weight to your qualification.

Don't take everything you read at face value; check out the facts about each course yourself. Ask course tutors as many questions as you want.

How can I be sure I'm making the right choice?

Be clear of your goal. If you've decided on a particular job, get an idea of what the job's about and if you'll like it. Read careers information, buy trade magazines, and speak to people currently working in the job. This research is well worth it. It's better to take your time rather than do a course that leads to a job you might not really want. You'll ensure that you don't waste any time or money.

What am I going to do after the course?

Plan for when you finish. If you're aiming for a particular job, do voluntary work while studying. If you're doing an English course and want to be a journalist, you could write for the student newspaper or work on the radio. Having a plan will help you make the most of the opportunities that come your way when you're on the course.

Questions 1–5

*Complete each sentence with the correct ending **A–F** from the box below.*

*Write the correct letter **A–F** next to Questions **1–5**.*

1 Students who want to do law ....

2 Mature students ....

3 Students who are motivated by self-development ....

4 Students who have young children ....

5 Students who choose a career in journalism ....

> **A** will not need any experience to start a course
> **B** will benefit from open-learning courses
> **C** could get relevant work experience while they study
> **D** can be accepted onto a course without qualifications
> **E** should enquire about the other students on their course
> **F** must have certain qualifications

Questions 6–9

Classify the following statements as applying to
   A *academic courses*
   B *vocational courses*
   C *both academic and vocational courses*

*Write the correct letter **A–C** next to Questions **6–9**.*

6 These courses are available through further education colleges. ....

7 You must take this kind of course if you wish to have a career in plumbing. ....

8 You will learn research methods on this type of course. ....

9 You will learn practical skills on this course. ....

Grammar focus task

These are extracts from the text. Without looking back at the text, fill in the gaps with the correct form of the verbs in brackets and then answer the questions that follow.

1 Your motives .... (*help*) you choose the best course for your aims and goals.

2 If you are career-driven, you .... (*need*) a course relevant to your profession.

3 You .... (*ensure*) that you don't waste any time or money.

4 What .... (*I/do*) after the course?

5 Having a plan .... (*help*) you make the most of the opportunities that come your way when you're on the course.

Which future forms are used? ....

Why? ....

6

Future 2

present simple; *be about to*;
future continuous; future perfect

A   Context listening

1 Janet is a university lecturer. She gets nervous when she gives talks at conferences. Look at the pictures. Which do you think would help Janet feel more confident and relaxed?

2 🎧 **6** Listen to Janet's conversation with her colleague, Phil. What advice does Phil give her?

3 **6** ◀◀ Listen again and complete the sentences below. Write no more than three words for each answer.

1 Janet .... on the report all next week.

2 By the end of the year, Janet .... the same talk at six conferences.

3 When she gets to Rome, Janet .... very nervous.

4 Before he gives his talk in London, Phil .... it at least ten times.

5 Janet is in a hurry because the train to the airport .... in 20 minutes.

4 Look at the sentences used in Exercise 3 and answer these questions.

1 Which sentences talk about events that will be over before a time in the future?

....

2 Which sentences talk about events or situations in progress at a particular time in the future? ....

3 Which sentence talks about a scheduled event? ....

B Grammar

1 Present simple

We use the present simple with a future meaning
◆ to talk about timetables or schedules:
*The conference only **lasts** three days.*
*The train to the airport **leaves** in 20 minutes.*

◆ after conjunctions such as *when, as soon as, after, before, until, as long as*:
*I'll be feeling really nervous **when I get** to Rome.* (**not** ~~when I will get to Rome~~)
*Can you do it **before** we **have** the departmental meeting?* (**not** ~~before we will have the meeting~~)
Note that other present tenses are also possible:
*I won't be able to relax **until** I'm actually **giving** my talk.*

2 *Be about to*

+	*am/is/are about to* + verb	*I'm **about to go** to Rome.*
–	*am/is/are not about to* + verb	*I'm **not about to go** to Rome.*
?	*am/is/are ... * + verb?	***Are** you **about to go** to Rome?*

We use *be about to* to talk about something likely to happen in the immediate future:
*I'm **about to go** to Rome for a conference.* (I will be leaving very soon)

⚠ The negative form suggests the speaker has no intention of doing something:
*I'm **not about to cancel** my trip.* (= I have no intention of cancelling my trip)

3 Future continuous

+	*will be* + verb + *-ing*	*I'll **be feeling** nervous.*
–	*will not (won't) be* + verb + *-ing*	*She **won't be feeling** nervous.*
?	*will ... be* + verb + *-ing?*	***Will** you **be feeling** nervous?*

We use the future continuous
◆ to describe or predict events or situations continuing at a particular point in the future or over a period of time in the future:
*I'll **be working** on the report all next week.*

*I'll **be working** on the report*

NOW   N E X T   W E E K

*I'll **be thinking** of you in Rome.*
*By the year 2015 it is estimated that well over one billion people **will be learning** English.*

◆ to talk about events that are planned or already decided (this use is similar to the present continuous for future arrangements):
*I'll **be seeing** Sarah at lunch.*

4 Future perfect simple

+	*will have* + past participle	*I'll **have done** it by then.*
–	*will not (won't) have* + past participle	*We **won't have done** it by then.*
?	*will ... + have* + past participle?	***Will** you **have done** it by then?*

We use the future perfect simple to talk about a future event that will finish before a specified time in the future, often with *before, by* + fixed time, or *in* + amount of time:
*By the end of the year I **will have given** the same talk at 6 conferences!*
*I'**ll have finished** it by next Friday.*
*In a week's time I'**ll have written** the report.*

5 Future perfect continuous

+	*will have been* + verb + *-ing*	*I'll **have been studying** here for three months.*
–	*will not (won't) have been* + verb + *-ing*	*We **won't have been studying** here for long.*
?	*will ... + have been* + verb + *-ing?*	*How long **will** you **have been studying** here?*

We use the future perfect continuous to show how long an activity or situation has been in progress before a specified time in the future. We usually mention the length of time:
*By the end of the month I'**ll have been working** here for three years.*

Grammar extra: The future in the past

We use *was/were going to, was/were planning to, was/were about to* + verb to talk something planned which did not or will not happen:
*I **was going to leave** this morning but they cancelled my flight.*
*We **were about to leave** when the phone rang.*

C Grammar exercises

1 The following chart shows the results of a class survey about planned activities for Saturday afternoon. Complete the sentences using the future continuous tense.

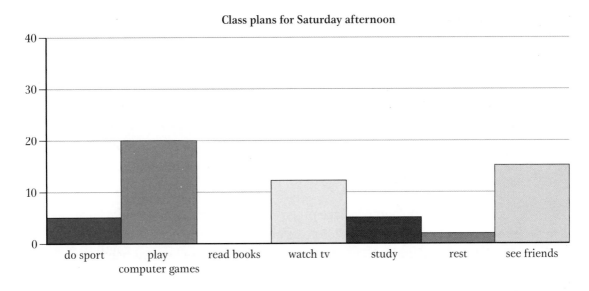

Class plans for Saturday afternoon

1 Twelve students _will be watching TV_ on Saturday afternoon.
2 The students .... books on Saturday.
3 The largest group of students .... this Saturday afternoon.
4 A similar number of students .... and .... this weekend.
5 A very small number of students .... this weekend.
6 Approximately 15 students .... this weekend.

Write what you will be doing at the following times.

7 At six o'clock tomorrow I'll ....
8 Next Saturday afternoon I won't ....
9 On Sunday morning ....
10 In a year's time ....

2 Read the following projections about the future population of Australia.

Population projections

According to the latest available projections (which are based on several combinations of assumptions reflecting past trends in births, deaths and migration), the total population of Australia is likely to have increased to between 22.3 and 23.3 million by 2021.

The projected population will increase at a declining rate. The average annual growth rate is predicted to be between 0.5 and 0.8 during 2011–2021. Without overseas migration, the projected total population should peak at about 23.3 million in 2041, and then start to decline marginally.

Age distribution
The projected population will age progressively due to the increasing proportion of the elderly (aged 65 years or more) and the decreasing proportion of children (aged under 15 years). In brief, the number of persons aged under 15 is projected to be between 3.7 and 4.1 million in 2031; the population of working age (15–64 years) is projected to increase to between 14.4 and 15.0 million in 2031; and the number of persons aged 65 years or more is projected to increase to between 2.94 and 2.98 million in 2031. The projections also show significant increases in the number of persons aged 80 years or more.

Write the verbs in brackets in the future perfect tense. Then choose the correct ending for each sentence.

1 By the year 2021 the population of
   Australia _will have reached_ (*reach*)

2 The population of Australia
   .... (*peak*)

3 By the year 2031 the number of children
   aged under 15 .... (*rise*)

4 By 2031 the number of people of working
   age in Australia .... (*grow*)

5 By 2031 the number of people aged 65
   and over .... (*go up*)

6 By the year 2031 the number of people
   aged over 80 .... (*increase*)

a by the early 2040s.

b to almost 2.98 million.

c a maximum of 23.3 million.

d to between 3.7 and 4.1 million.

e significantly.

f to around 15 million.

3 In six of these sentences there is a verb in the wrong tense. <u>Underline</u> each mistake and write the correction.

1   When <u>I'll find</u> the answer I'll let you know. ....<u>I find</u>..........

2   My exams <u>finish</u> on 27th June. ....

3   I'll be fine in the interview as long as they <u>won't ask</u> me technical questions. ....

4   What time is your meeting <u>about to start</u> tomorrow? ....

5   I'll hand in my notice for this job after <u>I'll get</u> the contract for my new one. ....

6   I'll text you before we <u>set off</u> ....

7   The bus <u>doesn't arrive</u> until 7.30 in the evening. ....

8   I've got my schedule for the Japan trip. We're about to fly to Tokyo at 10 am on Monday, and then travel by train to Kyoto for one night. ....

9   The moment <u>I'll receive</u> my results I'll phone you. ....

4 Fill in the gaps with a future form from this unit and the verbs in brackets.

Teacher: What ...<u>will you be doing</u>.. (**1** *you/do*) this time next year?

Student 1: Well, that's difficult to say but I hope that I .... (**2** *travel*) round the world. Before then I .... (**3** *hopefully/save up*) enough money for the ticket. I plan to end up in Australia and when I .... (**4** *get*) there I'll get a job and earn some money. So, in a year's time I .... (**5** *probably/travel*) for a few months already. I hope that I .... (**6** *visit*) quite a lot of different countries by then too.

Teacher: What do you plan to do when you graduate?

Student 2: Well, my plans have changed a bit. I .... (**7** *do*) a journalism course, but I didn't get accepted. So I've sorted something else out and I .... (**8** *start*) a hospitality course tomorrow, actually. It's for six months, so I .... (**9** *not/finish*) in time to go travelling next spring, unfortunately. However, as soon as I .... (**10** *find out*) if I've passed the course, I can apply for a job in a hotel in Australia.

D Test practice

Academic Writing Task 2

You should spend about 40 minutes on this task.

Write about the following topic:

> *The birth rate in most developed countries is predicted to begin to fall over the next 50 years. By 2030 it is estimated that over one third of the population in most developed countries will be aged 65 and over.*
>
> *What effects will these predictions have on developed countries if they prove true? What can be done now to deal with this situation?*

Give reasons for your answer and include any relevant examples from your own knowledge or experience.

You should write at least 250 words.

Grammar focus task

Look at the extract from a model answer below. Fill in the gaps with the verbs in the box in the correct future tense.

be	pay	rise	work

... By 2030 the percentage of the population aged 65 or older **1** .... significantly, to more than 30%. This means that fewer people **2** ...., and therefore fewer people **3** .... income tax. In the future it may be necessary for governments to increase the official retirement age to 70 or even older. When today's 30-year-olds **4** .... in their sixties it is unlikely that they will enjoy the relaxed lifestyle that today's older generation can expect when they give up work.

Countable and uncountable nouns

countable and uncountable nouns; quantity expressions
(*many, much, a lot of, some, any, a few, few, no*)

A Context listening

1 You are going to hear Alan and Sara talking about advertising a spare bedroom to rent. Before you listen look at the types of furniture below. Tick the furniture you think might be in the room.

- ☑ shelves
- ☐ a wardrobe
- ☐ a lamp
- ☑ a bedside table
- ☐ a filing cabinet
- ☑ a bed
- ☑ a desk
- ☑ a mirror
- ☐ a sofa
- ☐ a towel rail
- ☐ a coffee table
- ☐ a rug

2 🎧 **7** Listen and answer the questions below.

1 Which three pieces of furniture are in the room?

   A a bed   **C** a desk   **F** a mirror

   B a bedside table   **E** a lamp   **G** a wardrobe

2 What does the desk look like?

A    **B**    **C**

3 **7** ◀◀ Listen again and fill in the gaps in the advertisement.
Write no more than one word or a number for each answer.

> **Accommodation for rent**
>
> Small, furnished **1** .... available. Sunny with a nice view of the **2** .... Good location close to two types of **3** ....
> Rent **4** £................... per **5** .... Rent includes **6** .... and all other bills.

4 Look at the two groups of nouns in the table below. How are they different? Add the nouns from Exercises 2 and 3 into the table in the correct group.

Group 1	Group 2
advertisement *newspaper* *windows*	*money* *news* *accommodation*

B Grammar

1 Countable and uncountable nouns

Countable nouns

- generally have a singular and plural form: *a window, lots of windows*
  ⚠ Some countable nouns only have a plural form: *clothes, trousers, jeans, scissors*
- take a singular or plural verb form: *The window **is** big. The windows **are** big.*
- can be replaced by a singular or plural pronoun: *I'd like that **desk**; **it**'s better than mine. It's got **shelves** as well. **They**'re really handy.*
- can be measured with weights and measures: ***two kilos of** potatoes* or numbers: *It's got **three** drawers.*

- can be used with *a/an*: ***a** desk, **an** apple*

Uncountable nouns

- cannot be plural: *advice (**not** ~~advices~~), furniture (**not** ~~furnitures~~), data*
  ⚠ Some uncountable nouns look plural but they are not: *news, economics, physics*
- take only a singular verb form: *The natural light **is** really nice.*
- can be replaced by a singular pronoun: *'What shall we say about **the furniture**?' 'Well, **it**'s not luxurious but **it** is very comfortable.'*
- can be measured with weights and measures: ***two kilos of** sugar* or with words like *a piece of, cup of, bit of, slice of*: ***a piece of** information*
- cannot be used with *a/an*: *information (**not** ~~an information~~)*

2 *Some* and *any*

Some

- is generally used in positive statements: *There are **some shelves** above the desk.*
- can also be used in questions and particularly in requests and offers: *Would you like **some biscuits**?*
- means 'an unspecified (not large) amount': *It would be great to get **some money** to help with the rent.* (we don't know how much money)

⚠ We use *some of* with other determiners (e.g. *my, the, these*) to refer to a particular group: ***Some of my** students have part-time jobs.*

Any

- is usually used in negatives and questions: *My desk has**n't** got **any drawers**.*   *Has your desk got **any drawers?***
- can also be used in positive statements to mean 'it doesn't matter who/which/where/when': *Call me **any time** if you need further help.* (= it doesn't matter when you call)

⚠ We can also use *no* + noun to mean the same as *not ... any*: *My desk has got **no drawers**.* (= my desk hasn't got any drawers)
We use *no* when the noun is a subject: ***No applicants** had the necessary experience for the job.* (**not** ~~Not any applicants~~)

Words like *something/anything, somebody/anybody*, etc. follow the same rules as *some* and *any*.

3 Quantities

We can use the following words to say how many or how much:

	Plural countable nouns	Uncountable nouns
everything	*all (of)*	*all (of)*
large quantities	*lots of / plenty of / a lot of* *many (of)* *most (of)* *a large/considerable/substantial number of*	*lots of / plenty of / a lot of* *much (of)* *most (of)* *a large/considerable/substantial amount of*
medium quantities	*some (of)/a certain number of*	*some (of)/a certain amount of*
small quantities	*(a) few (of)* *a small/limited/tiny number of*	*(a) little (of)* *a small/limited/tiny amount of*
nothing	*no / not any / none of*	*no / not any / none of*

A few and **a** *little* are different from *few* and *little*. Compare:
Few rooms have such good natural light. (= not many, so you are lucky)
*We have **a few** rooms available with a sea view.* (= a small number)

Little research has been done in this area. (= not enough)
A little *research has already been carried out in this area.* (= a small amount)

⚠ We use *a few of* with other determiners (e.g. *my, the, these*) to refer to a particular group:
A few of the rooms *have a sea view.*

Lots of / a lot of are less formal than *much/many*:
*There are **lots of advertisements** for accommodation in the paper.*
Many scientists *believe that global warming is having a negative impact on our climate.*

⚠ We do not usually use *lots of* with negative statements:
*We don't have **a lot of/much** time so we'll have to be quick.* (**not** ~~we don't have lots of time~~)

⚠ We do not usually use *much* in positive sentences:
*I found **a lot of** information on the Internet.* (**not** ~~much information~~)

Grammar extra: Nouns that can be both countable and uncountable

Sometimes the same noun can be either countable or uncountable depending on the meaning (e.g. *light, room, cake, time*). Materials and liquids can also be either (e.g. *glass, paper, coffee, wine*). Compare:
*The natural **light** is really nice.* (uncountable)
*Both of the **lights** in the ceiling are really old.* (countable)
*There isn't much **room** for a desk.* (uncountable = space)
*We have two spare **rooms**.* (countable = rooms in a house)
*Do you drink much **coffee**?* (uncountable = in general)
*I'd like to order **a coffee**, please.* (countable = a cup of coffee)

C Grammar exercises

1 Fill in the gaps with a word from the box below in the correct form. If the word is countable, you may need to change it to a plural form.

| advice | cake | ~~challenge~~ | electricity | information | situation | size |

1 I've faced many ...challenges... in my life, but none as difficult as this.
2 Some of the best .... I heard while I was a student was to take regular breaks when studying so that you don't lose concentration.
3 A dictionary is a wonderful source of ....
4 I've made some little .... for Claire's birthday party.
5 One hundred years ago cars all looked the same but these days they come in lots of different shapes and ....
6 My job as a journalist means I can find myself in difficult .... at times, but at least it's never boring.
7 There was no .... in the remote cottage, so they had to cook over the fire.

2 <u>Underline</u> the correct form of the verbs.

1 Despite the recent improvement in the economy, unemployment <u>*has continued*</u> / *have continued* to rise.
2 Our company hasn't changed its products for over 30 years but now the time *has come* / *have come* for a rethink.
3 The ideas in the report *was* / *were* presented in a very clear way.
4 The data *show* / *shows* that the numbers of people buying mobile phones has remained stable for the past two years.
5 Transport to and from the airport *is included* / *are included* in the price.
6 There *was* / *were* no facilities like running water or electricity in the village.
7 All the information *is* / *are* interesting and well presented, but we need to consider the whole situation very carefully before we reach a decision.
8 There *was* / *were* some important news about the proposed new hospital in the local paper today.

3 Fill in the gaps with *amount, number, few, little, many* or *much*.

How much sleep do we need?

The 1 ...*amount*... of sleep each person needs depends on 2 .... factors, including age. Infants generally require about 16 hours a day. For most adults, seven to eight hours a night appears to be the ideal 3 .... of sleep, although a 4 .... people may need as 5 .... as five hours' sleep or as 6 .... as ten hours' sleep each day. Getting too 7 .... sleep creates a sleep debt, and eventually, your body will demand that the debt be repaid.

A large 8 .... of people over 65 have frequent sleeping problems, such as insomnia, and deep sleep stages in 9 .... elderly people often become very short or stop completely. Microsleeps, or very brief episodes of sleep in an otherwise awake person, are another mark of sleep deprivation. In 10 .... cases, people are not aware that they are experiencing microsleeps. The widespread practice of burning the candle at both ends in western industrialized societies has created so 11 .... sleep deprivation that what is really abnormal sleepiness is now almost the norm.

4 Read the extract from a talk about a holiday destination. Decide if the underlined quantity expressions are correct or not. Tick (✓) them if they are right and correct them if they are wrong.

The island is beautiful. Don't be dismayed when you get off the plane and find yourself in a large, rather ugly city with **1** <u>a little</u> sense of the old way of life you have read about. Just a short car ride away is the island you have been promised with its small villages and slow pace of life. And there really is **2** <u>anything</u> for everyone. For those that like sunbathing, it has **3** <u>some</u> of the most beautiful beaches in the world. If you like walking, the paths take you through some breathtaking scenery. **4** <u>Little</u> other places can match the stunning landscape of this island. For water sports enthusiasts, there are **5** <u>any</u> unusual activities such as diving for pearls or turtle spotting, along with **6** <u>few</u> of the more common sports such as waterskiing or windsurfing. If history is your thing, don't worry. There's **7** <u>much</u> history round every corner. Ruins from the ancient civilisations that lived here over 3000 years ago are everywhere, and although **8** <u>a lot of</u> people come here just to see the palace, you can find some lesser remains scattered around the surrounding hills.	1 ...*a little*... 2 .... 3 .... 4 .... 5 .... 6 .... 7 .... 8 .... 9 .... 10 .... 11 ....
Visit it **9** <u>some</u> time of the year and you will not be disappointed. Not **10** <u>many</u> places in the world can offer so much. **11** <u>Not any</u> holiday will ever match this one – our island has got it all!	

Academic Reading

*You should spend about 20 minutes on **Questions 1–14** which are based on the Reading Passage below.*

Dressed to dazzle

As high-tech materials invade high-street fashion, prepare for clothes that are cooler than silk and warmer than wool, keep insects at arm's length, and emit many pinpricks of coloured light.

The convergence of fashion and high technology is leading to new kinds of fibres, fabrics and coatings that are imbuing clothing with equally wondrous powers. Corpe Nove, an Italian fashion company, has made a prototype shirt that shortens its sleeves when room temperature rises and can be ironed with a hairdryer. And at Nexia Biotechnologies, a Canadian firm, scientists have caused a stir by manufacturing spider silk from the milk of genetically engineered goats. Not surprisingly, some industry analysts think high-tech materials may soon influence fashion more profoundly than any individual designer.

A big impact is already being made at the molecular level. Nano-Tex, a subsidiary of American textiles maker Burlington, markets a portfolio of nanotechnologies that can make fabrics more durable, comfortable, wrinkle-free and stain-resistant. The notion of this technology posing a threat to the future of the clothing industry clearly does not worry popular fashion outlets such as Gap, Levi Strauss and Lands' End, all of which employ Nano-Tex's products. Meanwhile, Schoeller Textil in Germany, whose clients include famous designers Donna Karan and Polo Ralph Lauren, uses nanotechnology to create fabrics that can store or release heat.

Sensory Perception Technologies (SPT) embodies an entirely different application of nanotechnology. Created in 2003 by Quest International, a flavour and fragrance company, and Woolmark, a wool textile organisation, SPT is a new technique of embedding chemicals into fabric. Though not the first of this type, SPT's durability (evidently the microcapsule containing the chemicals can survive up to 30 washes) suggests an interesting future. Designers could incorporate signature scents into their collections. Sportswear could be impregnated with anti-perspirant. Hayfever sufferers might find relief by pulling on a T-shirt, and so on.

The loudest buzz now surrounds polylactic acid (PLA) fibres – and, in particular, one brand-named Ingeo. Developed by Cargill Dow, it is the first man-made fibre derived from a 100% annually renewable resource. This is currently maize (corn), though in theory any fermentable plant material, even potato peelings, can be used. In performance terms, the attraction for the 30-plus clothes makers signed up to use Ingeo lies in its superiority over polyester (which it was designed to replace).

As Philippa Watkins, a textiles specialist, notes, Ingeo is not a visual trend. Unlike nanotechnology, which promises to transform what clothes can do, Ingeo's impact on fashion will derive instead from its emphasis on using natural sustainable resources. Could wearing synthetic fabrics made from polluting and non-renewable fossil fuels become as uncool as slipping on a coat made from animal fur? Consumers should expect a much wider choice of 'green' fabrics. Alongside PLA fibres, firms are investigating plants such as bamboo, seaweed, nettles and banana stalks as raw materials for textiles. Soya bean fibre is also gaining ground. Harvested in China and spun in Europe, the fabric is a better absorber and ventilator than silk, and retains heat better than wool.

Elsewhere, fashion houses – among them Ermenegildo Zegna, Paul Smith and DKNY – are combining fashion with electronics. Clunky earlier attempts involved attaching electronic components to the fabrics after the normal weaving process. But companies such as SOFTswitch have developed electro-conductive fabrics that behave in similar ways to conventional textiles.

Could electronic garments one day change colour or pattern? A hint of what could be achieved is offered by Luminex, a joint venture between Stabio Textile and Caen. Made of woven optical fibres and powered by a small battery, Luminex fabric emits thousands of pinpricks of light, the colour of which can be varied. Costumes made of the fabric wowed audiences at a production of the opera *Aida* in Washington, DC, last year.

Yet this ultimate of ambitions has remained elusive in daily fashion, largely because electronic textiles capable of such wizardry are still too fragile to wear. Margaret Orth, whose firm International Fashion Machines makes a colour-changing fabric, believes the capability is a decade or two away. Accessories with this chameleon-like capacity – for instance, a handbag that alters its colour – are more likely to appear first.

Questions 1–6

Look at the following list of companies (1–6) and the list of new materials below.

Match each company with the correct material.

Write the correct letter A–H next to the companies 1–6.

NB *You may use any answer more than once.*

1 Corpe Nove ....
2 Nexia Biotechnologies ....
3 Nano-Tex ....

4 Schoeller Textil ....
5 Quest International and Woolmark ....
6 Cargill Dow ....

New materials

A material that can make you warmer or cooler
B clothing with perfume or medication added
C material that rarely needs washing
D clothes that can change according to external heat levels
E material made from banana stalks
F material that is environmentally-friendly
G fibres similar to those found in nature
H clothes that can light up in the dark

Questions 7–14

Complete the summary below.

*Write **NO MORE THAN TWO WORDS** from the Reading Passage for each answer.*

Major changes in fabrics

Using plants

Nanotechnology will bring changes we can see, while the brand called **7** .... will help the environment. Fibre made from the **8** .... plant has better qualities than silk and wool.

Electronics

In first attempts to use electronics, companies started with a material made by a standard **9** .... method and then they fixed **10** .... to the material.

Luminex fabric

• needs a **11** .... to make it work.
• has already been used to make stage **12** ....
• is not suitable for everyday wear because it is too **13** ....

The first products that can change colour are likely to be **14** ....

Grammar focus task

Which of these nouns from the text are countable (C) and which are uncountable (U)? Which is an example of a noun that can be both countable and uncountable? How is it used in the text?

1 materials (paragraph 1) ....C......
2 shirt (paragraph 2) ....
3 heat (paragraph 3) ....
4 technique (paragraph 4) ....
5 sportswear (paragraph 4) ....
6 fibre (paragraph 5) ....
7 clothes (paragraph 6) ....
8 choice (paragraph 6) ....

Referring to nouns

articles; other determiners (demonstratives, possessives, inclusives: *each, every, both, all, either, neither* etc.)

A Context listening

1 You are going to hear a speaker at an environmental awareness conference talking about a European satellite called Envisat. Before you listen, put the words below into two groups: *the environment* and *satellites*.

climate	fully-equipped	global warming	instrument
launch	monitoring	observation	operational costs
outer space	ozone depletion	precise	

2 🎧 **8a** Now listen to the talk and complete the notes below. Write no more than two words or a number for each answer.

> Envisat satellite
> - Envisat was launched **1** ....
> - Envisat has **2** .... instrument systems.
> - In 1990s ESA launched **3** .... and **4** ....
> - ESA will spend 2.3 billion euros over **5** ....
> - This is the same as **6** .... of coffee per person per year.

3 <u>Underline</u> the correct words. **8a◄◄** Listen again to check your answers.

1 Envisat is *a/the* fully equipped observation satellite.

2 *A/The* satellite was launched in 2002.

3 With its ten instrument systems it is equipped with *−/the* best eyes possible and offers everything that *−/the* scientists could wish for.

4 The total cost of the Envisat Programme is 2.3 billion euros over 15 years. Included in *that/this* sum is development and construction of the instruments.

5 *Neither/None* of our countries can afford to let down their environmental guard.

4 Look at your answers to Exercise 3 and answer these questions.

1 Why do we say *a satellite* in sentence 1 and *the satellite* in sentence 2?

2 In sentence 3, why do we use an article before *best*? Why don't we use an article in front of the word *scientists*?

3 In sentence 4, what does *this sum* refer to?

4 In sentence 5, why can't we use *neither*?

B Grammar

1 Articles

a/an

We use *a/an*

- to refer to something for the first time:
  *I'd like to talk to you today about **an exciting development**.*

- to refer to any one from a group of several:
  *Climate protection is **a challenge** for our entire society.* (one of many challenges)

- to classify people or things as belonging to a group:
  *Envisat is **a fully-equipped observation satellite**.* (there are different kinds of satellite)

- to say what job somebody does:
  *My brother is **an engineer**.*

⚠ We can only use *a/an* with singular countable nouns.

the

We use *the*

- when the listener/reader knows which thing we mean (it may have been mentioned before):
  *Envisat is **a fully-equipped observation satellite** ... **The satellite** was launched in 2002.*
  or it is understood which thing we mean:
  *As part of **the conference** on environmental awareness ...* (we are at the conference now so it is clear which one I mean)
  Compare:
  *I went to **a conference** on Environmental awareness last week.* (the person I am talking to does not know which conference I am talking about)

- when there is only one of this thing:
  the earth, the sun, the twentieth century, the sixties, the Government, the Prime Minister (there is only one government and one prime minister in each country)

- for superlatives (see Unit 11):
  *It is equipped with **the best eyes** possible.*

- to talk about playing a musical instrument:
  *He plays **the piano** and she plays **the guitar**.*

- with certain proper nouns:
  nationalities (*the British, the Chinese, the Egyptians*)
  rivers (*the Thames, the Yangtze, the Nile*)
  island groups (*the Maldives, the Philippines, the Seychelles*)
  mountain ranges (*the Alps, the Himalayas*)
  seas and oceans (*the Black Sea, the Mediterranean, the Pacific*)
  country names that represent a group (*the United Kingdom, the United States of America*)
  many famous/historical buildings (*the White House*)
  noun phrases with *of* (*the Great Wall of China, the Temple of Heaven*)
  ⚠ With university names we can say ***the** University **of** Bath* or *Bath University*.

No article

We use no article
- with plural or uncountable nouns to talk generally about things:
  *It will deliver **information** about our changing environment.*
  *It offers everything that **scientists** could wish for.* (scientists in general not a specific group of scientists)

- with certain proper nouns:
  continents (*Europe, Asia*)
  countries (*Australia, China*)
  states or counties (*Michigan, Cambridgeshire*)
  towns and cities (*Tokyo, Jeddah*)
  mountains (*Everest, Kilimanjaro*)
  lakes (*Lake Superior*)
  companies (*Microsoft, Sony*)
  buildings and places with the name of a town (*Heathrow Airport*)

- with mealtimes:
  *I have **lunch** at 12.30.*

- in common expressions after prepositions:
  to/at school/university; to/in class; in prison/hospital/bed

  ⚠ We can use *the/a* if we want to be specific. Compare:
  *When I was a child I used to walk **to school**.*
  *When I was a child I went **to the school on the other side of town**.*

  However, we cannot use an article with the following expressions:
  at home; at/to work; at night; by bus/bicycle/car/train/plane; on foot

2 Demonstratives: *this, that, these, those*

We use these words to show whether something is near or remote, in terms of time or place:

	near	remote
time	*I'd like to talk to you **this morning** about an exciting development.* (today)	*My mother called me later **that day**.* (I am telling you this on a different day)
place	*I like **these pictures**.* (here)	*Oh, I prefer **those** pictures.* (over there)

We can use *this/that/these/those* to refer back to something previously mentioned in the text:
*The total cost of the Envisat programme is 2.3 billion euros over 15 years. Included in **this sum** ...* (this sum = 2.3 billion euros)

We can refer back to whole sentences or ideas with *this* and *that*:
*Seeing the earth from outer space highlights how tiny and fragile our planet is. Envisat helps people to understand **that**.* (= understand how tiny and fragile our planet is)

There is often very little difference between *this* and *that* when used in this way, so we could say:
*Envisat helps people to understand **this**.*

3 Possessives

We use possessive determiners (*my/your/his/her/its/our/their*) to tell us what or who something belongs to:
our blue planet; **their** *children*

⚠ We cannot use possessive determiners after other determiners (e.g. *a*, *the*). We use determiner + noun + *of* + possessive pronoun:
this planet of ours (**not** ~~this our planet~~)

We use *'s* with singular nouns and irregular plural nouns. We use *s'* after regular plural nouns:
Europe's technological showpiece; the children's toys; my parents' house

We usually use noun + *of* instead of *'s* when the thing we are referring to is not a person or animal:
the price of the hotel (**not** ~~the hotel's price~~)

4 Inclusives

each, every

Each and *every* are used with a singular noun and verb.

Each is used for things or people in a group of two or more, with a focus on the individuals in the group:
Each European citizen *has therefore invested seven euros in the environment.*

Every is used for three or more things, with a focus on the group. Often the difference in focus between *each* and *every* is very small:
Every citizen *will have access to precise information about changes in the environment* (= *Each citizen ...*)

We can use *each* (but not *every*) + *of* + noun/pronoun:
Each of the students *gave the teacher a present.* (**not** ~~every of the students~~)

all, most, some

We use *all/most/some* + plural noun and verb to talk about things in general:
Most children *like sweets.*
Some people *believe space exploration is a waste of money.*

We use *all/most/some* + *of* + pronoun or determiner + noun or to refer to a specific group:
Most of the children *at my school play football.*

⚠ We do not need to use *all* + *of* before a noun, but we need *of* before a pronoun:
All the children *at my school play a musical instrument.*
All of them *like music.* (**not** ~~all them~~)

⚠ When *all* is followed by a singular noun referring to time the meaning is different. Compare:
I worked hard **all day**. (= I worked hard for one whole day)
I worked hard **every day**. (= I regularly worked hard)

Both, neither, either, none

Both, *neither* and *either* refer to two people or things. We use *both* + plural noun and *either/neither* + singular noun:

Both *satellites were launched in the 1990s.*
Neither *person knew very much about Envisat before the conference.* (= not one or the other)
I don't mind where we go. **Either** *restaurant is fine.* (= one or the other is fine)

⚠ We use *both* + *of* + determiner + plural noun (or pronoun) with a plural verb. We can use *either/neither* + *of* + determiner + plural noun (or pronoun) with a singular or a plural verb:
Neither of my sisters **lives/live** *in the same town as me.*
Both of them **are** *married.* (**not** ~~Both of them is married.~~)

None means 'not one' (of a group). It can be followed by a singular or plural verb:
None *of our countries* **is/are** *able to ignore the implications of global warming.*

C Grammar exercises

1 In some of these sentences there is a mistake with articles. <u>Underline</u> each mistake and write the correction.

1 My father likes <u>the classical music</u> and listens to it all the time. .....~~the classical music~~.....

2 I saw a man sitting in a restaurant. A woman came and joined him, but the man got up and left without speaking to her! ....✓...............

3 Sun was shining and it was a lovely day. ....

4 I can play piano. ....

5 I come from United Arab Emirates. ....

6 I've applied to study at the University of Edinburgh. ....

7 I usually go to work by the bus. ....

8 My husband is doctor. ....

9 Sorry I'm late – car wouldn't start this morning. ....

10 I'm going to take a cruise down river Nile. ....

11 I once saw a cat wearing a pink coat and boots! ....

12 My husband collects the antiques. He's always going to auctions. ....

2 Fill in the gaps with *a/an* or *the* or put a cross (✗) if no article is needed.

BORNEO BORN AND BRED

1 ....✗.... Local legends say that 2 .... Borneo's few thousand wild elephants are descendants from those brought to 3 .... island from India or Malaysia as 4 .... gift to 5 .... sultan in 6 .... eighteenth century. Biologists from 7 .... Columbia University's Centre for Environmental Research and Conservation compared

DNA samples from Borneo elephants with Asian elephants in Sumatra, India and elsewhere. 8 .... findings confirmed their suspicions: Borneo's elephants are genetically different. In fact 9 .... DNA differences are so great between them and their closest relatives (elephants in Peninsular Malaysia) that 10 .... populations may have separated up to 300,000 years ago, say 11 .... scientists. The animals became isolated when 12 .... island became totally cut off from the mainland due to 13 .... rise in sea level. Borneo's elephants are, therefore, 14 .... important, separate population.

3 Underline the most suitable words.

> **Report on holiday survey**
>
> **1** *This/That* survey aimed to find out about **2** *people's / the people's* ideal holidays. We
> used **3** *the interviews / interviews* and **4** *the questionnaires / questionnaires* to collect
> **5** *our/their* data. **6** *Both/All* of **7** *those/these* methods of data collection were quick and
> simple to carry out and **8** *neither/none* of them were too demanding of the public.
> **9** *Our findings / Findings* show that many people like to take their holidays in the
> summer. **10** *This/The* view was reinforced by the destinations suggested by
> **11** *the people / people* involved in **12** *a survey / the survey*. **13** *The beach holidays /*
> *Beach holidays* were the most popular, particularly in **14** *the Spain / Spain* or **15** *the*
> *France / France*. **16** *Most/Both* people in the survey said they looked forward to their
> holiday. **17** *Each/All* person we interviewed agreed that it was important to have at
> least one holiday **18** *every/all* year. **19** *The price of the holiday / the holiday's price* was
> important to most people, with general agreement that value for money was a
> primary consideration.

4 Fill in the gaps with words from the box.

~~both~~	each	every	my	neither	none	this	that
that	their	those					

My home town is smaller than London, but there are some similarities. **1** *Each* of the
two cities is famous for its architecture. For example, **2** .... Kuala Lumpur and London
have tall, modern buildings, set amongst older historical buildings. Although both cities
have rivers running through them, **3** .... city is by the sea, which is a shame, as I think
some of the most beautiful cities in the world are by the sea.
4 .... major city in the world has one thing in common – being large and busy – and
5 .... is true of both London and Kuala Lumpur. In fact, some people don't like my
city because it is so noisy and busy, but **6** .... is one reason why I love it.
A lot of city markets take place in the day-time, but in **7** .... home city they don't
open until it's dark! Malaysians tend to buy all their groceries at the night markets. In
London people tend to use supermarkets for **8** .... food shopping.
It is always hot in Kuala Lumpur, but London can get very cold. **9** ....'s probably why
you get outdoor restaurants all over Kuala Lumpur all year round whereas in London
there are almost **10** .... in the winter. In some restaurants in Kuala Lumpur, you can
go to the kitchen and point at the food and say, 'I'll have one of **11** ...., please!' You
can't do that in London!

D Test practice

Listening Section 4

Questions 1–2

*Choose the correct letter **A**, **B** or **C**.*

1 Health club membership in Europe
  A has reached 36 million.
  B has declined in recent years.
  C has followed a similar trend to America.

2 If people today ate the same amount as their parents did
  A they would gain weight.
  B they would have more energy.
  C they would feel healthier.

Questions 3–4

*Choose **TWO** letters **A–E**.*

According to the speaker which **TWO** factors have contributed to the change in our fitness levels?

A availability of better food
B different working conditions
C labour-saving devices
D changes in healthcare
E diets which do not work

Question 5

*Choose the correct letter, **A**, **B** or **C**.*

5 Which of the following machines has been available for less than ten years?

A 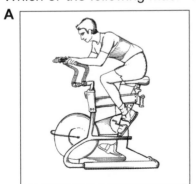   **B**    **C**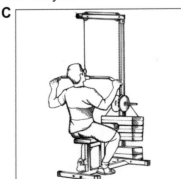

Questions 6–10

Which exercise method do the following statements apply to?
   A using an elliptical trainer
   B running on the road
   C using a treadmill

*Write the correct letter **A**, **B**, or **C** next to Questions 6–10 below.*

6 The impact on the body is more than twice your own body weight.
7 The impact on the body is almost the same as your own body weight.
8 It has the same impact on the body as walking does.
9 It is the best method for losing weight at speeds over 14 kph.
10 It has the highest impact on the joints.

Grammar focus task

Look at the following extracts from the recording. Which words or ideas do the underlined words refer to in the text?

1 Unfortunately, instead of eating less than their parents did, many consume a lot more.
2 On top of this, the change in employment patterns over the past ...
3 And this is where exercise machines come in.
4 That's an amazing number of people
5 As its name implies, the machine delivers an elliptical motion ...
6 In that respect, ellipticals are superior.
7 After that, just keep going and going and going ...

Pronouns and referencing
personal, possessive and reflexive pronouns;
avoiding repetition

9

A Context listening

1 You are going to hear a conversation between Chi Wen, a student from Hong Kong who is studying in Australia, and her homestay host Mrs Smith. Which household chores do you think Chi Wen will have to do?

2 🎧 **9** **Listen and write**

A if Mrs Smith will do this	B if Chi Wen will do this	C if both of them will do it

1 cook dinner   4 make lunches   6 wash sheets

2 make breakfast   5 wash clothes   7 clean the house

3 buy food

3 **9 ◀◀** **Listen again and fill in the gaps.**

1 I can introduce .... to a friend of ...., Yi Ling.

2 I know ....'s really enjoying .... here in Australia.

3 Now, I have had a lot of students staying with .... over the years and I do have a few rules.

4 First of all, my husband and .... want everyone to feel at home so .... treat everyone like ....'re a member of our own family.

5 And what about other meals? Can I cook for ....?

6 Yes, everyone makes their own breakfast and I always make sure there is plenty of food in the fridge so .... can prepare .... a packed lunch if you like.

7 I expect everyone to wash and iron for ....

8 Can I use .... to make local calls?

4 **Put the words you wrote in Exercise 3 into four groups.**

I, ...   me, ...

myself, ...   mine, ...

B Grammar

1 Personal and possessive pronouns

Subject personal pronouns:	*I, you, he, she, it, we, they*
Object personal pronouns:	*me, you, him, her, it, us, them*
Possessive pronouns:	*mine, yours, his, hers, ours, theirs*

We use pronouns to replace nouns and avoid repetition of the noun:
I can introduce you to my friend, Yi Ling. **She***'s a student from Taiwan.* (**not** ~~Yi Ling's a student~~)

We use subject pronouns before verbs:
I *only arrived last month.*

and object pronouns after verbs or prepositions:
I have had a lot of students staying **with me** *over the years.*

We use possessive pronouns to replace a possessive determiner and a noun:
I don't have a phone here. Can I use **yours***?* (= your phone)

⚠ *Its* is not used as a possessive pronoun.

2 Reflexive pronouns

Reflexive pronouns: *myself, yourself, himself, herself, itself, ourselves, yourselves, themselves*

We use reflexive pronouns
◆ when the subject and the object of the verb are the same:
You *can prepare* **yourself** *a packed lunch if you like.*

◆ to add emphasis to the subject or object:
I clean the kitchen and the living areas **myself***.* (= I do it, not anybody else)

◆ with *by* to mean *on my own/on your own* etc.:
I clean the kitchen and the living areas **by myself***.* (= on my own)

◆ after some set expressions in the imperative with *yourself/yourselves*:
Help **yourself***.*   *Look after* **yourself***.* (= be careful)   *Enjoy* **yourselves***.*

⚠ Notice the use of *each other/one another* below:
The boys taught **themselves** *English.* (= each boy taught himself English)
The boys taught **each other/one another** *some new words.* (= each boy taught the other boy some new words)

3 Some special situations

It

We can use *it*

♦ as a subject to start a sentence without carrying any meaning. Often the sentences are about the weather, the time or distance:
It didn't always rain.   It's five o'clock.   It's 10 km from the sea.

♦ to start sentences when the real subject is an infinitive or an *-ing* form:
*It won't take long **to settle in**.* (= to settle in won't take long)

♦ to refer to phrases, whole sentences or ideas:
*I only arrived last month and I am still finding **it** all a bit strange, actually.* (= living in a foreign country)

⚠ We use *there* + *be* + noun phrase to show something exists (or doesn't exist), not *it*:
There's a good coffee shop near here. (**not** ~~It is a good coffee shop near here.~~)

You and *we*

To talk about everybody in general we can use

♦ *you*:
*In Australia **you** often eat sandwiches for lunch.* (= people in Australia)

♦ *we* (when we include ourselves in the group):
We often eat lunch in a bit of a hurry. (= Australian people in general, and the speaker is Australian)

They

We can use *they*

♦ to mean experts or authorities:
They have changed the law recently. (= the government)
They have discovered a new kind of beetle. (= scientists)

♦ when we do not know or do not need to say if the person is male or female:
*I asked a student if **they** liked learning English and they said no!*

One/ones

We can use *one/ones* to avoid repetition of a countable noun:
*I do have a few rules. The most important **one** is that I want everyone to feel at home.* (= the most important rule)

C Grammar exercises

1 Fill in the gaps with *it, its, itself, they, their* or *themselves*.

Anatomy of a bat

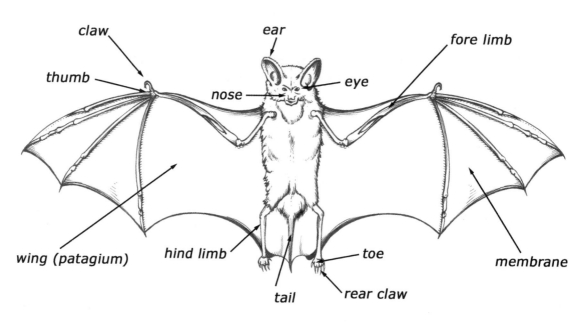

The entire wing of a bat is called the *patagium*. Many species also have a membrane between 1 ......*their*...... hind limbs enclosing the tail. The *patagium* is full of fine blood vessels, muscle fibres and nerves. When it is cold, these bats wrap 2 .... up in 3 .... wings like a coat. In warm weather 4 .... flap 5 .... wings in order to cool 6 .... bodies.

The bat has claws on 7 .... thumbs and sometimes on the toes of 8 .... fore and hind limbs. The rear claws enable 9 .... to hang 10 .... on to a tree branch or ledge.

All bats are active at night or at twilight, so 11 .... eyes are poorly developed. Instead 12 .... use 13 .... nose and ears to orientate 14 ....

2 Find and correct 13 places where nouns could be replaced with the pronouns in the box to make the email sound more natural.

> He   He   he   he   he   him   himself   ~~it~~   it   it   mine
> They   us   yours

To: **Liz Jenkins**

From: **Sandy Moore**

Subject: **University life**

Dear Liz

I'm sorry I haven't emailed you for a while. I'm really busy with my studies at the moment. My course is going well and I'm enjoying ~~my course~~ ^it^ a lot. The trouble is that my course takes up all my time. How is your course going?

I hope you will be able to visit me soon. I'd like you to meet my friends. My best friend here is Paul. Paul lives in the flat next to my flat, and I usually eat most of my meals with Paul. At the moment I'm doing most of the cooking though, because Paul had an accident last week. One of the reasons for the accident is connected to some changes at the university recently. The university authorities have decided that students shouldn't be allowed to bring cars up to the campus, so more and more of the students are cycling. Because of this new rule, Paul was riding his bicycle to the university. While he was cycling along a car driver drove into the back of his bike. The car driver didn't stop and check if he was okay. Luckily Paul was not badly hurt and managed to pick up his bike and get to the doctor's surgery. The doctor said his finger was probably broken and strapped his finger up, so he can't hold anything in his right hand at the moment and Paul can't really cook for Paul.

Anyway, he'd like to meet you, so we must arrange a time for you to come here.

Get in touch soon.
Love, Sandy

---

3 Fill in the gaps with a suitable pronoun or *there*.

Teacher: Do you think that governments spend too much on space exploration nowadays?

Student: Well, I think that **1** ....*there*........ are a lot of different factors to take into consideration. For example some countries want to show the rest of the world that **2** .... are successful and **3** .... can do this with a space exploration program. **4** .... seems that **5** .... is more important for these countries to impress the world than to look after their own people. Sometimes **6** .... is difficult to understand this because every country in the world has **7** .... problems and has poor people that need to be looked after because they can't look after **8** .... So, yes, I do think that these countries should look after people first before **9** .... start trying to send men to the moon! **10** .... are too many other problems here on earth that we need to sort out.

4 <u>Underline</u> the correct words.

There are many reasons why **1** <u>we</u> / they should recycle household waste. The main reason is to avoid using up valuable resources making new things when **2** it is / we are not necessary. However, I do not think the government should make **3** it / the law compulsory for people to recycle their waste.

If the government makes a law that all households must recycle **4** their / its rubbish, **5** the law / it could lead to more problems. For example, how can **6** you / people check that people are recycling everything? **7** It is not practical to do this. / To do this is not practical. In addition, there is the argument that individuals should be allowed to decide for **8** each other / themselves whether to throw something away or to recycle **9** it / something.

I believe the most sensible approach is for the government to put more money into recycling schemes. The most successful are **10** the ones / them where the government gives each household special boxes to put different kinds of waste in, and **11** the government / they provide a regular collection service. **12** They / There are separate boxes for plastic, metal, glass etc. This makes **13** to recycle easier for people / it easier for people to recycle and **14** they / there are therefore less likely to throw things in the rubbish bin.

D Test practice

Academic Writing Task 2

You should spend about 40 minutes on this task.

Write about the following topic.

> *Governments spend millions of dollars each year on their space programmes. Most recently, Mars is the focus of scientists' attention. Some people think this money would be better spent on dealing with problems closer to home.*
>
> *Do you agree or disagree?*

Give reasons for your answer and include any relevant examples from your own knowledge or experience.

You should write at least 250 words.

Grammar focus task

Look at these extracts from a model answer. Match the pronouns (1–5) to the uses (A–E).

... However, some people believe this cannot justify the huge amount of money spent on space research when there is a greater need for **1** <u>it</u> here on earth ...

... For example, the United States and the USSR raced each other to see who could put a man on the moon first. **2** <u>It</u> would have been much easier and cheaper if **3** <u>they</u> had pooled resources and information, and made a joint expedition into space ...

... **4** <u>It</u> is very difficult to argue against these criticisms ...

... In my opinion, **5** <u>we</u> need a balance between how much money is spent on space exploration and how much money is invested into solving problems here on earth. With continued co-operation between nations over space travel more will be achieved for less money. This should leave more money to be spent on problems at home ...

A a subject which doesn't carry a specific meaning

B to refer to *the United States and the USSR*

C to refer to *money*

D to refer to people in general

E to replace an infinitive as a subject

A Context listening

1 You are going to hear a man talking about a recent trip. Look at the following pictures and try to guess which three countries the man visited.

2 🎧 10 Listen to check if you were right.

3 10◀◀ Listen again and complete the table below. Write no more than two words for each answer.

Countries visited	Interesting facts
1	◆ many 2 .... and beautiful mosques
3	◆ travelled there by 4 .... ◆ good for 5 .... ◆ bought a beautiful 6 ....
7	◆ visited Gujarati Textile 8 .... ◆ great examples of 9 .... embroidery ◆ lots of wildlife in 10 .... areas ◆ saw incredible 11 .... birds and several poisonous 12 ....

4 Look at Exercise 3 and make a list of all the adjectives.

......interesting...... ....

....

....

....

B Grammar

1 Adjectives
Adjectives describe nouns.

How adjectives are used
We can use adjectives

◆ before nouns:
*There are so many **historical buildings**.*
*It was well worth the trip, especially if you like **local crafts**.*

◆ after the following verbs: *be, become, get, seem, appear, look, smell, taste, feel*
*The mosques in particular **are very beautiful**.*
*They always **seem pleased** to see you.*

◆ after *find/make/keep* + object:
*Work hard on your research if you want to **make your trip enjoyable** and **rewarding**.*
*I **found the insects** rather **frightening**.*

◆ with other adjectives or with other nouns to describe a noun:
*a **long**, **tiring boat ride*** (adjective + adjective + noun + noun)

The order of adjectives
When we use adjectives together, we put words which express opinion before words which describe the characteristics or type of what we are talking about:
*a **beautiful Turkish** carpet* (*beautiful* = opinion + *Turkish* = type: **not** *a Turkish beautiful carpet*)

We often use nouns as adjectives to add information about type:
*the Gujarati **Textile Museum***

When we use more than one adjective to describe characteristics or type, they usually follow this order:
size → temperature → age → shape → colour → nationality → material → type
Indian silk embroidery   *small mountain villages*
hot black coffee   *a beautiful old round table*

When there are two or more adjectives after a verb or noun, we use *and* between the last two:
*The people are very **welcoming and friendly** towards visitors.*
We use *and* between two colours:
*vivid **blue and green** feathers*

Adjectives ending in *-ed* and *-ing*
Some adjectives connected with feelings are formed from verbs and have two possible forms, usually *-ed* or *-ing* e.g. *tired/tiring*. We use *-ed* forms to talk about how we feel:
*I was **fascinated** to see the extraordinary range of patterns.*
*I was **amazed** at the variety of wonderful animals.*
We use *-ing* forms to describe the things or people that cause the feelings:
*It's an absolutely **amazing** city to visit.*
*India is a **fascinating** country.*

2 Adverbs

Adverbs give information about verbs, adjectives or other adverbs. Adverbs tell us *how* (manner), *where* (place), *when* (time), *how often* (frequency), or *how much* (intensity) something happens or is done. An adverb can be a single word (*sometimes*) or a phrase (*from time to time*).

How adverbs are used

Adverbs which tell us about

♦ **manner** are often formed by adding *-ly* to the adjective form:
   careful → carefully happy → happily
   They usually come after the verb (and object, if there is one):
   I plan my trips **very carefully**. (**not** *I plan very carefully my trips*)

♦ **place** usually come after the verb:
   It was the first time I had been **there**.
   Try to stay **near the old part of the city**.

♦ **time** such as *today, tomorrow, now, since 2003, for three minutes* can go at the beginning or the end of a clause:
   I had a very memorable trip **last year**. (**or** **Last year** *I had a very memorable trip.*)

♦ **frequency** usually come before the verb but after *be* or an auxiliary verb:
   I **often travel** *for my job.*
   I **have always enjoyed** *my visits there.*
   He's **never** *late.*

♦ **intensity** affect the strength of adjectives or adverbs:

fairly, quite,	*very, extremely,*	*absolutely,*
rather, pretty	*highly, really*	*completely, totally*

weaker ⟶ stronger

The adverbs at the stronger end of the scale (*absolutely, completely, totally*) can only be used with some adjectives. These tend to be 'extreme' adjectives that suggest a limit in their meaning (e.g. *terrifying, excellent, exhausted*). Other 'non-extreme' adjectives (e.g. *frightened, good, tired*) never collocate with these stronger adverbs. Compare:
There are some **absolutely stunning** *examples of Indian silk embroidery.* (**not** *fairly stunning*)
The people are **very friendly**. (**not** *absolutely friendly*)
Really collocates with most adjectives.

⚠ We cannot intensify adjectives or nouns which describe type (**not** *a very Textile Museum*).

The order of adverbs

When two or more adverbs are used together at the end of a clause the order is usually manner → place → time:

I'll meet you **outside the station at six o'clock**. (*outside the station* = place, *at six o'clock* = time)

Irregular adverbs

Some adverbs of manner look the same as the adjective form (e.g. *hard, fast, straight, late, early*):

Work **hard** *on your research.* (adverb)
This is a **hard** *exercise.* (adjective)

Hard is an adjective and an adverb, and *hardly* is an adverb meaning *very little*:
He **hardly** *had time to say hello.* (= he had very little time to say hello)

Good is an adjective, and *well* is the adverb:
He spoke **very good** *English.* (describes *English*)
He spoke English **very well**. (describes how he spoke)

However, *well* can also be an adjective when talking about health:
She's not **well** *– she's got a cold.*

Grammar extra: Adjectives

Some adjectives can be followed by *to* + infinitive to add to their meaning (e.g. *able, likely, right, wrong, lucky*) and some adjectives describing feelings (e.g. *surprised, afraid, happy, delighted*):

I'll be **happy to answer** *questions.*
I was **fascinated to see** *the extraordinary range of patterns.*

Some adjectives can be followed by a preposition + *-ing* (see Unit 19):

People are **tired of hearing** *politicians' promises.* (**not** *tired to hear*)
I am not very **good at taking** *photographs.* (**not** *good to take photographs*)

C Grammar exercises

1 Read the test task and the students' responses. Some of the adjectives they used are underlined. If they are used correctly, put a tick (✓). If they are wrong, write the correct answer.

> **Describe a favourite place.**
> **You should say:**
>   **where it is**
>   **what kind of place it is**
>   **what makes it special**
> **and explain why you like it so much.**

My favourite place is a **1** <u>quiet little</u> wood near my home town in Indonesia. I like it because it is a **2** <u>green peaceful</u> place. It is full of **3** <u>old tall</u> trees and there are lots of **4** <u>wild interesting</u> animals.	1 .... ✓ .... 2 .peaceful..green. 3 .... 4 ....
I'm going to tell you about my bedroom. I love it because it is full of my things. The walls are painted with **5** <u>blue yellow</u> stripes, and there is a **6** <u>wooden dark</u> floor. There is a **7** <u>lovely old</u> photo of my family by my bed, and all my precious books are on the shelves.	5 .... 6 .... 7 ....
My favourite place is the town I grew up in. It has **8** <u>an ancient beautiful ruined</u> castle and lots of **9** <u>historical old</u> buildings. The streets are **10** <u>narrow winding</u>, and there are lots of good shops. It is **11** <u>busy noisy</u>, but I like that. I feel good there because I have so many **12** <u>childhood happy</u> memories.	8 .... 9 .... 10 .... 11 .... 12 ....

2 Write the missing adjectives and adverbs.

..dramatic.. – *dramatically*   ..impressive.. – ....slight.... – ....

....steady.... – ....sharp.... – ....steeply.. – ....

Now use the words to fill in the gaps on the next page. Use one pair of words for each question.

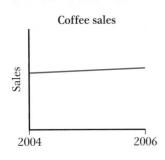

Coffee sales

1 a Sales of coffee showed a ....slight........ increase between 2004 and 2006.

   b Sales of coffee increased ....slightly........ between 2004 and 2006.

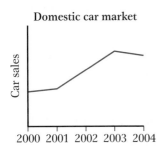

Domestic car market

2 a The domestic car market showed an .... growth of 50% for three consecutive years from 2001 to 2003.

   b The domestic car market grew .... by 50% for three consecutive years from 2001 to 2003.

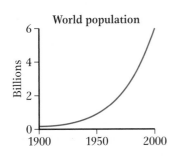

World population

3 a The world population grew .... between 1950 and 2005.

   b The world population experienced a .... growth between 1950 and 2005.

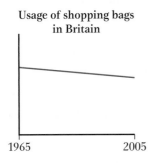

Usage of shopping bags in Britain

4 a The number of British households using their own shopping bags when shopping fell .... between 1965 and 2005.

   b There was a .... fall in the number of British households using their own shopping bags when shopping between 1965 and 2005.

Average house prices

5 a House prices climbed .... during the first half of the year before falling .... in August.

   b There was a .... climb in house prices during the first half of the year before a .... fall in August.

3 Match the beginnings (1–8) and the endings (a–h) of the sentences. Join them by adding a suitable *-ed* or *-ing* adjective formed from one of the verbs in the box. Use each verb once.

excite   frighten   interest   ~~please~~   relax   surprise   tire   satisfy

1 I was really   pleased ..c..   a adventure I've ever had. I can't
                                                        wait to go back!
2 Martin's excellent exam results
   were very   ....   b as he had hardly had time to
3 The jungle was full of strange   study.
   noises and I felt   ....   c when I opened my present
4 After so much hard work, it was   because it was just what I wanted.
   a very   ....   d after exercise.
5 Paula wasn't   ....   e moment when I finally finished
6 Having a warm bath can be very ....   the project.
7 My trip through the jungle was   f so I had a warm bath.
   the most   g during the whole trip.
                          ....   h in the lecture so she fell asleep.
8 After walking so far I felt very ....

4 Underline the correct words.

Environmentalists and conservationists tell us that there are ways that each of us can help to **1** *very reduce / greatly reduce* our impact on the planet. We can **2** *work hard / hardly work* to conserve energy and we can invest in equipment to help us create our own power. People **3** *say often / often say* that they want to save the planet, but the only way to do this is to **4** *take immediately action / take action immediately*.

It is **5** *really important / important really* for individuals to **6** *responsibly act / act responsibly* and try to reduce their contribution to greenhouse gases. There are several ways we can do this. For example there are mini wind turbines that you **7** *can install easily / easily can install* on your roof as well as very efficient solar panels that **8** *work good / work well* all year round to provide electricity.

But if this is all too expensive, there are other ways to conserve energy that actually save you money. In cooler weather, simply keep the heat **9** *inside safely / safely inside* by closing doors after you so that the warmth doesn't escape. It is **10** *absolutely essential / very essential* that we all take this seriously and do our best to lead a more sustainable life.

D Test practice

General Training Reading

Questions 1–8

*Look at the information about five museums **A–E** in Seoul, South Korea.*

For which museum are the following statements true?

*Write the correct letter **A–F** next to Questions 1–8.*

NB *You may write any letter more than once.*

1 This museum also functions as an occasional venue for performing arts. ....

2 You can learn about natural history in this museum. ....

3 This museum is the only one of its kind in Korea. ....

4 This is the most high-tech of the museums. ....

5 A historical building once stood where this museum stands today. ....

6 This museum contains something for the very distant future. ....

7 The exhibits in this museum include objects from the distant past. ....

8 You can take classes one day a week at this museum. ....

A Namsangol Traditional Folk Village

Located just north of Namsan Park, this re-creation of a small village depicts the architecture and gardens of the Chosun Dynasty (1393–1910). There are five restored traditional houses from that era. A large pavilion overlooks a beautiful pond and an outdoor theatre hosts dance and drama performances on weekends. There is also a hall displaying traditional handicrafts and a kiosk selling souvenirs. Recently, a time capsule containing 600 items representing the lifestyle of modern-day people of Seoul was buried to celebrate the city's 600th anniversary. In 2394, it will be opened!

B Eunan Museum

This privately-owned museum displays rare specimens of animals, ores, and species of insects collected from around the world. The building comprises six floors, one under ground and five above. Among the fauna on exhibition are shellfish, insects, butterflies and birds. The collection is housed on the lower floors. On the third floor is a library and the fifth floor has a study room and an ocean exhibition hall. One aim of the museum is to bring animal extinction to the attention of the public.

C National Museum of Korea

This is one of the most extensive museums in Seoul, housing art and archaeological relics from Korean prehistory through to the end of the Chosun Dynasty (1910). Throughout the three-floor museum, there are 4,500 artefacts on display in 18 permanent galleries. Audio guides, touch screens, and video rooms all help to bring the ancient world alive here. In addition to regular exhibitions, the museum offers special educational programs such as public lectures, arts and crafts classes, and special tours.

D Seoul Metropolitan Museum of Art

Established in 1988, this museum is located on the former site of Kyonghee-gung palace. There are four floors with six exhibition halls. The collections include more than 170 Korean paintings, Western paintings and prints. Spend a peaceful and relaxing day amidst beautiful works of art. If you are an art enthusiast and would like to learn, the museum offers art courses every Friday.

E Korea Sports Museum

This is the sole museum in Korea dedicated to sports. It displays about 2,500 items tracing back to 1920, when Korea's first sports organization was founded. You can browse through sports memorabilia such as badges, medals, photographs, trophies, and mascots related to national and international sports events. Make sure not to miss the taekwondo-related exhibits.

Questions 9–14

Read the information below and answer Questions 9–14.

Gear Guide – Buying a Backpack

Most walkers will know the value of a good backpack. Choosing one is a different matter, as any trip to an outdoor shop will reveal. To help, gear expert Peter Hawkins examines the ins and outs of a backpack.

A quick glance through my outdoor trade directory reveals 49 companies that sell or make rucksacks. If they all produce ten backpacks then we have a frightening number for the humble beginner to choose
5 from. So before you set foot in an outdoor shop consider what you want your rucksack for.

The first and most vital consideration is your anticipated load. If your walks are short summer evening strolls then a small sack would be fine, but if your walks are day-long and year-round then your sack will need to be bigger. Mine typically contains a flask, packed lunch, waterproofs, clothing I've peeled off during the day, first aid kit and an emergency shelter. In winter I add a sleeping bag and a torch. I need
10 a sack with a reasonable capacity.

My current backpack is a Craghopper AD30 (30 litres) which is just big enough. Admittedly I do often lead walking parties in remote places so perhaps my added responsibilities cause me to carry more. Compare my list with yours to see if you need as much carrying space.

The second consideration is weight. Choose a light sack, but make sure it can take the weight of what
15 you are carrying and it supports the load comfortably on your back.

The next thing to consider is the rucksack's features. Today you can get quite technically advanced backpacks boasting excellent features: advanced fabrics, a variety of side and lid pockets, loops for walking poles, internal frames, adjustable straps, hip belts and clever ventilation systems to keep your back cool.

You also need to look inside. It may seem obvious, but you should choose a backpack that allows you
20 easy access. Some have narrow necks that make removing bulky items difficult. It's also important to choose a backpack that fits the length of your back. Being six feet I need a long, thin rucksack rather than a short, wider one. If I use the latter, I have a hip belt round my stomach!

Last, and probably least, we have the look of the sack to consider. Obviously you can't see it when it's on your back, but why buy something that won't look good on you? After all, there's no shortage of
25 colours or designs to choose from.

Questions 9–14

Do the following statements agree with the opinions of the writer in the Reading passage?

Next to Questions 9–14 write

YES　　　　*if the statement agrees with the opinions of the writer*
NO　　　　*if the statement contradicts the opinions of the writer*
NOT GIVEN　*if it is impossible to say what the writer thinks about this*

9 Few companies make backpacks. ....

10 When choosing a backpack, people should think about their needs. ....

11 The Craghopper AD30 is more comfortable than other brands. ....

12 Manufacturers still need to solve the problem of backpacks causing your back to get hot. ....

13 A person's physical shape and size is an important consideration when choosing a backpack. ....

14 The style of a backpack is less important than other considerations. ....

Look at the adverbs taken from the second reading passage and say whether each one gives information about time, place, manner, intensity or frequency.

a often (*line 11*)　　..............................

b comfortably (*line 15*)　..............................

c today (*line 16*)　　..............................

d quite (*line 16*)　　..............................

e inside (*line 19*)　　..............................

11 Comparing things

**comparative and superlative adjectives and adverbs;
other ways of comparing; comparing nouns and quantities**

A Context listening

1 You are going to hear a talk comparing the performance of older and younger athletes. Before you listen look at the phrases from the talk. Which ones would you associate with young athletes and which ones would you associate with older athletes?

breaking records	strongest in the world	greatest increases in speed
peak fitness	physical improvement	four minutes quicker each year
Olympics	complete a marathon	set record running times

2 🎧 11 Listen and check if you were right.

3 11◀◀ Listen again and say whether these sentences are true or false. Correct the sentences that are false.

1 Older athletes are getting faster and fitter.

2 Runners aged 50+ are speeding up less rapidly than young runners.

3 Women aged 60–68 running the New York marathon run on average two minutes faster each year.

4 Older athletes are less likely to achieve their peak fitness than younger athletes.

5 People grow weaker because they are less active than when they were younger.

4 Underline the language used to compare in Exercise 3.

1 Which sentences contain adjectives?

2 Which sentences contain adverbs?

3 Which word is used as both an adjective and an adverb?

B Grammar

1 Comparing adjectives

adjective	comparative	superlative
one syllable: *hard*	adjective + *-er*: *harder*	*the* + adjective + *-est*: *the hardest*
one syllable ending in *-e*: *nice*	adjective + *-r*: *nicer*	*the* + adjective + *-st* : *the nicest*
one syllable ending in vowel + consonant: *fat*	adjective with last consonant doubled + *er*: *fatter*	*the* + adjective + consonant doubled + *-est*: *the fattest*
two syllables ending in *-y*: *happy*	adjective ~~y~~ + *ier*: *happier*	*the* + adjective ~~y~~ + *iest*: *the happiest*
two or more syllables: *enjoyable*	*more* + adjective: *more enjoyable*	*the most* + adjective: *the most enjoyable*
Irregular: *good, bad, far*	*better, worse, further/farther*	*the best, the worst, the furthest/farthest*

Comparative adjectives

We use comparative adjectives to compare two or more things, people or places:
*Younger runners will always be **faster** than older runners.*

or the same thing, person or place at two different times:
*I'm much **fitter** than I was last year.*

We use *than* after comparative adjectives to say what we are comparing something with. Sometimes we leave out the *than*-clause if it is clear from the context what we are comparing something with:
*Older athletes are getting **faster and fitter**. (than in the past)*

Superlative adjectives

We use superlative adjectives to compare one thing in a group with all the others in that group:
*The Olympics is probably **the most exciting** sports event in the sports calendar.*

We can modify superlatives with
◆ *one of the / some of the* + superlative + plural noun:
   *It's one of the few chances we get to see **some of the best athletes** in the world competing against each other.*
   *Tamsin is **one of the most generous people** I know.*
◆ ordinal numbers:
   *Our team was **the third best** in the competition.*

We can replace *the* with a possessive:
***my** best friend*
***his** greatest achievement*

2 Comparing adverbs

We can compare how things are done by using *more/most* + adverb:
*Runners aged 50 and over are speeding up **more rapidly** than younger people.*
*Women aged 60 to 68 improved **the most markedly**.*

Adverbs that have the same form as the adjective (e.g. *hard, fast, straight, late, early, quick*) add
-er/-est:
*Women aged 60 to 68 run on average four minutes **faster** each year.*

There are some irregular adverbs (e.g. *well, better, best; badly, worse, worst; far, further, furthest; little, less, least*):
*I did **worse** than I had expected in the exam, so I was disappointed.*

3 Other ways of comparing

We use *less/the least* to mean the opposite of *more/the most*:
*You might imagine that the Masters Games would be **less** exciting to watch.*
*That was probably **the least** enjoyable meal I've ever had!*

We can add emphasis
♦ with words like *even, far, a great deal, a little, a lot, much* + comparative:
  *Older women showed **much greater** increases in speed than expected.*

♦ in formal English with words like *slightly, considerably, significantly* + comparative:
  *The figures for 2003 were **significantly higher** than those for the year 2000.*
  *The number of women in higher education was **only slightly lower** than the number of men.*

⚠ We cannot use *very* with comparatives (**not** ~~the number of women was very lower~~).

We can say two things are the same or similar with *as* + adjective/adverb + *as*:
*My car is **as old as** yours.* (= the two cars are the same age)
*Older athletes are **as likely** to achieve their peak fitness **as** younger athletes.* (= they have the same chance of achieving this)

We can add to the meaning by using *just, almost, nearly, half, twice, three times* etc.:
*In 2005, our team was **almost as successful as** in 2003.*
*He can run **twice as fast as** the others in his team.*

We can say two things are different with *not as* + adjective/adverb + *as*:
*While they may **not** be **as fast as** their younger counterparts ...*

We can show that a change is happening over time by repeating the comparative:
*Each year athletes seem to be getting **better and better**.*
*Our atmosphere is gradually becoming **more and more polluted**.*
*It seems **less and less likely** that there will be a general election this year.*

We use *the* + comparative + *the* + comparative to show that two things vary or change at the same time:
*It would seem that **the longer** athletes keep competing **the greater** their chances of setting new records are.*
The sooner the better.

4 Comparing quantities

quantifier	comparative	superlative
a lot / much / many	more	the most
a few	fewer (+ plural countable noun)	the fewest (+ plural countable noun)
a little	less (+ uncountable noun)	the least (+ uncountable noun)

For plural or uncountable nouns we can compare quantities with *more* or *most*:

*Today's top sportspeople receive a lot **more money** than in the past.*

We can use *fewer* or *the fewest* with plural countable nouns, and *less* or *the least* with uncountable nouns:

*25 years ago few 60-year-old men and even **fewer women** would have considered running a marathon.*
*There used to be **less information** available about fitness.*

We can add emphasis
◆ with *a lot / many* + *more / fewer* + plural countable noun:
  *Increased sponsorship has given today's athletes **many more opportunities** to succeed.*

◆ with *a lot / much* + *more / less* + uncountable noun:
  *Today's athletes need to do **much more training** than in the past.*

◆ by repeating *more/less/fewer*:
  *So much in our society is about making **more and more money**.*

We can say something is the same or different using (*not*) *as many/much* + plural/uncountable noun (+ *as*):

*There aren't **as many people** doing sports at school (as there used to be).*

We can add more specific information about quantity by using *half, twice, three times* etc. with *as many/much ... as*:

*In 2004 China won nearly **twice as many** silver medals **as** the US.*
*The US won more than **three times as many** medals **as** Great Britain.*

Grammar extra: Comparing nouns
We can compare how similar things are using *like, the same (as), similar to*:
*Older athletes can achieve **the same** degree of physical improvement **as** those in their twenties and thirties.*
*He swims **like** a fish.*
*This film is **similar to** this director's last one.*

C Grammar exercises

1 Fill in the gaps with the adjectives in the box in a comparative or superlative form.

| brave | effective | exciting | expensive | ~~fast~~ | happy | good | heavy | small |

1 I travelled through Turkey by train because it was _the fastest_ way to cross the country.
2 Scientists have discovered a tiny bacteria living in the deep ocean. They say it is .... living organism known to man.
3 It is almost impossible to find a parking space in the city centre so it is .... to travel by public transport if you need to go there.
4 Pain killers are much .... now so they reduce pain a lot faster than in the past.
5 I like all kinds of sports, but I think football is .... game to watch because it is so fast-moving.
6 Nick did a bungee-jump, but I was too scared. He's much .... than me.
7 I think people from the north of my country are .... than people from the south. In the south no one ever seems to smile, but it's the opposite in the north.
8 The website listed hotels in a wide price range. I was amazed that the .... ones cost over $500 a night.
9 Weightlifters these days are lifting .... weights than ever before.

2 Fill in the gaps with the words in brackets in a comparative or superlative form.

Teacher: What are 1 _the most obvious_ (obvious) differences you have noticed between your own country and this one?

Student: Oh there are so many! In my country people are 2 _not as interested_ (not/interested) in foreigners as people here, who are much 3 .... (friendly). They are always kind and welcoming. Also, the weather is very different. It's much 4 .... (hot) in my country. It's only autumn but I am feeling cold here already and it's getting 5 .... (cold) every day. I don't like that. Then there's the food. Your food is 6 .... (not/good) ours. Our food is 7 .... (spicy) and 8 .... (delicious). I think it's 9 .... (good) in the world! It is 10 .... (not/expensive) either. I've also noticed that people here eat slightly 11 .... (early) and they eat their meals 12 .... (quickly). And I am beginning to change my own habits too! 13 .... (long) I stay here 14 .... (fast) I seem to be eating.

3 Fill in the gaps in the model answer below. Use one word in each gap.

The charts below show the number and types of books bought by men and women and four different age groups in the UK.

Summarise the information by selecting and reporting the main features, and make comparisons where relevant.

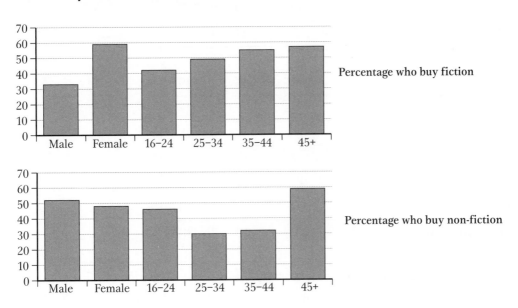

The charts give information about the types of books that British men and women and different age groups buy. The initial impression from the charts is that women tend to buy **1** .... *more* .... books than men overall, although they buy slightly **2** .... non-fiction books. The people that buy the **3** .... books are in the 45+ age group.

Nearly 60% of women buy fiction, which is almost **4** .... as many as the number of men who choose this type of book. Nevertheless, most age groups buy **5** .... fiction books than non-fiction ones showing that non-fiction is generally **6** .... popular than fiction.

The number of people buying fiction increases steadily from ages 16 to 45 with the **7** .... number of books, at just over 40% of the age group, bought by 16- to 24-year-olds and the **8** .... number, at just over 50%, bought by the over 45s.

However, the pattern is different for non-fiction. The number of books bought by 25- to 44-year-olds is **9** .... lower than the number bought by 16- to 24-year-olds and those over 45. Just over 40% of 16- to 24-year-olds buy non-fiction, but this number is not **10** .... high as the number of people aged 45 and over buying non-fiction, at nearly 60%. Only 31% of 35- to 44-year-olds buy non-fiction, and the number of 24- to 34-year-olds is **11** .... lower at 28%.

4 Read the description of the table below. Decide if the <u>underlined</u> comparisons are correct or not. Tick (✓) them if they are right and correct them if they are wrong.

2004 Olympic Games Medal Table					
Rank	Country	Gold	Silver	Bronze	Total
1	United States	35	39	29	103
2	China	32	17	14	63
3	Russia	27	27	38	92
4	Australia	17	16	16	49
5	Japan	16	9	12	37
6	Germany	14	16	18	48
7	France	11	9	13	33
8	Italy	10	11	11	32
9	South Korea	9	12	9	30
10	Great Britain	9	9	12	30

The table shows the number of medals won by the top ten countries in the 2004 Olympic Games. The USA won **1** <u>greatest</u> number of medals overall with a total of 103. They won **2** <u>more silver medals as gold</u> and **3** <u>more medals than</u> any other country in both categories. China had **4** <u>the second high</u> number of medals at 63, but unlike the USA, China won **5** <u>less silver medals than gold medals</u>. While Russia's silver medal total was **6** <u>more good than</u> China's, they did not do **7** <u>well as</u> China in the gold medals, winning just 27. In fact China had a **8** <u>more lower</u> overall medal total than Russia but, as the table is based on the number of gold medals won, they were placed second. Similarly, Germany was **9** <u>significantly successful</u> at winning medals than Japan, with a total of 48 compared to Japan's 37, but because Japan won **10** <u>two more gold medals that</u> Germany they were ranked **11** <u>higher</u>. Great Britain gave **12** <u>the worse</u> performance in this group, winning only nine gold and nine silver medals.

1 *the greatest*
2 ....
3 ....
4 ....
5 ....
6 ....
7 ....
8 ....

9 ....
10 ....
11 ....
12 ....

D Test practice

Academic Writing Task 1

You should spend about 20 minutes on this task.

> **The chart below shows the average hours worked per day by married men and women in paid employment.**
>
> **Summarise the information by selecting and reporting the main features, and make comparisons where relevant.**

You should write at least 150 words.

Hours worked by married men and women in paid employment

Grammar focus task

Fill in the gaps in the following sentences using the correct form of the words in brackets and any other words you need.

1 The total number of hours worked by married women with children is .... (great) the total number of hours worked by men.

2 Whilst women aged 45 to 64 may work .... (few) hours inside the home than younger women, overall they work .... (great) number of hours per day due to the extra hours of paid work that they do.

3 Men aged 25 to 44 spend only .... (slight/more) time working outside the home than men aged 45 to 64, but this figure is .... (significant/high) the number of hours of paid work that women of the same age do.

4 Women in the 25 to 44 age group work almost .... (many) hours inside the home as outside, and there is only a slight difference in the 45 to 64 age group.

5 However, men work on average .... (three/long) outside the home than inside.

12 The noun phrase
noun + prepositional phrase; noun + participle clause; noun + *to*-infinitive clause

1 You are going to hear a woman giving a talk about a project she is involved in. Before you listen look at the pictures and the words below. What do you think the purpose of the project is?

> abundance   analyze   calculate   car tyres   conservation   debris   diver
> habitat   harbour   reef   rope   rubble   seahorses   species   submerged

2 🎧 **12** Listen and see if you were right. What did the study show? What did the woman's team decide to do?

3 **12◀◀** Listen again and match the beginnings (1–8) and endings (a–h) of these phrases. Stop the recording when you need to.

1 this horrible rubbish		a	with bright red bodies
2 the idea		b	of the past
3 the areas		c	of putting rubbish into the harbour
4 other debris		d	with submerged rubbish
5 sea tulips		e	to expand our study
6 a decision		f	lying on the sea floor
7 the rubble		g	cleared of rubbish
8 other possible sites		h	lying at the bottom of the harbour

4 Add the phrases from Exercise 3 to the table below.

noun + preposition	noun + past participle	noun + -*ing*	noun + *to*-infinitive
the idea of putting rubbish into the harbour		this horrible rubbish lying at the bottom of the harbour	

B Grammar

The noun phrase

A noun phrase is a group of words with a noun as its main part. Information about the noun can be before the noun and/or after the noun.

Information that comes before the noun in a noun phrase is usually expressed through
- determiners (see Unit 8):
  this horrible rubbish
- adjectives and adverbs (see Unit 10):
  a *rich* habitat

Information that comes after the noun is usually expressed through
- prepositional phrases:
  an abundance **of** creatures
- past participle clauses:
  the rubbish **contained** in the harbour
- present participle (-*ing*) clauses:
  the rubbish **lying** at the bottom of the harbour
- *to*-infinitive clauses:
  a decision **to expand**

1 Noun + prepositional phrase

We can add information after a noun by using a prepositional phrase. Common prepositions in these phrases are *of, in, for, on, to, with*:
possible sites **with submerged rubbish**
a rich habitat **for an abundance of creatures**

Of is the most common preposition used in prepositional noun phrases. It is used after nouns of quantity or containers:
the **number of** fish   an **abundance of** creatures (quantities)
a **bottle of** water   a **packet of** biscuits (containers)

We also use *of* to show belonging or possession (see Unit 8):
the rubble **of the past** (**not** ~~the past's rubble~~)
particular areas **of the harbour**

We often use *at, in* and *on* to talk about physical location:
this rubbish lying **at the bottom** of the harbour
different species living **in Sydney Harbour**

Prepositional phrases containing *with* often express the same information as a relative clause with the main verb *have*:
harbour sites **with submerged rubbish** (= harbour sites which have submerged rubbish)
sea tulips **with bright red bodies** (= sea tulips which have bright red bodies)

2 Noun + past participle clause

A past participle clause gives the same information as a relative clause (see Unit 20) with a passive verb:

*all of the rubbish **contained in the harbour*** (= rubbish which is contained in the harbour)
*areas **cleared of rubbish*** (= areas which have been cleared of rubbish)
*the data **collected from the sites*** (= the data which is collected from the sites)

In both spoken and written English using a noun + past participle clause is more common than the equivalent relative clause because it can express the same information in fewer words.

3 Noun + present participle (*-ing*) clause

A present participle clause can give the same information as a relative clause with an active verb, often in the present or past continuous:

*the other debris **lying on the sea floor*** (= the other debris which is lying on the sea floor)

As in section 2 above, the noun + present participle clause is more common than the equivalent relative clause.

4 Noun + *to*-infinitive clause

To-infinitive clauses are used to show a purpose or intention and usually follow nouns of time, place, manner and quantity:

*time **to go***
*the place **to visit***
*a way **to look at it***
*a lot **to look at***

Nouns followed by the *to*-infinitive are related to verbs also followed by the *to*-infinitive (e.g. *decide/decision*; *plan/plan*):

*a decision **to expand*** (decide to)
*our plan **to build** a new hospital* (plan to)

C Grammar exercises

1 Fill in the gaps with *of, in, for, on, to* or *with*.

1 My family live in an old, wooden house ...with... shutters.
2 Our main meal .... the day usually includes rice and vegetables.
3 She got the best exam results .... the whole school.
4 At a wedding reception in Britain, all the guests usually get a piece .... the cake.
5 In my country there are special universities .... talented sportsmen and women.
6 You need a large amount .... money if you want to travel around the world.
7 My recent business trip .... Florida was a great success.
8 The house .... the corner is for sale.
9 The weather .... Greece is wonderful compared with here.
10 You should buy a grammar book .... answers, so that you can practise by yourself.

2 Fill in the gaps with the present or past participle of the verbs in brackets.

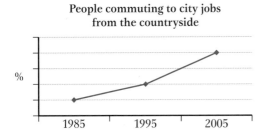

People commuting to city jobs from the countryside

1 The information ....given........ (*give*) in the graph shows that more and more people .... (*work*) in towns and cities prefer to live in the countryside and commute to work. The number of people .... (*move*) out of towns and cities increased significantly between 1985 and 2005.

2 Our awareness of food quality has changed recently with more people .... (*buy*) organic food and eggs and meat .... (*produce*) from animals that live in natural, comfortable conditions. Since 1980 the quantity of food .... (*grow*) organically in the UK has risen steadily.

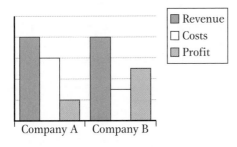

Revenue
Costs
Profit

Company A   Company B

3 The graph gives information .... (*concern*) sales and profits of two manufacturing companies. Company A sells pencils .... (*make*) in the UK, whereas Company B sells pencils .... (*manufacture*) overseas. Company B has lower costs .... (*result*) in a higher annual profit.

3 Join the two sentences to make one sentence using a noun phrase. Add prepositions where necessary.

1 I live in Malaysia. I live in the capital city.

   I live in the .... *capital city of* .... Malaysia.

2 Many people buy their own home. The number is increasing.

   The number of .... increasing.

3 A proposal was made by the education department. It was rejected by the government.

   The proposal .... the government.

4 We have computer software. The software's purpose is to predict future earthquakes.

   We have computer software .... earthquakes.

5 A new dictionary is about to be published. The dictionary contains more words than ever before.

   A new dictionary .... to be published.

6 My favourite novel is a story. The story is based on the author's own experience.

   My favourite novel .... own experience.

4 Use noun phrases to replace the underlined sentences.

> **Describe a holiday you have had that was successful.**
> **You should say:**
>   **when the holiday took place**
>   **who you went with**
>   **why it was successful.**

with my friends

I recently had a wonderful holiday in Crete ∧. **1** ~~I went with my friends.~~ When we arrived we saw a bus. **2** The bus was waiting to take us to our hotel. The hotel was nice with good views. **3** The views were of the sea. The location was also very good. **4** There was lots to do nearby. There are lots of Minoan sites. **5** You can visit them. It's a lovely island.

6 It has beautiful beaches. We spent our time sightseeing, lying on the beach and walking. Actually, it was the walking that I liked best. We did one amazing walk. **7** It was through the Samarian Gorge. It took all day, but was well worth it. We saw a snake. **8** The snake was curled up on a rock. And lots of lizards and birds. We got really hot and were very tired when we arrived at the beach at the end of the long walk. It was great to see the sea. **9** It was sparkling in the sun. We ran into the water to cool down. It was the best holiday ever.

Academic Reading

*You should spend about 20 minutes on **Questions 1–12** which are based on the Reading Passage below.*

Practical intelligence lends a hand

Dr Rajendra Persaud explains how practical intelligence is linked to success.

This year, record numbers of high school students obtained top grades in their final exams, yet employers complain that young people still lack the basic skills to succeed at work. The only explanation offered is that exams must be getting easier. But the real answer could lie in a study just published by Professor Robert Sternberg, an eminent psychologist at Yale University in the USA and the world's leading expert on intelligence. His research reveals the existence of a totally new variety: practical intelligence.

Professor Sternberg's astonishing finding is that practical intelligence, which predicts success in real life, has an inverse relationship with academic intelligence. In other words, the more practically intelligent you are, the less likely you are to succeed at school or university. Similarly, the more paper qualifications you hold and the higher your grades, the less able you are to cope with problems of everyday life and the lower your score in practical intelligence.

Many people who are clearly successful in their place of work do badly in standard IQ (academic intelligence) tests. Entrepreneurs and those who have built large businesses from scratch are frequently discovered to be high school or college drop-outs. IQ as a concept is more than 100 years old. It was supposed to explain why some people excelled at a wide variety of intellectual tasks. But

IQ ran into trouble when it became apparent that some high scorers failed to achieve in real life what was predicted by their tests.

Emotional intelligence (EQ), which emerged a decade ago, was supposed to explain this deficit. It suggested that to succeed in real life, people needed both emotional as well as intellectual skills. EQ includes the abilities to motivate yourself and persist in the face of frustrations; to control impulses and delay gratification; to regulate moods and keep distress from swamping the ability to think; and to understand and empathize with others. While social or emotional intelligence was a useful concept in explaining many of the real-world deficiencies of super intelligent people, it did not go any further than the IQ test in measuring success in real life. Again, some of the most successful people in the business world were obviously lacking in social charm.

Not all the real-life difficulties we face are solvable with just good social skills – and good social acumen in one situation may not translate to another. The crucial problem with academic and emotional intelligence scores is that they are both poor predictors of success in real life. For example, research has shown that IQ tests predict only between 4% and 25% of success in life, such as job performance.

Professor Sternberg's group at Yale began from a very different position to traditional researchers into intelligence. Instead of asking what intelligence was and investigating whether it predicted success in life, Professor Sternberg asked what distinguished people who were thriving from those that were not. Instead of measuring this form of intelligence with mathematical or verbal tests, practical intelligence is scored by answers to real-life dilemmas such as: 'If you were travelling by car and got stranded on a motorway during a blizzard, what would you do?' An important contrast between these questions is that in academic tests there is usually only one answer, whereas in practical intelligence tests – as in real life – there are several different solutions to the problem.

The Yale group found that most of the really useful knowledge which successful people have acquired is gained during everyday activities – but typically without conscious awareness. Although successful people's behaviour reflects the fact that they have this knowledge, high achievers are often unable to articulate or define what they know. This partly explains why practical intelligence has been so difficult to identify.

Professor Sternberg found that the best way to reach practical intelligence is to ask successful people to relate examples of crucial incidents at work where they solved problems demonstrating skills they had learnt while doing their jobs. It would appear that one of the best ways of improving your practical intelligence is to observe master practitioners at work and, in particular, to focus on the skills they have acquired while doing the job. Oddly enough, this is the basis of traditional apprentice training. Historically, the junior doctor learnt by observing the consultant surgeon at work and the junior lawyer by assisting the senior barrister.

Another area where practical intelligence appears to resolve a previously unexplained paradox is that performance in academic tests usually declines after formal education ends. Yet most older adults contend that their ability to solve practical problems increases over the years. The key implication for organizations and companies is that practical intelligence may not be detectable by conventional auditing and performance measuring procedures. Training new or less capable employees to become more practically intelligent will involve learning from the genuinely practically intelligent rather than from training manuals or courses.

Perhaps the biggest challenge is in recruitment, as these new studies strongly suggest that paper qualifications are unlikely to be helpful in predicting who will be best at solving your company's problems. Professor Sternberg's research suggests that we should start looking at companies in a completely different way – and see them as places where a huge number of problems are being solved all the time but where it may take new eyes to see the practical intelligence in action.

Questions 1–5

*Choose the correct answer, **A**, **B**, **C** or **D**.*

1 Professor Sternberg's study showed that
  A qualifications are a good indicator of success at work.
  B education can help people cope with real-life problems.
  C intelligent people do not always achieve well at school.
  D high grades can indicate a lack of practical intelligence.

2 What is the 'deficit' referred to in the fourth paragraph?
  A People with high IQ scores could not score well in EQ tests.
  B EQ tests were unable to predict success at work.
  C High IQ scores did not always lead to personal success.
  D People with high EQ scores could not cope with real life.

3 Professor Sternberg's research differed from previous studies because
  A he used verbal testing instead of mathematics.
  B he began by establishing a definition of intelligence.
  C he analyzed whether intelligence could predict success in real life.
  D he wanted to find out what was different about successful people.

4 Part of the reason why practical intelligence had not been identified
  before Professor Sternberg's study is that
  A the behaviour of successful people had never been studied.
  B successful people are too busy with their everyday lives.
  C successful people cannot put their knowledge into words.
  D successful people are unaware of their own abilities.

5 In order to increase the practical intelligence of employees, companies need to
  A adopt an apprentice-style system.
  B organise special courses.
  C devise better training manuals.
  D carry out an audit on all employees.

Questions 6–12

Classify the following characteristics as belonging to

   A academic intelligence (IQ) tests
   B emotional intelligence (EQ) tests
   C practical intelligence tests

*Write the correct letter **A**, **B** or **C**, next to Questions 6–12 below.*

6 measures skills which are likely to improve with age
7 assesses people's social skills
8 measures the ability to deal with real-life difficulties
9 the oldest of the three tests
10 high scorers learn from their actions
11 high scorers are more likely to stay calm in difficult situations
12 questions have more than one possible answer

Grammar focus task

Look at the first paragraph of the text and find one example of each of the following types of noun phrase:

1 noun + prepositional phrase

2 noun + past participle clause

3 noun + *to*-infinitive

A Context listening

1 You are going to hear two doctors discussing a patient. Before you listen look at the newspaper headline and guess how it relates to the patient.

THE **Morning Herald**

Does anyone know who this man is?

Today's top stories

2 🎧 **11** Listen and check if you were right.

3 **11◄◄** Listen again and say whether the sentences below are true or false. Correct the sentences that are false.

1 The patient could remember all his personal details.

2 The patient definitely came from Yorkshire.

3 The patient could speak French and Italian.

4 Joe thinks that the patient might have been running away from something.

5 Joe thinks that the patient was definitely unmarried.

6 The patient has been unable to make contact with anyone he knows.

7 Deborah thinks that the patient can't have hit his head.

8 Deborah thinks that the patient will never recover his memory.

4 <u>Underline</u> these words in the questions and answers in Exercise 3.

could	couldn't	might	be able to	must	can't	will

1 Which words refer to ability?

2 Which words refer to certainty or impossibility?

3 Which words refer to possibility?

B Grammar

Modal verbs (*can, could, may, might, must, will, would, shall, should, ought to, need*) are auxiliary verbs that give information about ability, possibility or necessity.

Modal verbs are followed by the infinitive without *to* and their form doesn't change:
*He **could speak** French and Italian.* (**not** ~~He coulds speak~~)
***Could** you **speak** French before you lived there?* (**not** ~~Did you could speak~~)

1 Ability

We use the following verbs to talk about ability:

Present	*can, can't, be able to, manage to*	*I **can't** swim.*
Past	*could, couldn't, be able to, manage to*	*They **weren't able to** find out his name.*
Perfect	*be able to, manage to*	***Have** you **managed to** finish the report yet?*
Future	*be able to, manage to*	*I **won't be able to** meet you later.*

It is more common to use *can/could* to talk about general ability in the present and past than *be able to*:
***Can** you remember much about it?* (= Are you able to remember?)
*He **could** speak French and Italian, but he couldn't remember his name.*

To talk about ability on one specific occasion in the past we use *couldn't, was(n't)/were(n't) able to*, but not *could*:
*The police **were able to** find out that he could speak French and Italian.* (**not** ~~The police could find out~~)
*He **couldn't** remember who he was.*

We sometimes use *manage to* to show that something is difficult to achieve:
*I've finally **managed to** give up smoking after all these years!*

We use *be able to* or *manage to* with perfect or future forms:
*Apparently he's **been able to** find his family.*
*Within a year he'll probably **be able to** remember quite a lot.* (**not** ~~Within a year he can probably remember quite a lot.~~)

2 Other uses of *can*

We use *can* to mean *sometimes*:
*People **can do** funny things when they've experienced something terrible.* (= people sometimes do funny things)

We also use *can* to ask for and give permission:
***Can I** borrow the car this afternoon?*
***You can** borrow it, but I need it later this evening.*

3 Possibility

We use *must, may, might, could, couldn't* and *can't* when there is some evidence, information or belief that something is probably or possibly true (or not true). The modal verb we choose depends on the strength of the evidence we have to support our ideas.

very likely	*must*
possible	*might, may, could, may not, might not*
very unlikely	*can't, couldn't*

Could, may and *might* express the same degree of possibility:
*He **may/might/could** remember some things already.*

Couldn't expresses the same probability as *can't*. It is usually used to talk about the past:
*The police realised he **couldn't** be Canadian.* (= it was very unlikely that he was Canadian)

⚠ *May not* and *might not* do not express the same probability as *couldn't*:
*The supermarket **may/might not** be open today because it's a Bank Holiday.* (**not** ~~the supermarket couldn't be open~~)

Present

We use *may (not), might (not), could(n't), must, can't* + infinitive without *to* to talk about possibility in the present:
*He **may remember** some things already.* (= it is possible he remembers some things now)
*It **can't be** very easy living with someone who doesn't remember any of the past.* (= it is very unlikely that it is easy)

We use *may (not), might (not), could(n't), must, can't* + be + -ing to talk about things (possibly) happening or in progress at the time of speaking:
*They **must be having** a difficult time adjusting to it all.*
*The phone is engaged. She **might be talking** to her sister on the phone.*

Past

We can use *may (not), might (not), could(n't), must, can't* + have + past participle to talk about possibility in the past:
*In the attack he **must have hit** his head.* (= there is strong evidence that he hit his head)
*He **could have had** a wife and children.* (this is a possible situation)
*He **can't have been** married.* (= there is strong evidence that he wasn't married)

We can use *may (not), might (not), could(n't), must, can't* + have been + -ing to talk about things possibly happening or in progress in the past:
*He **might have been trying** to run away from his past.*

Future

We can use *may (not)*, *might (not)*, and *could (not)* + infinitive without *to* to talk about possibility or uncertainty in the future:
He could make a total recovery one day.

We can use *may (not)*, *might (not)*, *could (not)*, *must*, *can't* + *be* + *-ing* to talk about things possibly happening at a time in the future:
I might be meeting John later.

4 Expressing possibility and opinions in written texts

Modals are very important in written texts because they 'soften' the message and help to show that the author is expressing an opinion rather than a proven fact. *May* is very common in these kinds of texts as well as *can* used to mean 'sometimes'. (see B3)

Compare these sentences and the teacher's comments:

Student's work	Teacher's comment
People are unkind about their colleagues but it is simply because they are feeling insecure at work.	How do you know this?
People can be unkind about their colleagues but it may simply be because they are feeling insecure at work.	Good sentence.
Banning cars with high fuel consumption is a good idea, as it will result in less pollution.	This is a very strong opinion.
Banning cars with high fuel consumption may be a good idea, as it could result in a less pollution.	Good sentence. You are making your opinion 'softer'.

5 Alternatives to modals

Adverbs like *certainly*, *probably*, *possibly*, *perhaps* and *maybe* can be used to express similar ideas to modal verbs:
He had probably been attacked and robbed. (= he must have been attacked)

We can use *it* + *be* + *certain/likely/probable/possible/impossible* to express ability, probability and possibility:
It is possible to program your computer to translate texts automatically. (= you can program your computer)
It is possible that the train will be late. (= the train might be late)

C Grammar exercises

1 Underline the most suitable words. Sometimes both options are possible.

1 He's a concert pianist and he <u>can</u> / *manages to* play all Beethoven's sonatas.

2 When I lived in a small town I *was able to* / *could* walk almost everywhere, but now I live in the capital city I need a car.

3 They worked all night and *could* / *managed to* finish the report just in time.

4 The protestors *didn't manage to* / *couldn't* persuade the president to change the law.

5 Next year she *can* / *will be able to* join the club, but she's not old enough yet.

6 In my country it *can* / *is able to* get very cold in the winter.

7 I was nearly late as the bus didn't come, but luckily I *could* / *managed to* get a taxi.

8 I hope that I *will be able to* / *will manage to* do some sightseeing when I'm in New York next week on business, but I've got a busy schedule.

9 She didn't get good enough grades to go to her first choice of university but she *could* / *was able to* get a place at another one.

2 Tick (✓) the sentence, a or b, which best matches the sentence on the right.

1a He might be British.	He has a British passport.
b He must be British. ✓	
2a Our teacher can't be off sick.	I just saw him in the corridor talking to a student.
b Our teacher may not be off sick.	
3a It can be cold in Delhi in December.	I advise you to take some warm clothes just in case.
b It must be cold in Delhi in December.	
4a John can't have been working late last night.	He wasn't home when I called at seven.
b John might have been working late last night.	
5a He can't be a millionaire.	He has shares in the most successful company of all time.
b He must be a millionaire.	
6a I may come to the lecture this afternoon.	It depends if I finish my essay before then.
b I must come to the lecture this afternoon.	
7a The exam may have been very difficult.	Not many people passed it.
b The exam must have been very difficult.	
8a John couldn't know how to get here.	We will have to give him directions.
b John might not know how to get here.	

3 Replace the underlined phrases with a suitable past modal phrase.

The mummy of Djedmaatesankh, a young woman from the ninth century BC, lies behind a glass display in the Royal Ontario Museum. 2,800 years ago she lived in Thebes with her husband on the east bank of the river Nile. They were well-off, although as a double-income couple without children 1 ~~it is likely they were~~ rather unusual. Djedmaatesankh was a musician at the great Temple of Amun-Re at nearby Karnak, where her husband was a temple doorkeeper. 2 <u>It is possible that their jobs at the temple provided</u> the couple with a small wage and other benefits to supplement their main income from a piece of fertile Nile land on which 3 <u>it is possible that they grew</u> crops of barley, sesame, or dates.

We can only guess at what Djedmaatesankh's life would have been like, and try to imagine what her problems were. 4 <u>It is possible she was</u> anxious about her inability to have children and certainly, as she approached her thirties, 5 <u>it is highly likely that she worried</u> about her health.

Looking upon a face from so long ago, a face not unlike that of any other young woman in Egypt today, ties us more personally to history. In a way that 6 <u>was impossible for her to imagine</u>, Djedmaatesankh has achieved a degree of fame in our 21st century, appearing in dozens of newspapers and magazines.

1 <u>they must have been</u>

2 ....

3 ....

4 ....

5 ....

6 ....

4 Read the following essay. Find seven places where you can add *may*, *can* or *can't* to soften the verbs.

'Children can be adversely affected by the influence of television.'
To what extent do you agree with this statement? Give reasons for your answer.

Almost every family has a television these days, and many children watch a whole range of programmes every day. Some people believe that television is͜harmful to children, saying that it influences behaviour in a negative way.

can be
....

There are a lot of programmes on television that are not educational and that contain violence and bad language. However, watching violence on television encourages violent behaviour in children. This is true in cases of children who have already exhibited violent tendencies, but it isn't true of all children, otherwise we would have an epidemic of child crime. It is also argued that bad language on television encourages the same in children.

....
....
....
....

Nevertheless, overall I believe that restricting children's television viewing to mainly educational programmes shown at a time of day when there is no violence or bad language will overcome any risks of television being a bad influence.

....

D Test practice

Listening Section 4

Questions 1–10

Complete the summary below.

*Write **NO MORE THAN TWO WORDS** for each answer.*

The history of soap

In ancient times soap was used to clean **1** .... Soap was not seen as a means of personal hygiene until **2** .... times. Ancient people had little technology but many **3** .... so were probably able to discover soap by chance. Soap was probably only used in **4** .... societies. There is no evidence that tribespeople at the time of the British **5** .... used soap.

The history of soap has mostly been discovered from **6** .... The earliest known use of soap in 2500 BC was to wash **7** .... The Egyptians made soap by mixing salts with oil taken from **8** .... The Romans saw washing themselves as a social activity. They removed dirt using steam and a **9** .... When Pompeii was excavated, they discovered a **10** .... for making soap.

Grammar focus task

Listen to the first part of the recording again and fill in the gaps with a modal and the verb in brackets in the correct form.

1 While you .... (*find*) some information on the origins of soap, it is not a substance which has excited a great deal of study so far.

2 We can only assume that other activities .... (*provide*) the basis from which this key concept arose.

3 So, how is it that these primitive people from over two thousand years ago .... (*discover*) soap?

4 I carried out some experiments using basic techniques to try to find out what people without any chemical knowledge .... (*observe*).

5 I was able to demonstrate that they would indeed .... (*make*) a soap that is not dissimilar to the one we know today.

Decide whether the modals are used to show ability or possibility in these sentences.

A Context listening

1 You are going to hear a man asking a colleague for advice about living in Hong Kong. Before you listen, look at the pictures and guess which of these topics they talk about.

accommodation | clothes | food | language lessons

social life | transport | weather | work permits

2 🎧 14 Listen and check if you were right.

3 14◄◄ Now listen again and fill in the gaps in the colleague's advice.

1 You .... a few days to recover from jet lag.

2 You .... the underground system as much as possible.

3 You .... some Cantonese to travel on the public light buses.

4 You .... loose change on the ferries and the buses.

5 You .... to speak Cantonese in some market stalls.

6 You .... a work permit before you go.

7 You .... too casually for work.

8 You .... any guide books in England.

9 You .... lots of passport photos with you.

4 Complete the table below with words from Exercise 3.

strong obligation or necessity	advice or suggestions	no obligation or necessity
need to		

B Grammar

We use expressions of obligation and necessity when there is a need to do something. This need can be internal (the speaker feels it is necessary) or external (rules or the situation make it necessary).

1 Obligation and necessity

The verbs *must* (*mustn't*), *have to*, *have got to*, and *need to* express obligation and necessity:
*You'll **need to** allow a bit of extra time to get over jet lag.*
*You **have to** get a work permit before you go.*
*You **mustn't** dress too casually for work.*

Must is a modal verb and its form doesn't change:
*He **must** try a bit harder.* (**not** ~~he musts~~)

We use *must* when the obligation comes from the speaker:
*You **must** invite me to visit you.* (the speaker wants this)

When there is an institutional rule or a law *have to* or *need to* are more common than *must*:
*You **have to** get a work permit before you go.* (this is a rule)

Have to is more common in spoken English than *must*, but in written English either is used.
Have got to is more common in spoken English than written English:
*I've **got to** find somewhere to live quite quickly.*

Must is usually used on signs, notices and printed information:
*All employees **must** hold a valid work permit.*

To talk about obligation and necessity in the present we can use *must*(*n't*), *have to*, *have got to* or *need to*. We use *have to* or *need to* with past and future tenses:
*You **will have to learn** some Cantonese.* (**not** ~~You will must learn~~)
*He **had to get up** really early to catch the ferry to work.* (**not** ~~He must got up early~~)

⚠ We do not usually make questions with *must* and *ought to*:
*What sort of things **do you need to** know?* (**not** ~~What sort of things must you / ought you to know?~~)

2 No obligation

We use *not have to*, *not need to* and *needn't* to suggest that there is no obligation or necessity to do something:
*You **needn't** buy lots of guide books before you go.* (= it is not necessary to buy guide books before you go)

⚠ *Mustn't* does not mean the same as *don't have to*, *don't need to* and *needn't*:
*You **don't have to** wait for ages.* (= it is not necessary to wait)
*You **mustn't** wait here.* (= it is not allowed to wait here)

To talk about lack of obligation in the past we can use *needn't have* + past participle, *didn't need to* or *didn't have to*:

We **didn't have to** worry about work permits when I was there.
I **needn't have bothered** to get a work permit. (= it wasn't necessary)

There is a difference between *didn't need to* and *needn't have*:

John picked me up from the station so I **didn't need to get** a taxi home. (= it wasn't necessary so I didn't get a taxi)
I **needn't have got** a taxi because John's flat wasn't far from the station. (= I got a taxi but it wasn't necessary)

To talk about the future we use *not have to* or *not need to*:

I hope I **won't have to** work late tonight.
He's **not going to need to** come to the meeting after all.

3 Suggestions and advice

We can use modal verbs *should(n't)* and *ought (not) to* to make suggestions or give advice:
You **should** try and use it whenever you can. (= I think it is a good idea)
You **ought to** take lots of passport photos with you.
You **shouldn't** dress casually for work.

We can use *must* to give strong advice:
You **must** phone me when you get there.

4 Adverbs

Adverbs like *also, always, never, sometimes, just* and *only* come after modal verbs:
You **should always** carry plenty of loose change.
You **must never** do that again.

To add extra emphasis we can use *really* before the verb:
You **really have to** see it to believe it.

5 Formal written English

Verbs of obligation, necessity and suggestion are common in formal and academic writing when giving opinions:
Governments **should** take advice from the experts before making new laws.
Companies **need to** consider cultural differences when engaging in business with overseas organisations.

C Grammar exercises

1 Underline the correct words. Sometimes both options are possible.

1 In my office you *have to / don't have to* wear a suit but lots of people do.

2 These pills *must not / don't have to* be taken if you are under twelve years old.

3 I *must / have to* leave now because I have a meeting.

4 I *didn't need to go / needn't have gone* to the station to pick her up because she decided to get the bus, so I finished my essay instead.

5 Notice to all conference participants: Please note that you *must / have got to* register before entering the conference hall.

6 You *mustn't / don't have to* smoke inside but you can smoke outside.

7 When I was at university I *must / had to* write my assignments by hand because there weren't any computers then.

8 British dog-owners *have to / must* have passports for their dogs when they travel abroad.

9 Next year I'*ll have to / 'll must* get a job to pay back all the money I've borrowed from the bank for my university fees.

10 The interview went really well so I *didn't need to worry / needn't have worried* about it so much beforehand.

2 Fill in the gaps below with the correct form of (*not*) *have to*, *must*, (*not*) *need* or *should*.

1 A: I'm going to Florence next week so I __'ll have__ to buy a guidebook.

  B: Ah, well, you're in luck. You .... buy a book because I've got a small guide to Florence I can lend you.

2 A: What's Mike doing these days?

  B: He's studying really hard. He .... pass his exams in order to get the promotion his company have promised him.

3 A: .... (*you*) wear a uniform at work?

  B: Yes, and I find it rather strange because I've never worn one before. When I was at school we .... wear a uniform although the girls .... wear skirts and not trousers.

4 A: The rules for university fees have just changed. I was really lucky because I .... pay for my education, but unfortunately my brother .... pay when he goes to university next year.

  B: Yes, I know. My sister will be affected too.

117

5　A: The bread's in the oven. Can you remind me to get it out in 20 minutes? I
.... forget like last time when I burnt the loaf.

B: I'm sorry. I'm afraid I .... go now, so I won't be able to remind you.
Can't you set a timer?

A: Oh, ... (*you/really*) go? I'd hoped you'd stay to lunch and have some of
my bread!

6　A: I've just joined the tennis club. They've got all sorts of rules, you know.

B: Really? Like what?

A: Well, you .... wear white clothes on the courts, of course. But the really
silly rule is that you .... turn your mobile off as soon as you arrive at
the club. I don't want to do that – what if I'm needed at work or something?

B: Perhaps they don't know you're a doctor. You .... tell them.

3　**Read the extract from an Academic Writing Task 2. Decide if the <u>underlined</u> phrases
are correct or not. Tick (✓) them if they are right and correct them if they are wrong.**

Pollution is causing enormous problems all over the world these days. Governments **1** <u>need to act</u> quickly
to stop this problem before it is too late.

The first thing I believe we **2** <u>absolutely should do</u> is reduce the amount we use our cars. Our
governments **3** <u>must to encourage</u> us to use public transport. In my country, public transport is not
very reliable, so the first thing that governments **4** <u>have to do</u> is to ensure that buses and trains are a
viable alternative to the car. They **5** <u>also should reduce</u> the costs to the public of travelling on public
transport.

However, it is not only the government that **6** <u>needs to make</u> an effort. All of us **7** <u>should make</u> some
effort to reduce pollution. First of all we **8** <u>ought try</u> to walk or cycle if we can, rather than using our
cars. In the past people **9** <u>must walk</u> or cycle because they did not have cars. It is a shame that we
have become so dependent on cars now. Secondly, we **10** <u>should trying</u> to share car use with our
friends and colleagues.

All of us **11** <u>will must make</u> some changes to our lives if we want to reduce pollution. Fortunately, we
12 <u>mustn't make</u> big changes to make big improvements in the situation.

1　..........✓..........	5　....................................	9　....................................
2　<u>absolutely must do</u>	6　....................................	10　....................................
3　....................................	7　....................................	11　....................................
4　....................................	8　....................................	12　....................................

4 Fill in the gaps with the correct form of (*not*) **have to**, **ought to** or **must**(*n't*) and the verbs in brackets.

Teacher: Do you think it's a good thing for young people to travel to different countries before settling down to a job?

Student: Yes, I think it's a really exciting and interesting thing to do.

Teacher: What **1** _do you have to think_ (*you/think*) about if you're going to go travelling?

Student: Well, you **2** .... (*consider*) lots of things first. For example, you **3** .... (*have*) enough money in the first place, so you **4** .... (*work*) a bit first to save some money. Then another important thing to consider is who to go with. You **5** .... (*travel*) with a friend, but it is probably safer and less lonely if you do. Also, you **6** .... (*learn*) a bit about the countries before you go. It's a good idea to research cultural issues, so that you don't offend people by your behaviour. If you go to Nepal, for example, you **7** .... (*shout*) or raise your voice in public, and you **8** .... (*always/walk*) around a Buddhist temple in a clockwise direction. You **9** .... (*find out*) these things before you go.

Teacher: What things **10** .... (*you/arrange*) before you travel?

Student: Well, to visit some countries you **11** .... (*have*) a visa, so you **12** .... (*organise*) that before you go.

General Training Reading Section 2

Questions 1–13

Read the passage below and answer Questions 1–6.

School rules

A Pupils are required to be in their classrooms by 8.30 a.m. each morning for registration. Pupils coming late will be punished accordingly. Pupils may not leave the school grounds during the normal working day without permission. During study periods and recreation students in the sixth form may leave the school grounds provided that parents have given written authorization at the beginning of the year.

B Students must come to school in proper attire. If this basic rule is not observed, the school reserves the right to refuse entry to any student.

C The school strongly disapproves of pupils taking paid employment. It should certainly never interfere with school activities, and will not be accepted as an excuse for missing any school commitment.

D In the case of a pupil being absent from school, please telephone on the first day in all instances. Messages can be left on the answering machine before 7.30 a.m. or you can send an email to the school address to reach us by 8.30 a.m. at the latest.

E Except in the case of illness, students are expected to be present for the entire school year. Routine medical and dental appointments should be arranged so as not to conflict with school commitments, as should family travel.

F The school regards the completion of careful and regular work at home as an indispensable part of the curriculum. Every pupil has a study plan outlining his/her evening obligations day by day and parents are asked to ensure that their child has a suitable place and time in which to do the work prescribed. If a pupil appears to be doing too little work, parents should contact the form teacher at once.

G Homework can be excused only after the receipt and approval by the teacher concerned of a letter from a parent setting out the reasons. Social engagements are not acceptable as an excuse. It is essential that pupils endeavour to catch up on any missed work as soon as possible.

H During the holidays the school and its grounds are out-of-bounds for all pupils, unless accompanied by a teacher. Pupils visiting the school's sports hall or any of the school's grounds or taking part in a school visit of any kind, whether in term or in the holidays, are subject to school rules.

I No pupil may drive a car or motorbike within the school grounds without permission from the headmaster. Permission to come by bicycle should be obtained from the form teacher. Bikes must be walked onto the school grounds. Cycle helmets must be worn and lights used after dark. Rollerblades, roller skates and skateboards are not permitted within the school grounds at any time.

J Bicycles must not be chained to the school railings. Any bicycles brought onto school grounds should be clearly labelled with the owner's name and must be left locked in the bicycle sheds provided.

K Parents are strongly advised to put name tags on their children's belongings. The school cannot be held responsible for any loss or theft of students' property. Students must keep track of their belongings and not leave them lying around unattended.

Questions 1–6

*The reading passage has eleven rules labelled **A–K**.*

Which rule contains the following information?

*Write the correct letter **A–K** next to Questions 1–6 below.*

***NB** You may use any letter more than once.*

1 information about what to do if your child cannot attend school
2 the person to contact about how much homework your child should be doing
3 advice about how students can keep their bicycles secure
4 the school's opinion about schoolchildren working to earn money
5 details of what parents should do if their child cannot complete their homework
6 rules about visiting the school property outside of school time

Questions 7–13

Read the passage below and answer Questions 7–13.

School of Independent Study

The University's Independent Study online and correspondence courses offer you the flexibility to reach your educational goals without giving up your life. The study materials you use in your course have been developed by the university faculty so the material you cover is the same as in the courses offered on campus. The only difference is that you can study and take tests when it's convenient for you!

Tuition and fees

The Independent Study tuition fee is $115 per course. Students may take as many courses as they want. There is a shipping and handling fee of $30 for each course. All Independent Study students must purchase a Study Guide at a cost of $30. The university also charges a connectivity fee of $12 per course. Students enrolling for the first time will be charged a $9 per course Academic Excellence fee; for returning students this fee is just $3 per course. A $15 Academic Records fee is charged once each term, regardless of the number of courses taken. This fee entitles a student to free replacement copies of end-of-course documentation for life. Tuition and fees for out-of-state students are the same as those of local residents.

Time limits

A course can be finished in a minimum of two weeks per module and must be finished in a maximum of four weeks. For example, if your course has three modules you must remain in it for a minimum of six weeks and a maximum of twelve weeks. If you need to meet a deadline, you should take these minimum and maximum periods into account. These periods are calculated from the date you receive your first lesson from the Independent Study office. Modules cannot always be completed in the minimum amount of time. You need to make sure that you know whether your instructors are on vacation at any stage during your enrolment, as this could affect the return of assignments, exams and final grades. Your enrolment is valid for nine months, which begins on the day we post your enrolment application.

Questions 7–13

Look at the following statements.

Next to Questions 7–13 write

> **TRUE**   *if the statement agrees with the information*
> **FALSE**   *if the statement contradicts the information*
> **NOT GIVEN** *if there is no information on this*

7 The course content offered through the School of Independent Study is different to the other courses the university offers.

8 Students will receive all course materials by post.

9 The Study Guide is optional for Independent Study students.

10 Students will need to pay for extra copies if they lose their final certificate.

11 Students are able to complete each module in less than two weeks.

12 Students may take four weeks to complete a module if necessary.

13 Some modules take longer than two weeks to complete.

Grammar focus task

This is an extract from the second text. Without looking back, fill in the gaps with the correct modal verb or *need to*.

A course can be finished in a minimum of two weeks per module and 1 .... be finished in a maximum of four weeks. For example, if your course has three modules you 2 .... remain in it for a minimum of six weeks and a maximum of twelve weeks. If you 3 .... meet a deadline, you 4 .... take these minimum and maximum periods into account. These periods are calculated from the date you receive your first lesson from the Independent Study office. Modules cannot always be completed in the minimum amount of time. You 5 .... make sure that you know whether your instructors are on vacation at any stage during your enrolment, as this could affect the return of assignments, exams and final grades.

Are the verbs used to show obligation, necessity or advice?

Reported speech
tense changes; time references;
reporting questions; reporting verbs

15

A Context listening

1 You are going to hear an interview with Christopher West, the Managing Director of a company called Angleside. Before you listen, look at the newspaper headlines below. Which of the topics in the box do you think Mr West mentions?

JOBS TO GO AT ANGLESIDE

DOUBTS OVER COMPANY'S FUTURE

| voluntary redundancy   early retirement   low profits   good business sense |
| a promising future   poor relationship between management and workers |

2 🎧15a Listen to the first part of the recording and check if you were right.

3 15a◀◀ Listen to the first part again and fill in the gaps.

Mr West: However, we **1** .... voluntary redundancy and early
               retirement and **2** .... to cover most of the jobs this way.

Interviewer: And what has led to this situation? **3** .... a result of
               Angleside's poor performance over the past five years?

Mr West: No, the company **4** .... badly. This **5** ....
               nothing to do with the figures. It just makes good business sense.

Interviewer: So **6** .... that your figures **7** .... the basis for
               this decision to cut jobs?

Mr West: Absolutely. We **8** .... the way we operate our business two
               years ago.

4 Here is the journalist's radio report. Fill in the gaps with the verbs in the box. **⌂15b** Then listen to the second part of the recording to check your answers.

announced	asked	assured	claimed	denied	hoped	promised	said

At local company Angleside, up to 150 employees will lose their jobs. Christopher West, the Managing Director, **1** .... they would be offering voluntary redundancy and early retirement and **2** .... to cover the job losses in this way. I **3** .... Mr West if these cuts were a result of Angleside's poor performance over the past five years but he **4** .... that the company had not been doing well and **5** .... that the job losses have nothing to do with the figures. West **6** .... that they decided to make changes two years ago. He **7** .... me that the company would continue to operate in the future and **8** .... to do his best for the employees.

5 What are the main differences between the texts in Exercise 3 and Exercise 4?

B Grammar

We can use reported speech to report in writing or speech what someone has said.

1 Tense changes

When we report what someone has said we sometimes change the tense of the main verb: we move tenses 'back' one tense.

Original tense of main verb	Tense in reported speech
present simple I **live** in Italy. →	**past simple** She said she **lived** in Italy.
present continuous I**'m living** in Italy. →	**past continuous** She said she **was living** in Italy.
past simple I **lived** in Italy. →	**past perfect** She said she **had lived** in Italy.
past continuous I **was living** in Italy. →	**past perfect continuous** She said she **had been living** in Italy.
present perfect I**'ve lived** in Italy. →	**past perfect** She said she **had lived** in Italy.
past perfect I**'d lived** in Italy. →	**past perfect** She said she**'d lived** in Italy.
be going to I**'m going to live** in Italy. →	*was/were going to* She said she **was going to live** in Italy.
will I**'ll live** in Italy. →	*would* She said she **would live** in Italy.
may / might I **may/might live** in Italy next year. →	*might* She said she **might live** in Italy next year.
can I **can live** in Italy. →	*could* She said she **could live** in Italy.
must I **must live** in Italy. →	*had to* She said she **had to** live in Italy.

However, we often choose not to change the tense. This may be because

◆ what we are talking about remains true:
   '*This **has** nothing to do with the figures.*'
   → *He said that the job losses **have** nothing to do with the figures.* (at the time of reporting this fact is still true)

◆ the original tense was past simple or past continuous:
   '*We **decided** to change the way we operate our business two years ago.*'
   → *West claimed that they **decided** to make changes two years ago.*

2 Reporting verbs

When we report what someone has said, we are unlikely to use exactly the same words as in the original speech. We can choose from many different reporting verbs to help us convey the general idea using fewer words than in the original speech. Here are some common reporting verbs:

reporting verb (+ *that*)
agree, admit, announce, argue, believe, claim, complain, deny, explain, insist, promise, propose, reply, request, say, state, suggest, think, warn: *The director **claimed** (**that**) they decided to make the changes two years ago.*

reporting verb + someone + *that*
assure, inform, persuade, remind, tell: *He **assured the interviewer that** the company would continue to operate in the future.*

reporting verb + *to*-infinitive
agree, ask, claim, offer, promise, propose, refuse: *He **promised to do** his best for the employees.*

reporting verb + someone + *to*-infinitive
advise, ask, encourage, invite, persuade, remind, tell, urge, warn: *They **urged the employees to stay** calm.*

reporting verb + preposition + *-ing* / noun
argue about, complain about: He **complained about the terrible food***.* *apologise for:* The company **apologised for** causing redundancies. *insist on:* The manager **insisted on** seeing the staff. *complain to:* He **complained to the manager.**

reporting verb + someone + preposition + *-ing* / noun
accuse of: They **accused the company of** planning badly. *advise about, remind about:* They **reminded her about the meeting.** *advise on, congratulate on:* He **advised me on the deal.** *blame for, thank for:* They **thanked her for** coming.

reporting verb + *-ing* / noun
accept, admit, deny, suggest: *The director **denied** having financial problems.* *The employees **accepted the offer** of early redundancy.*

reporting verb + someone (+ noun)
offer, promise, refuse: *He **offered her** a job.*

⚠ Some of the same verbs can be used in different ways (e.g. *admit, claim, offer, persuade*):
*West **claimed that they decided** to make the changes two years ago.*
*West **claimed to have decided** to make the changes two years ago.*

3 Time references etc.

We sometimes need to change other words or phrases in reported speech if they are reported at a different time from the original words:

today → that day   *tomorrow → the following day / the next day*
yesterday → the day before   *next week → the following week*
now → then / straight away   *this → that*
here → there

*He said he would see me **tomorrow**. (reported on the same day)*
*He said he would see me **the next day**. (reported at a later date)*

Sometimes the context requires pronouns to change:
*'I like **you**.' → **He** said **he** liked **her**.*
*'I like **you**.' → **I** said **I** liked **her**.*

4 Reporting questions

We use statement word order when reporting questions:
*I asked Mr West **how he was going to** deal with the problem.* (**not** ~~I asked Mr West how was he going to deal with the problem.~~)

To report questions with question words (*who, what, where, why, when, how*) we keep the question word:
*'**What** has led to this situation?'*
*→ The interviewer asked **what** had led to this situation.*

We can use *if* or *whether* to report yes/no questions:
'Are these cuts a result of Angleside's poor performance over the past five years?'
*→ I asked **if/whether** these cuts were the result of Angleside's poor performance over the past five years.*

⚠ We do not use a question mark for reported questions.

Grammar extra: Other ways of reporting
We can use other expressions to report speech e.g. *according to* (common in spoken and written English), *apparently, supposedly, seemingly* (more common in spoken English):
According to the radio programme, they are cutting 150 jobs.

15

C Grammar exercises

1 Here is a conversation between Tanya and her teacher.

> When are you taking the IELTS test? Have you registered yet?

> Yes. I'm doing it next Saturday.

> Do you feel prepared for it?

> Well, your classes have been really helpful, so I think so.

> You've made excellent progress.

> Thank you. I'm feeling very nervous though.

> Oh, try not to worry. You've worked very hard.

> Yes, I have. I think I'll be alright once I'm doing the test.

A week later, Tanya tells her friend about the conversation. Fill in the gaps.

To: Clara

From: Tanya

Subject: IELTS test on Saturday!

Hi Clara

I was talking to my teacher about my IELTS test last week. She asked
1 _me when I was taking_ the test. I said 2 .... Saturday. She asked
3 .... prepared for it. I replied 4 .... really helpful. She
told 5 .... excellent progress. I said 6 .... very nervous.
She told 7 .... worry and said 8 .... very hard. I said
9 .... alright once I 10 .... the test.

---

2 Underline the correct verb in each sentence.

1 Some people *argue*/*remind* that banning cars from city centres would reduce pollution.

2 The organisation campaigns against pollution and for the environment and they *insist*/*urge* people to start walking and cycling more.

3 My boyfriend is always forgetting things so it was a good thing I *reminded*/*suggested* him to bring his passport when we went on holiday.

4 I was very unhappy with the service so I *complained*/*insisted* to the manager and he gave me a discount on my meal.

5 I needed to talk to my boss so I *reminded*/*suggested* a meeting and we arranged one for later that day.

6 The students felt very strongly about the issue and *refused*/*insisted* on seeing the vice-chancellor to discuss it.

7 I asked him really nicely but he still *refused*/*denied* to help me.

8 The tennis player regretted his actions and *blamed*/*apologised* for his behaviour afterwards.

9 Jane was having difficulties sleeping and the doctor *advised*/*suggested* her to take some rest from her heavy work schedule.

10 The armed robbers *warned*/*announced* the bank staff not to move or they might use their guns.

3 Correct the mistakes in these sentences.

1 I met Annie and <s>she said me</s> she was getting married. *she told me / she said*

2 The education minister encouraged students take out a loan to cover their fees. ....

3 At the interview he asked did I want to start the job tomorrow! ....

4 The speaker urged people that they should vote for him. ....

5 We agreed making our presentation to the group first. ....

6 My tutor promised mark the first draft of my dissertation immediately. ....

7 Jacques invited us going to his house for dinner on Friday. ....

8 During the Speaking module the examiner asked me what were my hobbies. ....

9 The customers complained the quality of the food. ....

10 When the college announced about the changes, everyone was worried. ....

11 I wanted to pay for myself but my boyfriend insisted to pay. ....

12 The university sent me an email asking me when would I be arriving. ....

4 Report each of the sentences below using a verb from the box. Remember that you do not need to report the original words exactly.

agree   apologise   ask   ask   deny   encourage   persuaded   ~~promise~~
refuse   suggest

1 'We are going to lower taxes and reduce unemployment!'
The government promised to lower taxes and reduce unemployment.

2 'I really think you should apply for the job. You'd have a good chance of getting it.'
She ....

3 'No, I won't help you. Do it yourself!'
He ....

4 'Oh, okay, I'll go to the meeting.'
She ....

5 'I didn't cause the accident. It wasn't me.'
He ....

6 'We are very sorry that we lost your application form.'
They ....

7 'Why aren't there many poisonous snakes in Britain?'
He ....

8 'Are you going to the lecture tomorrow?'
She ....

9 'Why don't you have a day off? You could do with a rest.'
She ....

10 'Please come to the theatre with me, Dan. I really think you'll enjoy it.'
'Oh, alright then, Claire.'
Claire ....

D Test practice

Listening Section 3

Questions 1–3

*Complete the sentences. Write **NO MORE THAN THREE WORDS AND/OR A NUMBER** for each answer.*

1 Solar towers create energy from moving ....
2 The first ever recorded use of this type of energy was in the ....
3 The location of the first solar tower was ....

Questions 4–8

*Complete the flowchart. Write **NO MORE THAN TWO WORDS** for each answer.*

Solar tower flowchart

Towers are built using extra strong **4** ....
At the bottom they have a sunlight collector made of
5 .... spread over a large area of ground.

↓

The sunlight collector warms the air beneath it and
operates in a similar way to a **6** ....

↓

The air **7** .... through the tower causing
the turbines to turn.

↓

The turbines create **8** .... megawatts of
electricity.

Questions 9–10

*Circle **TWO** letters **A–E**.*

*What are **TWO** disadvantages of solar towers?*

    A they are too expensive to run
    B heat escapes from the solar collector
    C they require a great deal of land
    D they cannot produce electricity at night
    E they need to be able to withstand high winds

**Look at the extract from the recording and the summary of the discussion below.
Complete the summary using reporting verbs from this unit. Do not use *say*.**

Luke: But what about at night when there is no sun?

Millie: Well, they've managed to find a way to store the electricity produced during the
          day so it's no problem at night or even on cloudy days.

Tanya: So, there are no drawbacks then?

Millie: I didn't say that. One problem they do have is that a lot of the energy in the
          sunlight is lost in the form of heat from the collector, and then, of the
          remaining heat, a large proportion escapes from the top of the tower. But
          they're still worth the investment because, as I said, sunlight is free!

Luke 1 .... what happened at night when there is no sun. Millie
2 .... that they had managed to find a way to store electricity produced during
the day. She 3 .... having said that there were no drawbacks and 4 ....
that one problem was that a lot of the solar energy is lost from the collector. However, she
5 .... that they were still worth the investment because sunlight is free.

Verb + verb patterns

verb + *to*-infinitive; verb + *-ing*; verb + preposition + *-ing*; verb + infinitive without *to*

A Context listening

1 Freya is doing a course. What job do you think she wants to do?

2 🎧 **16** Listen and answer these questions.

1 What course is she doing?

2 What does she enjoy most?

3 What fear has she overcome?

3 Complete these sentences from the recording by using the verbs in brackets.
16◀◀ Listen again and check your answers.

1 I decided .... (*do*) an animal management course.

2 I chose .... (*study*) at Fairfield College because it's got a good range of animals and everyone's really friendly.

3 The course is only three days a week, so I've already started .... (*work*) part-time at a pet shop.

4 I prefer .... (*take*) time so I can get to know them.

5 I don't even mind .... (*clean*) them out.

6 They've let us .... (*treat*) some minor problems, like removing splinters from paws.

7 They make us .... (*handle*) all kinds of animals including spiders and snakes.

8 I remember .... (*feel*) really scared.

9 As long as you remember .... (*do*) it the way you've been taught, it's fine.

10 Before, if I heard him .... (*bark*), I just told him .... (*be*) quiet.

11 I'd really like .... (*work*) in either a zoo or a safari park.

4 All the verbs you have written in Exercise 3 follow other verbs. Which verbs are followed by:

1 (object +) *to*-infinitive ....

2 (object +) *-ing* ....

3 object + infinitive without *to* ....

Which verb is followed by two different patterns?

When you use two verbs together the form of the second verb depends on the first verb. The second verb can be the *to*-infinitive, the infinitive without *to*, or *-ing*.

⚠ Many verbs can also be followed by a *that*-clause e.g. *recommend, suggest, tell* (see Unit 15).

1 Verb + *to*-infinitive

Some verbs are followed directly by the *to*-infinitive and do not need an object:

> agree aim appear arrange attempt be able be likely claim decide deserve
> fail hope learn manage offer plan promise refuse seem tend try

*Was animal care something you always **hoped to do**?*
*I **decided to do** an animal management course during my last year at school.*

Some verbs are always followed by an object + *to*-infinitive:

> advise allow encourage force get persuade remind teach tell warn

*This course **has taught me to respect** all animals and overcome my fears.* (**not** ~~This course has taught to respect all animals~~)
*I just **told him to be** quiet.*

Get is used with an object + *to*-infinitive when it means *persuade* or *make*:
*If you want to **get your teachers to notice** your work you should make sure you hand it in on time.*

Some verbs can be used with or without an object + *to*-infinitive:

> ask choose dare expect help intend need prefer prepare want

*I didn't **want to touch** the snakes.*
*They **wanted us to touch** the snakes.*

2 Verb (+ preposition) + *-ing*

Some verbs are followed by *-ing*:

> avoid approve of can't help can't stand carry on consider deny don't mind
> enjoy feel like finish give up imagine include insist on involve keep mention
> mind practise put off recommend resist suggest think of/about

*I **prefer** deal**ing** with the customers but I **don't mind** clean**ing** out the animals and feed**ing** them.*
*We've **practised** handl**ing** animals.*

When a verb is followed by a preposition (except *to*) then the following verb is always *-ing*:
*I **was thinking about** do**ing** another course.*

3 Verb + *to*-infinitive or *-ing*

Some verbs are followed by either *to*-infinitive or *-ing* with little difference in meaning:

| attempt | begin | bother | continue | hate | like | love | prefer | start |

I've started working at a pet shop. (= I've started to work at a pet shop.)
I like feeding the animals. (= I like to feed the animals.)

⚠ *Would like / would love / would prefer* are followed by the *to*-infinitive:
I'd really like to work in either a zoo or a safari park.
I'd prefer to stop studying for a while.

Some verbs mean something different when they are followed by the *to*-infinitive or *-ing*:

| forget | go on | need | remember | stop | try |

verb	+ *to*-infinitive	+ *-ing*
go on	◆ one action follows another: *After university she went on to get a job as a vet.* (= she finished university and then she got a job as a vet)	◆ an action is repeated or continued: *She went on talking even though the film had started.* (= she continued talking)
remember	◆ you remember before you do the action: *As long as you remember to do what you've been told, it's fine.* (= 1 remember 2 do what you've been told)	◆ you remember after doing the action: *I remember feeling really scared.* (= 1 I felt scared 2 I remembered that feeling)
forget	◆ the action did not happen: *I forgot to post my application form.* (= I didn't post it)	◆ the action happened: *I'll never forget meeting you that cold winter's day.* (= we did meet) This form is usually in the negative.
stop	◆ there are two actions and the first stops so that the second can begin: *I stopped to ask the way.* (= I stopped and then I asked)	◆ there is one action which stops: *I'm going to stop studying for a while.*
try	◆ make an effort to do something. You may not always be successful: *I try to find out why he's barking.*	◆ experiment with doing something: *She tried adding a bit more sugar but it still tasted horrible.*
need	◆ the subject of the sentence will do the action: *I need to mend my jeans.* (= I will mend them)	◆ there is a passive meaning: *My jeans need mending.* (= we don't know who will mend them)

4 Verb + object + infinitive without *to*

| feel | hear | help | let | make | notice | see | watch |

Make and *let* are always followed by an object + infinitive without *to*:
*They **made us handle** all kinds of animals including spiders and snakes.*
*They **let us take** it slowly.*

⚠ When *make* is used in the passive we use the *to*-infinitive:
*I **was made to handle** all kinds of animals including spiders and snakes.*

Help can be followed by an infinitive with or without *to*:
*The course **helped me understand** my own dog better.* (= The course helped me to understand my own dog better.)

5 Negatives

If we want to make the second verb negative we use *not*:
*I chose **not** to study at this college.*
*I enjoy **not** working late.*

C Grammar exercises

1 Fill in the gaps with the correct form of the verbs in brackets.

Tutor: So have you managed **1** .to..finish. (*finish*) the assignment, Kumiko?

Kumiko: Well, I've nearly finished but I forgot **2** .... (*add*) a bibliography, so I'd like **3** .... (*have*) an extension, if that's possible?

Tutor: How long will you need **4** .... (*do*) it?

Kumiko: I aim **5** .... (*finish*) it today, but maybe two days would be the best thing.

Tutor: Yes, that's fine. Have you begun **6** .... (*work*) on your dissertation yet?

Kumiko: Yes, I started **7** .... (*write*) my questionnaire a couple of weeks ago, but I stopped **8** .... (*complete*) this assignment. I'm planning **9** .... (*get*) the questionnaire ready by the end of the week, and I'm hoping **10** .... (*show*) it to you for your comments before I use it. Could we meet next week?

Tutor: Yes, of course. I'm afraid I can't find my diary though. I remember **11** .... (*put*) it in my briefcase this morning, but it doesn't seem **12** .... (*be*) there. Why don't you email me with a suitable time?

Kumiko: Yes, okay.

Tutor: So, I'll see you in the seminar tomorrow. Don't forget **13** .... (*email*) me!

Kumiko: Thank you, I'll try **14** .... (*remember*).

2 Underline the correct form of the verbs.

1 Mario remembered *to give / giving* his assignment to his tutor because he had spoken to her about its length, but she insisted that she had never received it.

2 If you can't find the information at the library, try *to look / looking* on the Internet.

3 She studied medicine at university and went on *to become / becoming* a surgeon.

4 Look at Mum's car! It definitely needs *to clean / cleaning*!

5 I'll never forget *to fall / falling* off that swing when I was a child.

6 I was really nervous about the interview, and although I tried *not to worry / not worrying*, I was awake most of the night.

7 The new government needs *to take / taking* notice of the opinions of the people.

8 It seems that the new system of sending out reminders has worked, because this year 90% of members remembered *to renew / renewing* their membership in time.

9 Economists predict that house prices will go on *to rise / rising* for at least another year.

10 We weren't able to see the concert because Tamsin forgot *to bring / bringing* the tickets.

3 Decide if the <u>underlined</u> sections are correct or not. Tick (✓) them if they are right and correct them if they are wrong.

Teacher:	What impact do you feel a good learning experience at school can have on people in terms of future learning?
Student:	Oh, well, obviously, having a good experience as a student will **1** <u>allow you feel</u> positive about learning in general. If you've had supportive teachers at school who **2** <u>encouraged you to work</u> hard, you are more likely **3** <u>to go on to be</u> conscientious in your university studies.
Teacher:	Can you give me an example?
Student:	Well, with my art classes, my teacher was so supportive that I **4** <u>tried very hard pleasing</u> her. However, I have had other teachers who **5** <u>have made me to feel</u> useless, and that **6** <u>made me wanting</u> to give up.
Teacher:	How can teachers ensure that their students have a positive learning experience?
Student:	I think teachers **7** <u>need to be</u> interested in their students. If they aren't interested, their students **8** <u>will stop to make</u> an effort. Also, if students **9** <u>enjoy being</u> in class, they are more likely to learn. Students **10** <u>don't mind to work</u> hard if they like what they are doing. So teachers should **11** <u>try to make</u> their classes stimulating.
Teacher:	Do you think that the curriculum in schools allows teachers to be creative and make their lessons interesting?
Student:	Yes, in my country teachers must follow a curriculum, but the government **12** <u>doesn't force them teach</u> in a certain way. That means that teachers can **13** <u>decide to teach</u> the topic however they like. So, teachers can still be creative and **14** <u>let their students deciding</u> how they learn.

1 allow you to feel
2 ✓
3 ....
4 ....
5 ....
6 ....
7 ....
8 ....
9 ....
10 ....
11 ....
12 ....
13 ....
14 ....

4 Fill in the gaps in the letter using both of the verbs in brackets.

Dear Sir,

I am writing to complain about the service I received in your hotel at the weekend. I arrived at your hotel at lunchtime on Friday and your receptionist 1 told me to take (tell/me/take) a seat while she dealt with some other customers. I 2 .... (not feel like/wait) after a long journey but I sat down anyway. However, after your receptionist 3 .... (finish/talk) to the other customers she walked away and left no one behind the desk. After about ten minutes, I rang the bell, but still no one came. I 4 .... (try/find) someone else to help me, and when I 5 .... (fail/do) this I went behind the desk and called through the door. The receptionist was sitting in the back room at the computer. When she 6 .... (see/me/stand) in the doorway, she apologized and said she 7 .... (need/send) an urgent email and 8 .... (carry on/look) at her screen.

If this had been the only poor service I received during my stay, I would not 9 .... (bother/write) this letter. However, later that evening, in the dining room, I had another bad experience. Your menu only had one vegetarian dish, so I ordered this. Imagine my horror when I 10 .... (start/eat) and discovered meat in the dish. I 11 .... (consider/leave) immediately, but instead I explained the situation to the waiter. I 12 .... (expect/him/get) me another vegetarian meal, but instead he simply shrugged his shoulders, removed the plate and walked away.

I 13 .... (hope/receive) a full apology from you for this poor service and some recompense for the unpleasant time I experienced whilst staying in your hotel. I 14 .... (advise/you/give) your staff some customer care training in the immediate future.

Yours faithfully,
Geraint Rees

D Test practice

Academic Reading

*You should spend about 20 minutes on **Questions 1–13** which are based on the Reading Passage below.*

How consumers decide

Professor John Maule from the University of Leeds describes new research into the way that consumers choose a product.

Understanding consumers

Consumers are creatures of habit: they buy the same products time and time again, and such is their familiarity with big brands, and the colours and logos that represent them, that they can register a brand they like with barely any conscious thought process. The packaging of consumer products is therefore a crucial vehicle for delivering the brand and the product into our shopping baskets.

Having said this, understanding how consumers make decisions, and the crucial role of packaging in this process, has been a neglected area of research so far. This is surprising given that organisations invest huge amounts of money in developing packaging that they believe is effective – especially at the retail level. Our Centre for Decision Research at Leeds University's Business School, in collaboration with Faraday Packaging, is now undertaking work in this area. It has already led to some important findings that challenge the ways in which organisations think about consumer choice.

The research has focused on two fundamental types of thinking. On the one hand, there's 'heuristic processing', which involves very shallow thought and is based on very simple rules: 1) buy what you recognize, 2) choose what

you did last time, or 3) choose what a trusted source suggests. This requires comparatively little effort, and involves looking at – and thinking about – only a small amount of the product information and packaging. One can do this with little or no conscious thought.

On the other hand, 'systematic processing' involves much deeper levels of thought. When people choose goods in this way, they engage in quite detailed analytical thinking – taking account of the product information, including its price, its perceived quality and so on. This form of thinking, which is both analytical and conscious, involves much more mental effort.

The role of packaging is likely to be very different for each of these types of decision making. Under heuristic processing, for example, consumers may simply need to be able to distinguish the pack from those of competitors since they are choosing on the basis of what they usually do. Under these circumstances, the simple perceptual features of the pack may be critical – so that we can quickly discriminate what we choose from the other products on offer. Under systematic processing, however, product-related information may be more important, so the pack has to provide this in an easily identifiable form.

Comparing competition

Consumers will want to be able to compare the product with its competitors, so that they can determine which option is better for them. A crucial role of packaging in this situation is to communicate the characteristics of the product, highlighting its advantages over possible competitors.

So, when are people likely to use a particular type of thinking? First, we know that people are cognitive misers; in other words they are economical with their thinking because it requires some effort from them. Essentially, people only engage in effort-demanding systematic processing when the situation justifies it, for example when they are not tired or distracted and when the purchase is important to them.

Second, people have an upper limit to the amount of information they can absorb. If we present too much, therefore, they will become confused. This, in turn, is likely to lead them to disengage and choose something else.

Third, people often lack the knowledge or experience needed, so will not be able to deal with things they do not already understand, such as the ingredients of food products, for example.

And fourth, people vary in the extent to which they enjoy thinking. Our research has differentiated between people with a high need for thinking – who routinely engage in analytical thinking – and those low in the need for cognition, who prefer to use very simple forms of thinking.

Effectiveness varies

This work has an important impact on packaging in that what makes packaging effective is likely to vary according to the type of processing strategy that consumers use when choosing between products. You need to understand how consumers are selecting your products if you are to develop packaging that is relevant. Furthermore, testing the effectiveness of your packaging can be ineffective if the methods you are employing concern one form of thinking (e.g. a focus group involving analytical thinking) but your consumers are purchasing in the other mode (i.e. the heuristic, shallow form of thinking).

For the packaging industry it is important that retailers identify their key goals. Sustaining a consumer's commitment to a product may involve packaging that is distinctive at the heuristic level (if the consumers can recognize the product they will buy it) but without encouraging consumers to engage in systematic processing (prompting deeper level thinking that would include making comparisons with other products).

Conversely, getting consumers to change brands may involve developing packaging that includes information that does stimulate systematic processing and thus encourages consumers to challenge their usual choice of product. Our work is investigating these issues, and the implications they have for developing effective packaging.

Questions 1–6

Do the following statements agree with the information given in the Reading Passage?

Next to Questions 1–6 write

> **TRUE**   *if the statement agrees with the information*
> **FALSE**   *if the statement contradicts the information*
> **NOT GIVEN**   *if there is no information on this*

1 Little research has been done on the link between packaging and consumers choosing a product.
2 A person who buys what another person recommends is using heuristic thinking.
3 Heuristic processing requires more energy than systematic processing.
4 The concept of heuristic processing was thought up by Dr Maule's team.
5 A consumer who considers how much a product costs is using systematic processing.
6 For heuristic processing, packaging must be similar to other products.

Questions 7–8

*Choose the correct answer **A**, **B**, **C** or **D**.*

7 When trying to determine how effective packaging is, testing can be made 'ineffective' if
  A you rely upon a very narrow focus group.
  B your consumers use only heuristic thinking.
  C the chosen consumers use only shallow thinking.
  D your tests do not match the consumers' thinking type.

8 If a retailer wants consumers to change brands their packaging needs to be
  A informative.
  B distinctive.
  C familiar.
  D colourful.

Questions 9–13

Complete the summary below.

*Write **NO MORE THAN TWO WORDS** for each answer.*

Write your answers next to Questions 9–13 below.

Comparing competition

For consumers who want to compare products it is important that your packaging stresses the **9** .... of your product.

We know that people only use systematic processing if the **10** .... makes it necessary or desirable. We also know that too much **11** .... could make consumers choose another product. Furthermore, consumers may not fully understand details such as the **12** .... of a product. While some people like using systematic processing, others like to think in a **13** .... way.

Grammar focus task

Look at these sentences from the text. Without looking back, fill in the gaps using the correct form of the verbs in brackets.

1 This is surprising given that organisations invest huge amounts of money in .... (*develop*) packaging that they believe is effective.

2 This requires comparatively little effort, and involves .... (*look at*) – and .... (*think about*) – only a small amount of the product information and packaging.

3 Under heuristic processing, for example, consumers may simply need .... (*be able to*) distinguish the pack from those of competitors.

4 Consumers will want .... (*be able to*) compare the product with its competitors.

5 The role of packaging is likely .... (*be*) very different.

6 People vary in the extent to which they enjoy .... (*think*).

7 Prompting deeper level thinking that would include .... (*make*) comparisons with other products.

8 Conversely, getting consumers .... (*change*) brands may involve .... (*develop*) packaging that does stimulate systematic processing and thus encourages consumers .... (*challenge*) their usual choice of product.

143

A Context listening

1 Simon Brown has just inherited $10,000 from his grandfather and is talking to his father about what to do with it. Look at these pictures. What would you do with the money?

2 🎧**17** Listen to the recording. Which of the things in the pictures do Simon and his father talk about? Do you agree with Simon or his father?

3 Match the first and second halves of these sentences from the recording. **17◀◀** Listen again and check your answers.

1 Unless you invest it properly, ...

2 If I invest it, ...

3 If I went travelling, ...

4 If you were to spend a year travelling around the world, ...

5 If you own a car, ...

6 It would be great ...

7 You won't lose any money ...

8 As long as you get a second-hand one, ...

a you'd probably need an awful lot more money than this!

b if I could drive to work instead of travelling on the bus.

c you won't earn much interest.

d provided that you think of it as a long-term investment.

e you should still be able to invest some money as well.

f I'd lose a year of study.

g you also have to pay for insurance and road tax every year.

h I won't be able to access the money quickly.

4 Look at the sentences in Exercise 3 above. Which words or phrases have a similar meaning to *if*? Do any of the sentences talk about events in the past?

B Grammar

Conditional sentences talk about a condition (usually introduced by *if*) and a possible result or consequence. The *if*-clause can be before or after the result clause. We use a comma between clauses when the *if*-clause comes first. Either clause can be positive or negative.

1 Zero conditional

if + present tense, + present tense	*If* you **heat** water to 100°C, it **boils**.
present tense + *if* + present tense	Water **boils** *if* you **heat** it to 100°C.

We use the zero conditional to talk about something that is a general truth or fact (*if* has a similar meaning to *every time*):
If you **own** a car, you also **have** to pay for insurance and registration every year.

If it is no longer a fact we use the past tense:
When I was a child, **if** I **helped** my mother, she **gave** me extra pocket money.

2 First conditional

if + present tense, + *will/won't (might/could/going to)* + verb	*If I* **invest** my money, it **will grow**.
will/won't (might/could/going to) + verb + *if* + present tense	*My money* **will grow** *if I* **invest** it.

We use the first conditional to talk about something we feel is a probable future result:
If you **leave** your money in the bank, you **won't earn** any interest and it **may lose** value over time.

We can use *might, could*, or *may* instead of *will* to suggest something is less probable:
If I **invest** it, I **might lose** it all.

or *can* to mean *sometimes*:
If you **travel** at rush hour, the trains **can be** very crowded. (this sometimes happens)

3 Second conditional

if + past tense, *would(n't) (might/could)* + verb	*If I* **invested** my money, it **would grow**.
would(n't) (might/could) + verb + *if* + past tense	*My money* **would grow** *if I* **invested** it.

We use the second conditional to talk about imaginary, impossible or unlikely situations in the present or future. The past tense does not refer to past time:
If I **went** travelling, I **wouldn't have** any money left over.

⚠ With the verb *be* we can use *was* or *were* with *I/he/she/it*:
That's what I would do if I **were/was** *you.*

We can use *was/were + to-*infinitive to refer to unlikely actions in the future:
If you **were to spend** a year travelling around the world, you'd probably need an awful lot more money than this!

4 Other words to introduce a condition

We can use other words such as *when, provided that, in case, so/as long as* and *unless* instead of *if* in zero, first and second conditional sentences.

when; as soon as

We use *when* and *as soon as* instead of *if* to show that something is more likely:
*I'll give you a lift into town **if** I finish my work in time.* (= I am not sure if I will be able to give you a lift)
*I'll give you a lift into town **when/as soon as** I finish this work.* (= I will give you a lift)

unless

We use *unless* to show a negative condition, with a similar meaning to *if ... not*:
*You won't earn much interest **unless** you invest it properly.* (= if you don't invest it properly)

provided/providing that; so/as long as

These phrases can be used instead of *if* for emphasis. *Provided/providing that* are more common in written than spoken English:
*You won't lose any money **provided that** you think of it as a long-term investment.* (= if you think)
***As long as** you get a second-hand car, you should still be able to invest some money.* (= if you get)

in case

We use *in case* to talk about precautions. Compare:
*You should keep this reference number **in case** there are any problems.* (= keep the reference number because there might be problems later)
*You should quote this reference number **if** there are any problems.* (= quote this reference number at the time of any problems)
⚠ We don't usually start a sentence with *in case*.

C Grammar exercises

1 Match the beginnings (1–8) and the endings (a–h) of these sentences.

1 If I win the competition, ...c...
2 If you boil milk, ...
3 What will you do ....
4 What happens to the engine ....
5 If I get all my work done in time, ...
6 I might buy a new laptop computer ....
7 If you agree to enrol in the diploma course, ...
8 If you put the sofa there, ...

a we'll give you the job.
b if you don't get accepted at Macquarie University?
ⓒ I'll take you somewhere nice to celebrate.
d if you put diesel fuel into a petrol-driven car?
e it forms a skin on the top.
f I'll be home by six o'clock tonight.
g you won't be able to open the cupboard.
h if my boss allows me to work from home sometimes.

2 Fill in the gaps in the extracts below using the verbs in brackets in the correct form.

1 My parents ...would love... (love) it if I .... (become) a doctor but I'm not sure I'd be able to face all those years of study. Also if I .... (be) a doctor, I .... (hate) all those hours you have to work.

2 These days I use the Internet more and more to do my shopping. If I .... (not/have) my computer, I .... (not/know) what to do. I buy clothes, books and DVDs online as well as holidays. If you .... (not/find) what you want in the shops, you .... (find) it on the Internet. I'm going to Barcelona in a few weeks and I'm going to buy my ticket on the Internet because it .... (save) me about £50 if I .... (do) it that way.

3 This production of Shakespeare's play .... (surprise) you, unless you .... (be used to) seeing all the characters being played by just two people!

4 Eggs are best kept at a cool room temperature, so I don't keep my eggs in the fridge. If I .... (keep) them in the fridge I .... (take) them out half an hour before cooking. However, not everyone has somewhere cool to keep eggs. If you .... (not/have) a cool place to store them in your home, you .... (have to) use the fridge, but just remember to take them out in time.

3 Decide if the underlined verbs are correct or not. Tick (✓) them if they are right and correct them if they are wrong.

Teacher: Is it better to have one special friend or lots of good ones?	
Student: I think that if you have lots of friends, you **1** <u>will be lucky</u>. However, I feel that everyone should have someone special. If you **2** <u>won't have</u> a special friend, you won't have someone to talk to at difficult times in your life.	1 ... *are lucky* ... 2 ....
Teacher: When do people make most friends?	
Student: Well, everyone makes friends when they are at school. If you **3** <u>are</u> in an environment where everyone is your own age, you **4** <u>would probably</u> make friends.	3 .... 4 ....
Teacher: Do you think that friends need to be similar ages?	
Student: Well, generally friends from school are similar ages. But when you **5** <u>started</u> work, for example, you meet people of different ages. If you get on well with someone and you **6** <u>will have</u> a lot in common, then age **7** <u>won't be</u> important.	5 .... 6 .... 7 ....
Teacher: Do people need to have things in common to be friends?	
Student: Well, yes. If you **8** <u>like</u> the same things, you will probably get on well. But having said that, I have a very good friend who is completely different from me. She loves sport and I hate it. If you asked me why we were friends, I **9** <u>am not able</u> to say! Maybe it's just chance – if you are in a certain place at a certain time you **10** <u>become</u> friends, but if you **11** <u>will meet</u> the same person at a different time in a different place it **12** <u>didn't</u> happen.	8 .... 9 .... 10 .... 11 .... 12 ....
Teacher: What different roles do friends play in people's lives?	
Student: Well, your friends are the people you choose to be with. And if you **13** <u>will need</u> help, you often turn to your friends. It works the other way too. When your friends need you, you **14** <u>will help</u> them.	13 .... 14 ....

4 Underline the correct words.

1 I'll put my umbrella in my bag *in case* / *provided that* it rains later.

2 *Unless* / *As long as* you pay me in advance, I'll buy the tickets for you.

3 I'm going to get fat *if* / *unless* I stop eating so much chocolate.

4 You must follow the instructions accurately *in case* / *unless* you want to risk damaging the machine.

5 When I travel on planes I always put my toothbrush in my hand luggage *in case* / *if* my suitcase gets lost.

6 Ice skating is fun *as long as* / *when* you are willing to fall over a lot!

7 Dear Mr Brown, I am writing to inform you that your library books are overdue. *Provided that* / *When* you return them immediately, you will not be fined.

8 I've just signed the contract for the job in Indonesia, starting in April. *When* / *If* I move there, I'll have to sell my car.

9 I wouldn't stay out in the sun too long *as long as* / *if* I were you.

10 I don't really like going to parties *unless* / *as long as* I know most people there.

Academic Reading

*You should spend about 20 minutes on **Questions 1–13** which are based on the Reading Passage below.*

Endangered chocolate

A The cacao tree, once native to the equatorial American forest, has some exotic traits for a plant. Slender and shrubby, the cacao has adapted to life close to the leaf-littered forest floor. Its large leaves droop down, away from the sun. Cacao doesn't flower, as most plants do, at the tips of its outer and uppermost branches. Instead, its sweet white buds hang from the trunk and along a few fat branches which form where leaves drop off. These tiny flowers transform into pulp-filled pods almost the size of rugby balls. The low-hanging pods contain the bitter-tasting, magical seeds.

B Somehow, more than 2,000 years ago, ancient humans in Mesoamerica discovered the secret of these beans. If you scoop them from the pod with their pulp, let them ferment and dry in the sun, then roast them over a gentle fire, something extraordinary happens: they become chocolatey. And if you then grind and press the beans, which are half cocoa butter or more, you will obtain a rich, crumbly, chestnut brown paste – chocolate at its most pure and simple.

C The Maya and Aztecs revered this chocolate, which they frothed up with water and spices to make bracing concoctions. It was edible treasure, offered up to their gods, used as money and hoarded like gold. Long after Spanish explorers introduced the beverage to Europe in the sixteenth century, chocolate retained an aura of aristocratic luxury. In 1753, the Swedish botanist Carolus Linnaeus gave the cacao tree genus the name *Theobroma*, which means 'food of the gods'.

D In the last 200 years the bean has been thoroughly democratized – transformed from an elite drink into ubiquitous candy bars, cocoa powders and confections. Today chocolate is becoming more popular worldwide, with new markets opening up in Eastern Europe and Asia. This is both good news and bad because, although farmers are producing record numbers of cacao bean, this is not enough, some researchers worry, to keep pace with global demand. Cacao is also facing some alarming problems.

E Philippe Petithuguenin, head of the cacao program at the Centre for International Cooperation in Development-Oriented Agricultural Research (CIRAD) in France, recently addressed a seminar in the Dominican Republic. He displayed a map of the world revealing a narrow band within 18° north and south of the equator, where cacao grows. In the four centuries since the Spanish first happened upon cacao, it has been planted all around this hot humid tropical belt – from South America and the Caribbean to West Africa, east Asia, and New Guinea and Vanuatu in the Pacific.

F Today 70% of all chocolate beans come from West Africa and Central Africa. In many parts, growers practise so-called pioneer farming. They strip patches of forest of all but the tallest canopy trees and then they put in cacao, using temporary plantings of banana to shade the cacao while it's young. With luck, groves like this may produce annual yields of 50 to 60 pods per tree for 25 to 30 years. But eventually pests, pathogens and soil exhaustion take their toll and yields diminish. Then the growers move on and clear a new forest patch – unless farmers of other crops get there first. 'You cannot keep cutting tropical forest, because the forest itself is endangered,' said Petithuguenin. 'World demand for chocolate increases by 3% a year on average. With a lack of land for new plantings in tropical forests, how do you meet that?'

G Many farmers have a more imminent worry: outrunning disease. Cacao, especially when grown in plantations, is at the mercy of many afflictions, mostly rotting diseases caused by various species of fungi, which cover the pods in fungus or kill the trees. These fungi and other diseases spoil more than a quarter of the world's yearly harvest and can devastate entire cacao-growing regions.

H One such disease, witches broom, devastated the cacao plantations in the Bahia region of Brazil. Brazil was the third largest producer of cacao beans but in the 1980s the yields fell by 75%. According to Petithuguenin, 'if a truly devastating disease like witches broom reached West Africa (the world's largest producer), it could be catastrophic.' If another producer had the misfortune to falter now, the ripples would be felt the world over. In the United States, for example, imported cacao is the linchpin of an $8.6 billion domestic chocolate industry that in turn supports the nation's dairy and nut industries; 20% of all dairy products in the US go into confectionery.

I Today research is being carried out to try to address this problem by establishing disease resistant plants. However, even the best plants are useless if there isn't anywhere to grow them. Typically, farmers who grow cacao get a pittance for their beans compared with the profits reaped by the rest of the chocolate business. Most are at the mercy of local middlemen who buy the beans then sell them for a much higher price to the chocolate manufacturers. If the situation is to improve for farmers, these people need to be removed from the process. But the economics of cacao is rapidly changing because of the diminishing supply of beans. Some companies have realised that they need to work more closely with the farmers to ensure that sustainable farming practices are used. They need to replant areas and create a buffer for the forest, to have ground cover, shrubs and small trees as well as the canopy trees. Then the soil will be more robust and more productive. They also need to empower the farmers by guaranteeing them a higher price for their beans so that they will be encouraged to grow cacao and can maintain their way of life.

17

Questions 1–3

*Choose the correct letter, **A**, **B**, **C** or **D**.*

Write your answers next to Questions 1–3 below.

1 The flowers of the cacao plant appear

    A at the end of its top branches.
    B along all of its branches.
    C mainly on its trunk.
    D close to its leaves.

2 In Africa, banana trees are planted with the cacao plants in order to

    A replace the largest trees.
    B protect the new plants.
    C provide an extra crop.
    D help improve soil quality.

3 In paragraph H, what is the writer referring to when he says 'the ripples would be felt the world over'?

    A the impact a collapse in chocolate production could have on other industries
    B the possibility of disease spreading to other crops
    C the effects of the economy on world chocolate growers
    D the link between Brazilian growers and African growers

Questions 4–9

*The Reading Passage has nine paragraphs labelled **A–I**.*

Which paragraph contains the following information?

*Write the correct letter **A–I** next to Questions 4–9 below.*

4 a list of the cacao growing areas
5 an example of how disease has affected one cacao growing region
6 details of an ancient chocolate drink
7 a brief summary of how the chocolate industry has changed in modern times
8 the typical lifespan and crop size of a cacao plantation
9 a reference to the scientific identification of the cacao plant

Questions 10–13

Complete the notes below.

*Write **NO MORE THAN TWO WORDS** from the passage for each answer.*

Write your answers in spaces 10–13 below.

Ways of dealing with the cacao plant's problems

- Need to find plants which are not affected by **10** ....
- Chocolate producers need to work directly with farmers instead of **11** ....
- Need to encourage farmers to use **12** .... methods to grow cacao plants
- Make sure farmers receive some of the **13** .... made by the chocolate industry

---

Grammar focus task

Without looking back at the exam task, fill in the gaps with the verbs from the box in the correct tense.

| become | dry | grind | happen | let | obtain | press | roast | scoop |

Somehow, more than 2,000 years ago, ancient humans in Mesoamerica, discovered the secret of these beans. If you **1** .... them from the pod with their pulp, **2** .... them ferment and **3** .... in the sun, then **4** .... them over a gentle fire, something extraordinary **5** .... They **6** .... chocolatey. And if you then **7** .... and **8** .... the beans, which are half cocoa butter or more, you **9** .... a rich, crumbly, chestnut brown paste – chocolate at its most pure and simple.

18

Likelihood based on conditions 2
third conditional; mixed conditionals; wishes and regrets; *should(n't) have*

A Context listening

1 You are going to hear Simon Brown talking to his friend, Anna, about his car. Look at the pictures below. Why do you think he regrets buying it?

2 🎧 **18** Listen and decide if the following statements are true or false.

1 Simon bought a second-hand car.

2 The price of petrol nearly doubled last month.

3 Simon has saved very little money from his job.

4 Simon took his father's advice about the car.

5 Simon has a lot of money.

3 **18◀◀** Listen again and complete these sentences.

1 If I .... a second-hand car, I .... to take out this big bank loan.

2 It probably .... so bad if the price of petrol .... last month.

3 If I .... a bit before buying the car, I .... to save quite a bit by now.

4 If only I .... to him, none of this ....

5 If I .... his advice, I .... a small fortune now.

4 Look at your answers to Exercise 4 and answer these questions.

1 Which tense is used in the *if* clause in sentences 1, 2, 4 and 5? ....
Does it refer to present or past time? ....

2 Which sentences refer to a past situation in the result clause? ....
Which structure is used? ....

3 Which sentences refer to a present situation in the result clause? ....
Which structure is used? ....

B Grammar

1 Third conditional

if + past perfect, *would(n't) have* + past participle	*If you'd asked me, I'd have done it.*
would(n't) have + past participle + *if* + past perfect	*I'd have done it if you'd asked me.*

The third conditional describes hypothetical situations in the past. We use the third conditional to imagine the result of something that did not happen:
If I'd bought a second-hand car, I wouldn't have taken out this big bank loan. (= he bought a new car so he did take out a bank loan)

We can use *might* or *could* instead of *would* to say that something was less certain:
If I'd saved more money, I might have gone on that college trip last week.

2 Mixed conditionals

if + past perfect, *would(n't)* + verb	*If I'd saved more, I'd be rich.*
if + past simple, *would(n't) have* + past participle	*If I was sensible, I'd have saved more.*
if + past perfect, *would(n't) be* + *ing*	*If I hadn't saved, I wouldn't be going on holiday.*
if + past continuous, *would(n't)* + verb	*If I was going on holiday soon, I'd be happy.*
if + past simple, *would(n't) be* + *ing*	*If I didn't have savings, I wouldn't be going on holiday.*

We use mixed conditionals when the time in the *if* clause is different from the time in the result clause.

We can mix past time and present time to imagine
◆ the present result of a hypothetical past situation or action:

      past situation   present result

If I'd taken his advice, I'd own a small fortune now instead of a big debt! (= I didn't take his advice so now I don't own a small fortune)
It wouldn't be so bad if the price of petrol hadn't almost doubled last month.

◆ the past result of a hypothetical situation in the present:

      present situation   past result

If you got on better with him, you might have listened to his suggestions. (= you don't get on with your father so you didn't listen to his suggestions)
If he had more qualifications, he would have got the job.

We can mix past time and future time to imagine
◆ the future result of a hypothetical past situation or action:

      past situation   future result

If I hadn't broken my wrist, I'd be playing tennis later. (= I did break my wrist so I am not playing tennis later)
If I'd bothered to get tickets, I'd be going to the concert tonight. (= I didn't bother to get tickets so I am not going to the concert)

We can mix future time and present time to imagine

◆ the present result of a hypothetical future situation or action:

future situation   present result

*If I **wasn't meeting** my manager later, **I'd be** at the conference now.* (= I am meeting my manager later, so I'm not at the conference now)

◆ the future result of a hypothetical situation in the present:

present situation   future result

*If I **was** at home in America, **I'd be seeing** my mother tomorrow because it's her birthday.* (= I am not at home in America, so I won't be seeing my mother tomorrow)

3 Wishes and regrets

We use *wish* + past verb to talk about situations that we would like to be different:
*I **wish** I **could** help you.* (= I can't help you and I am sorry about that)
*I **wish** my father **wasn't** always right!* (= he is always right and I find that annoying)

We use *wish* + something/someone + *would* + infinitive without *to* to show that we want something to happen or someone to change their behaviour. We do not use this with state verbs:
*I **wish they would stop** talking so loudly!* (= they are talking loudly and I want them to stop)
*I **wish this holiday would go on** forever.*

We use *wish* + past perfect to talk about past situations that we regret:
*I **wish I'd thought** about the other costs before I bought it.* (= I didn't think about the other costs and I regret it now)

We can use *never* for emphasis with a negative verb:
*I wish I'd **never** bought the car.* (= I did buy it and I really regret it now)

⚠ We can use *if only* in place of *wish* with the same meaning. It is a little more formal:
If only I had listened to my father!

4 Should(n't) have

We use *should(n't) have* + past participle to say that what did or did not happen was a mistake or a bad thing:
*I **should have listened** to him.* (= but I didn't)

We can use *never* for emphasis with a negative verb:
*I **should never have bought** it!* (= I did buy it and now I regret it)

> **Grammar extra: *If it wasn't for …***
>
> We can use *if it wasn't/weren't for* + noun phrase to say that a situation is dependent on another situation, person or thing:
> *If it **wasn't/weren't for the car**, I'd have no money worries now.* (the car is the reason for my worries)
>
> We can use *if it hadn't been for* to talk about a past situation:
> *If it **hadn't been for** your advice, I would have made the wrong decision.*

C Grammar exercises

1 Fill in the gaps with the correct form of the verbs in brackets.

Tutor: Tell me what you intend to write in your evaluation of your research.

Student: Well, firstly, if I 'd had........ (**1** *have*) a larger number of questionnaires returned, I .... (**2** *get*) more useful data.

Tutor: Is there anything you could have done to improve that?

Student: Well, I suppose I .... (**3** *receive*) more completed questionnaires if I .... (**4** *make*) the questions easier to answer, for example, 'yes/no' questions.

Tutor: Yes, I think you are right. People are too busy to answer complicated questions. Any other things you might change?

Student: Yes. I think I .... (**5** *be*) more successful with my interviews as well if I .... (**6** *plan*) the questions more thoroughly beforehand, although I'm not sure about that. If I .... (**7** *prepare*) the questions in more detail, it .... (**8** *restrict*) the interviewees too much. Oh, and another thing: if I .... (**9** *start*) collecting data sooner, it .... (**10** *not/be*) such a rush in the end.

Tutor: Good. I must admit that if you .... (**11** *not/leave*) it all so late, I .... (**12** *be able to*) support you more. If you .... (**13** *come*) to see me before you sent out your questionnaires, I .... (**14** *help*) you. It is a shame that your data was so disappointing because your research questions were very interesting.

2 Read about two scientific discoveries that were made due to chance and complete the sentences.

Alexander Fleming's most famous discovery happened entirely by accident. One day he was cleaning the culture dishes in his lab when he saw mould growing on one of the plates. There weren't any germs growing around the mould, so Fleming decided to grow more of it for experiments. He discovered that the mould acted against bacterial infections. However, Fleming's initial publication about his discovery was largely ignored by the medical community so he abandoned his research in 1932. It wasn't until 1935, when the researchers Florey and Chain saw Fleming's research papers, that the drug, penicillin, was developed.

1 If Fleming hadn't been cleaning the culture dishes, he <u>wouldn't have seen mould</u> growing on one of the plates.

2 Fleming wouldn't have grown more of the mould if there .... growing around it.

3 If his initial publication hadn't been received so poorly by the medical community, he .... in 1932.

4 Penicillin might not have been developed if Florey and Chain ....

Harold Ridley, an ophthalmologist, developed a revolutionary way of helping people with poor eyesight as a result of cataracts[1]. During World War II, Ridley worked with RAF pilots with eye injuries. He noticed that their eyes did not become infected when they had eye injuries caused by bits of Perspex from the windows of their planes. As a result of this observation he decided to implant plastic lenses in the eyes of people with cataracts. Surgeons had earlier tried replacing the lens in the eye with a glass one, but the operations always failed because the body rejected the glass lens. Ridley's operations with plastic lenses were successful. However, the medical community opposed Ridley's discoveries and it took many years for the technique to be accepted. Today over 200 million people have their sight because of Harold Ridley.

[1] Cataracts are regions of dead cells within the lens of the eye, and can cause blindness.

5 If Harold Ridley .... pilots during World War II, he wouldn't have noticed the effects of Perspex splinters on their eyes.

6 If the pilots' eye injuries had become infected from bits of Perspex, he .... to implant plastic lenses in cataract patients' eyes.

7 If earlier surgeons had used plastic lenses, the operations ....

8 It wouldn't have taken so many years for the technique to become widely available if the medical community .... Ridley's discoveries.

3 Find and correct the mistakes in the sentences below.

1 If I hadn't ~~ate~~ *eaten* so much I wouldn't have a stomach ache now.

2 What would you done if you'd failed the exam?

3 I am starting university next autumn if I hadn't had such bad exam results.

4 If the government would have kept their promise, taxes wouldn't have gone up last year.

5 I would have finished my essay on time if I didn't have the accident.

6 If I was getting married next weekend, I was very excited by now.

7 If the economic conditions had been better when I bought this house, I might make a fortune by now.

8 Life today will be very different if Thomas Edison hadn't invented the electric light.

9 If you were more considerate, you didn't make so much noise last night.

10 If I didn't go to university, I wouldn't be doing this job now.

4 Fill in the gaps using *wish* or *should* and the words in brackets in the correct form.

1 You _shouldn't have left_ (*not/leave*) school so young. You'd have a better job now.

2 I really .... (*you/ask*) me before borrowing the car yesterday. I needed to use it.

3 I'm not enjoying my degree course at all. I .... (*I/not/choose*) physics. I .... (*choose*) maths instead because I used to love it at school.

4 I .... (*I/study*) languages at school because now I travel regularly for work to Berlin and Paris.

5 That man is really annoying me. I .... (*he/stop*) whistling.

6 We're lost again. We always get lost when you have the map. You .... (*let*) me have the map from the start!

7 I .... (*I/have*) more time to work on this assignment. I'm worried I won't finish it by the deadline.

8 I .... (*it/stop*) raining. I want to go for a walk.

9 I have terrible problems with my knees. I .... (*I/not/do*) so much running when I was younger.

10 You .... (*not/tell*) Paula about the party – it was meant to be a surprise.

Academic Reading

You should spend about 20 minutes on **Questions 1–13** which are based on the Reading Passage below.

The Giant Panda

For more than 100 years, scientists have argued over exactly what a panda is. Now, finally, with the help of DNA testing, the panda has been admitted to the *ursidae* (bear) family, and the spectacled bear of South America has been confirmed as its closest living relative.

In 1869, French Jesuit missionary Pere David first described the giant panda to western science. With just a pelt and reported sighting to go on, he classified it as a bear. However, the following year, zoologist Alphonse Milne Edwards dissected the first specimen and concluded that it had more in common with the red panda, a member of the raccoon family. For more than a century, scientists quarrelled over whether the giant panda belonged to the bear family, the raccoon family or a separate family of its own.

They had good reason to be confused. The giant panda shares many physical characteristics with the red panda. Both have evolved to feed on bamboo, grasping and eating it in the same way, with similar teeth, skulls and forepaws. They also both have a distinctive cry which they use to communicate with others in their group.

In the mid-1980s there were several studies involving DNA comparisons between the species. The first investigations linked the giant panda with bears, but in 1991 further tests contradicted these findings and placed it in the raccoon family with the red panda. By the year 2000, approximately twelve studies had been completed, and all except two placed the panda in the bear family. The data from these two studies was reanalysed by other researchers, who finally concluded that the giant panda was indeed a bear.

Today, there are eight species of bear. Along with dogs, their closest relatives, cats, raccoons and weasels, they belong to the order *Carnivora*, a group of meat-eating predators that evolved some 57 million years ago. The ancestors of modern bears split from this group about 34 million years ago, and today the panda is our oldest living bear, followed by the spectacled bear. Both are survivors of an ancient lineage dating back 18 million years. The rest – the brown, black, polar, Asiatic black, sloth and sun bears – are relatively modern, dating back four to five million years.

Researchers have found that the spectacled bear and the panda have several physical features in common. The spectacled bear's muzzle is comparatively short and it has blunt molar teeth and large jaw muscles, which are good for grinding fibrous vegetation – vegetation such as bamboo. Indeed, scientists in Venezuela have found that bamboo makes up 70% of the diet of some spectacled bear populations. For most spectacled bears, however, the bromeliad, a tropical plant with fleshy leaves, is their main food source. Most species of bromeliad grow in trees, and spectacled bears therefore have to be adept tree climbers because they spend their lives foraging for these plants, as well as fruits, in the cloud forest of the Andes.

The giant panda's diet is famously dull, with bamboo representing 99% of its intake. This is rather strange given that its physiology is typical of a carnivore and it has no special adaptation for digesting cellulose, the main constituent of plant cell walls. A panda manages to digest only about 17% of the bamboo it eats (a deer living on grass achieves 80% efficiency). It typically feeds for 14 hours a day, consuming 20 kg or more of bamboo. Unable to store fat effectively, it continues eating in the bitterly cold winter, at a time when many other bears hibernate.

With such a specialised diet, the giant panda has evolved a sixth digit, a prehensile elongated wrist bone called the radial sesamoid. They use this 'false thumb' to roll bamboo leaves into fat, cigar-shaped wads which they then sever using their powerful jaws. They feed mainly on the ground but are capable of climbing trees as well. The spectacled bear is a more frequent climber and will even climb spiky cacti plants to reach fruit at the top. They also construct tree nests to act as a bed as well as a platform to feed from fruit-laden branches.

Very occasionally, the giant panda supplements its diet with meat which it scavenges. Spectacled bears eat carrion, too, and some have been known to kill small calves. Spectacled bears are highly adaptable and are found in a wide range of habitats including rainforest, dry forest and coastal scrub desert. In contrast, the giant pandas live at an altitude of between 1,200 and 3,500 metres in mountain forests that are characterised by dense strands of bamboo.

There have been many theories as to why the panda has such a distinctive coat, but the most convincing argument is that of George Schaller, one of the first western scientists to study wild pandas. He believes the contrasting coat may help prevent close encounters with other pandas. 'In pandas, a stare is a threat,' Schaller says. 'The eye patches enlarge the panda's small, dark eyes tenfold, making the stare more powerful. A staring panda will hold its head low, so presenting the eye patches. To show lack of aggressive intent, a panda will avert its head, cover its eye patches with its paws or hide its face.' Interestingly, the spectacled bear is the only other bear with comparably obvious markings around the eye.

Questions 1–8

Classify the following characteristics as belonging to

> **A** *the giant panda*
> **B** *the spectacled bear*
> **C** *both the giant panda and the spectacled bear*

*Write the correct letter **A**, **B** or **C** next to Questions 1–8 below.*

1 an extra thumb on each paw
2 a tendency to sleep in trees
3 their species originated 18 million years ago
4 the ability to adjust to different environments
5 the use of noises to socialise with each other
6 the ability to climb trees
7 the eating of meat
8 a similarity to a type of raccoon

Questions 9–13

Complete the sentences with words taken from the passage.

*Use **NO MORE THAN TWO WORDS** for each answer.*

Write your answers in spaces 9–13 below.

  9 The panda's digestive system is that of a ....
10 The giant panda must eat constantly because it can only .... a small amount of bamboo.
11 In winter, giant pandas cannot .... because of their feeding habits.
12 Spectacled bears build .... to help reach their food.
13 Giant pandas may use their .... to threaten other pandas.

Look at the following extracts from the passage. Complete the sentences below using verbs in brackets in the correct form.

> For more than 100 years, scientists have argued over exactly what a panda is. Now, finally, with the help of DNA testing, the panda has been admitted to the *ursidae* (bear) family.

1 If scientists .... (*have*) DNA testing 100 years ago, they
.... (*be able to*) discover what a panda was.

> However, the following year, zoologist Alphonse Milne Edwards dissected the first specimen and concluded that it had more in common with the red panda, a member of the raccoon family.

2 If Alphonse Edwards .... (*not/dissect*) a giant panda, scientists
.... (*not/think*) the giant panda was a raccoon.

> They had good reason to be confused. The giant panda shares many physical characteristics with the red panda; both have evolved to feed on bamboo, grasping and eating it in the same way, with similar teeth, skulls and forepaws.

3 If the giant panda .... (*not/resemble*) a red panda, there
.... (*not/be*) so many arguments among scientists.

> In the mid-1980s there were several studies involving DNA comparisons between the species. The first investigations linked the giant panda with bears, but in 1991, further tests contradicted these findings and placed it in the raccoon family with the red panda.

4 If the 1991 DNA tests .... (*not/contradict*) the earlier findings, then the
argument .... (*be*) resolved earlier.

19 Prepositions

prepositions after verbs, adjectives and nouns;
prepositional phrases

A Context listening

1 A student is being interviewed for a teacher training course. Which of the following do you think she says she's worried about?

finding accommodation

lots of hard work

controlling the class

pupils being rude to her

transport

finding maths difficult

having the right clothes

being unprepared to teach

2 🎧19a Listen and see if you were right.

3 19a◀◀ Listen again and complete the interviewer's notes below.

Notes

Reasons for applying for this course:
- has always been **1** .... teaching
- wants to gain a teaching qualification

Reasons for choosing our college specifically:
- can **2** .... accommodation **3** .... her brother
- was **4** .... the description of the course in the prospectus
- is keen on **5** .... teaching before doing it

Expectations of the course:
- a friend **6** .... her **7** .... the hard work

Concerns about the course:
- feels she is not very **8** .... maths
- has no **9** .... teaching
- **10** .... not being able to control the class
- unsure what to do if pupils **11** .... her

4 Look at your answers to Exercise 3. Find at least one example of each of the following:

1 verb + *about* ....

2 adjective + *about* ....

3 adjective + *at* ....

4 verb + *at* ....

5 adjective + *in* ....

6 noun + *of* ....

7 verb + *with* ....

8 adjective + *by* ....

B Grammar

The choice of preposition in a clause often depends on the adjective, verb or noun which comes before it.

1 Verb + preposition

Verb	Preposition
care, complain, hear, know, learn, say something, talk, think, warn, wonder, worry, write	*about*
aim, fire, laugh, look, point, shout, yell	*at*
choose, decide, differentiate, distinguish	*between*
aim, apologise, apply, forgive, hope, long, prepare, search, wait, watch, wish	*for*
learn, prevent, stop	*from*
assure, convince	*of*
concentrate, count, depend, insist, rely	*on*
apologise, explain, present, speak, talk, write	*to*
be, deal, go out, play, stay	*with*

⚠ We do not use a preposition with *marry*:
She married him last year. (**not** *She married with him*)

Verbs of saying or thinking (e.g. *complain, know, learn, say something, talk, think, warn somebody, wonder, write*) are often followed by *about* when we want to indicate the topic:
*That way you can **learn about** teaching before being asked to do it.*

⚠ Some other verbs of saying or thinking (e.g. *discuss, debate, consider, mention*) do not need a preposition:
*We need to **discuss** the problem.* (**not** *discuss about*)

Some verbs of saying (e.g. *apologise, explain, present, speak, talk, write*) are often followed by *to* + person to show who the speech is directed at:
*Have you **talked to anyone** who has done this course?*

We use *at* + person/thing after some verbs (e.g. *aim, fire, laugh, look, point, shout, yell*) to show who or what is the focus of the verb:
*If they **shout at me** in class, I'm not sure what I'll do.*

We often use *for* after verbs that show desire (e.g. *aim, hope, long, wish*) to introduce the thing we want:
*I'm **aiming for a good mark** in my next assignment.*

⚠ We use *to* after *aim, hope* and *long* if they are followed by a verb:
*I'm **hoping to** get a better mark than last year.*

2 Adjective + preposition

Adjective	Preposition
anxious, annoyed, concerned, depressed, excited, upset, worried	**about**
amazed, annoyed, astonished, awful, bad, clever, excited, good, skilled, surprised, terrible, useless	**at**
amazed, annoyed, astonished, concerned, disturbed, excited, impressed, inspired, shocked, surprised	**by**
bad, concerned, good, responsible	**for**
disappointed, interested	**in**
frightened, scared, terrified	**of**
aware, clever, cruel, generous, good, kind, mean, nasty, nice, polite, rude, selfish, true, typical, unkind	**of**
cruel, good, kind, mean, nasty, nice, polite, rude, unkind	**to**
annoyed, bored, concerned, disappointed, fed up, impressed, obsessed, pleased, satisfied, wrong	**with**

Adjectives talking about ability (e.g. *awful, bad, clever, good, skilled, terrible, useless*) are often followed by *at*:
*I'm not very **good at** maths.*

Some adjectives describing fear (e.g. *frightened, scared, terrified*) can be followed by *of*:
*There are some aspects of the course that I am a bit **scared of**.*
*Most people are **frightened of** being in front of a class for the first time.*

Adjectives describing behaviour (e.g. *clever, generous, good, kind, nice, selfish*) in a clause starting with *it, that* or *this* are often followed by *of*:
Would you like a cup of tea of coffee? **That's** *very **kind of** you.*

Adjectives describing behaviour directed towards others (e.g. *cruel, good, kind, mean, nasty, nice, polite, rude, unkind*) are often followed by *to*:
*I'm worried about the pupils being **rude to** me.*

3 Noun + preposition

Noun	Preposition
anything, information, nothing, something	**about**
excuse, explanation, ideas, in return, need, reasons, reputation, responsibility	**for**
change, decrease, drop, experience, fall, increase, rise	**in**
experience, knowledge, understanding	**of**
effect, impact, influence	**on**
in association, experience	**with**

4 Prepositional phrases: *by, in, at, on, of*

We use *by*

◆ to talk about who in a passive clause:
*But you will be taught how to deal with those things **by the tutors** on the course.*

◆ to explain how something is done:
*You can remove any dirty marks **by wiping** it with a wet cloth.*

◆ to talk about transport and communications e.g. *by plane, by email*:
*We'll be in touch **by email** soon if that's okay.*

◆ to talk about chance (e.g. *by chance, by accident, by mistake*):
*I saw the advertisement for the job **by chance** and decided to apply for it.*

We use *in* for the following expressions: *in love, in pain, in private, in touch, in debt, in danger, in a rush, in fashion, in luck, in the end.*
*Don't forget to keep **in touch** while you're away!*

We use *at* for the following expressions

◆ *at first, at large, at peace*:
***At first** I was impressed by the reputation of the university but I also like the course you offer.*

◆ *at work, at home, at school, at the airport, at university*:
*I've just finished my first degree **at Stamford University**.*

We use *on* to say why you are somewhere (e.g. *on holiday, on business, on duty*).

We use *of* with expressions of quantity (e.g. *all, any, both, either, neither*).

Grammar extra: Prepositions

We can use nouns, pronouns, or *-ing* after a preposition:
*I was really impressed **with the description** of the course in your prospectus.*
*If they shout **at me** in class, I'm not sure what I'll do.*
*Well, I've always been interested **in** teach**ing**.*

In negatives *not* comes between the preposition and *-ing*:
*I'm worried **about not** be**ing** able to control a class.*

C Grammar exercises

1 Choose the correct word (A, B or C) to complete each sentence.

1 I still haven't forgiven her .... her behaviour in front of my boss.

   (A) for   B of   C from

2 I'm going to .... to your parents about your exam results.

   A talk   B discuss   C ask

3 I'm scared .... making a fool of myself when I give the presentation.

   A for   B to   C of

4 I'm very .... in you. You've made a real mess of things.

   A concerned   B astonished   C disappointed

5 The new drug prevents the bacteria .... growing.

   A to   B from   C in

6 There are many things .... with our society today.

   A bad   B wrong   C disturbing

7 It was very generous .... you to offer to help me.

   A of   B about   C for

8 The president first became .... in politics as a student.

   A aware   B involved   C enthusiastic

2 In nine of these sentences there is a wrong preposition. <u>Underline</u> each mistake and write the correction.

1 There has been a rise in the number of people buying their own homes. .....✓.....

2 It is not difficult to distinguish amongst the emotional response to this crime and the law's response. ....

3 There is no need about a new school in this area. ....

4 We want the government to promise to make a change in the law. ....

5 I hate the way she always laughs to people. ....

6 I've decided to apply to that job in the newspaper. ....

7 Professor Ho has a good knowledge about his subject. ....

8 I'm afraid I broke this glass in accident. ....

9 My husband's staying at my cousin while he is on business in America. ....

10 I gave him one of my paintings in return for his help when I moved house. ....

11 Why do governments always insist in doing things that are unpopular? ....

12 When I was in school I did much more sport than I do these days. ....

3 Fill in the gaps in the conversation with a word from the box and a preposition.

| ~~anxious~~ | bad | choose | depend | effect | obsessed | rely | true | worried |

Teacher: Do you think that money can solve all problems?

Student: No, not really. Of course, I would be **1** ......*anxious*...... *about* money if I didn't have very much, but I believe that too much money can be **2** .... you.

Teacher: So you think it is possible to have too much money?

Student: Well, there are lots of stories in the media about people who have won lots of money in the lottery and realised that they are not happier as a result. I think that large amounts of money can have a negative **3** .... people.

Teacher: Do you think that people **4** .... modern technology like computers too much and that people are **5** .... having the latest high tech equipment?

Student: Well, yes, in some countries. But this isn't **6** .... many people in the world who are only **7** .... their next meal. In rich countries people always want a new gadget to make life easier but I'm not sure these machines do actually do that. When we go shopping we have to **8** .... hundreds of different brands of the same thing, and when these things go wrong we don't know what to do. I would prefer it if life were simpler and we didn't **9** .... expensive technologies so much.

169

4 Fill in the gaps in the letter with a preposition.

FIVE STAR HOTELS

★ ★ ★ ★ ★

Dear Mr Rees,

Thank you for your letter of 21 June. I was very disturbed 1 ....by.... your account of what happened in our hotel last week, and I am writing to apologise 2 .... this. I can understand that you were shocked 3 .... the way the employee spoke to you. There can be no excuse 4 .... such behaviour and I fully understand why you felt the need to complain 5 .... the situation. I can provide no explanation 6 .... the way the receptionist behaved.

Our hotel group has a reputation 7 .... being good 8 .... looking after our customers, and I am very sorry that your experience 9 .... our service did not confirm this. I intend to deal 10 .... the staff member appropriately and I will ensure that she does not repeat this behaviour 11 .... sending her on a retraining course next week. I would like to assure you that the behaviour you encountered is not typical 12 .... our staff.

As the manager, I am responsible 13 .... all of our employees so please accept my apologies again and this voucher worth £50 to spend in any 14 .... our hotels.

Yours sincerely,

Clive Martin
Hotel Manager

D Test practice

Listening Section 2

Questions 1 and 2

Choose the correct letter A, B or C.

1 How far away is the nearest big town to Greenville?
   A 10 kilometres
   B 25 kilometres
   C 500 kilometres

2 Which service came to the town recently?
   A fire service
   B medical service
   C weather station

Questions 3–10

Complete the notes below.

*Write **NO MORE THAN THREE WORDS AND/OR A NUMBER** for each answer.*

Volunteer storm spotters

Duties:
- Need to **3** .... the weather station as soon as the storm has passed
- Fill in a **4** ....
- Attach extracts from **5** ....

What to report:
- Hail which measures **6** .... across or larger
- Wind damage e.g. **7** .... that have been brought down
- Flooding caused by heavy rainfall

How do I become a volunteer?
- There will be a **8** .... day next month
- Contact local **9** .... if you want to attend
- Important to sign up before 31st **10** ....

These are some extracts from the recording. Without listening to the text again, fill in the gaps with the correct prepositions.

1 Today we're going to be talking .... what we as a community can do to help each other in severe weather.

2 The National Weather Bureau can provide a lot of helpful information and even warn us .... severe storms.

3 You don't have to be particularly skilled .... anything.

4 They'd also like to hear .... very heavy rainfall.

5 What should you do if you care .... our community and you want to help?

6 This will only take up a day so don't worry too much .... it.

7 You'll need to talk .... the police.

A Context listening

1 You are going to hear part of a radio programme about making sure your home is safe when you are away. Before you listen, look at the picture. What do you think the radio programme will mention?

2 🎧 **20** Listen and see if you were right.

3 **20◀◀** Listen again and complete the advice below using no more than three words from the recording.

How to protect your home

Outdoors
- If you live in an area **1** .... a lot of tall trees, cut off overhanging or dead branches.
- Put away objects **2** .... damaging missiles.

Indoors
- If you are away for a long time then find someone **3** .... on your home for you.
- Install lights **4** .... a timer so that it looks as though you are home.
- Find someone **5** .... your mail regularly.

---

4 Look at your answers and <u>underline</u> all of the relative pronouns (*where, which, who, that*).

Which relative pronoun refers to a place? ....

Which relative pronouns are used to refer to people? ....

Which relative pronouns are used to refer to things? ....

B Grammar

Relative clauses give information about a noun (or noun phrase). They are linked to the noun (or noun phrase) by a relative pronoun (e.g. *who*, *which*). The relative pronoun can be either the subject or the object of the clause, and we do not use another pronoun in the clause to refer to the noun:

*Why not install lights **which** have a timer?* (**not** ~~Why not install lights which they have a timer?~~)

⚠ We sometimes use a participle clause instead of a relative clause (see Unit 12):
the man sitting beside me (= the man who is sitting beside me)
the food kept in the fridge (= the food which is kept in the fridge)

1 Relative pronouns

We use
- *who* to refer to people:
  *Please welcome **Mike Bowers, who** is going to talk to us about how to look after your home.*
- *which* to refer to things:
  *These are dangerous if you live in **a flat which** is in a large high-rise building.*
- *that* to refer to people or things:
  *Find **someone that** can check on your home while you're away.*
  *Store away any **objects that** could become damaging missiles.*

  That is an alternative to *who* and *which* and is more common in spoken English.
  ⚠ *That* is not used in non-defining relative clauses (see below).
- *where* to refer to places:
  *This is your home, **the place where** you keep your most treasured possessions.*
- *when* to refer to times:
  *Programme them to come on at **times when** you would normally be home.*
- *whose* to show possession:
  *You're **a person whose job** involves a lot of travel.*
  *He lives in **an old house, whose roof** needs repairing.*
- *why* after *the reason* or *reasons*:
  *There are often very good **reasons why** one house is burgled and another is not.*

2 Defining relative clauses

Defining relative clauses give information after a noun to identify the noun more clearly:
*Find someone **who can collect your mail for you**.*
*Store away any objects **that could become damaging missiles** if it gets windy.* (the relative clause identifies the type of objects)

Without these relative clauses, it is unclear which person, place or thing we are referring to:
Store away any objects if it gets windy. (we do not know which objects)

We can leave out the relative pronoun when it refers back to the object of the defining relative clause. Compare:

*Maybe there's a neighbour **(that)** you can ask.* (*neighbour* is the object of the verb)
*In the evening, a house **that**'s very dark can really stand out.* (*house* is the subject of the verb: **not** ~~a house is very dark can really stand out~~)

3 Non-defining relative clauses

Non-defining relative clauses add extra, non-essential information about something. Compare:
*I applied to the university**,** which is located in the centre of the city.* (there is only one university, so its location is extra information: non-defining)
I applied to the university which is located in the centre of the city. (there is another university which is not in the centre of the city: defining)

Non-defining relative clauses are more common in written language than in spoken language.

With non-defining relative clauses
◆ we do not use the relative pronoun *that*:
  *The burglars got in through the kitchen window, **which** the owners had forgotten to shut.*
  (**not** ~~the kitchen window, that the owners~~)

◆ we separate the relative clause from the main clause with commas. There may be two commas or one comma depending on whether the relative clause comes in the middle of a sentence or at the end:
  *A letterbox can become full of uncollected letters, **which is a great help to a burglar**.*
  *Mr Smith, **who was my primary school teacher,** got married last week.*

◆ we cannot leave out the relative pronoun:
  *My new house, **which** I have just redecorated, is much larger than my old house.* (**not** ~~My new house, I have just redecorated~~)

◆ the relative pronoun can refer to a single noun phrase or to a whole clause:
  ***My neighbour, who** lives upstairs, often looks after my flat.* (*who* refers to my neighbour)
  ***Some people seem to think it's just a matter of locking all the doors, which** is fine as long as there are no nasty storms while you are away.* (*which* refers to the whole of the first phrase)

Compare the key differences between defining and non-defining relative clauses:

Defining relative clauses:
◆ identify the thing that you are talking about
◆ *that* can replace *who* or *which*
◆ the relative pronoun can be left out if it refers to the object
◆ no commas

Non-defining relative clauses:
◆ give additional, non-essential information
◆ *that* cannot be used
◆ the relative pronoun cannot be left out

◆ must have commas

4 Prepositions

When prepositions are used with relative clauses they usually come at the end of the clause in spoken English:

*You may have a neighbour that you can rely **on**.* (informal)

In formal style the preposition can be placed before the relative pronouns *which* or *whom*:

*I was unsuccessful in obtaining a place at any of the universities **to which** I applied.*

*My boss, **for whom** I have worked for over 30 years, has decided to retire.*

Grammar extra: Common collocations with relative pronouns

We often use the expression *the one* with defining relative clauses:

*He's **the one who** suggested I became a teacher.*

*My father is **the one that** taught me to play the piano.*

*That house is **the one where** I grew up.*

Where can be used after expressions such as *the situation*, *the stage* or *the point*:

*We were in **a situation where** there were no easy solutions.*

*I'm almost at **the stage where** I'm ready to quit my job and go into business for myself.*

*I've reached **the point where** I feel I should just give up.*

C Grammar exercises

1 Match the beginnings (1–10) and endings (a–j) of these sentences, and join them by adding a relative pronoun. In which two sentences can the relative pronoun be left out?

1 The college has many students ....who.... ..d...   a Mozart performed many of his operas.

2 My cousin Phillip is a solicitor; he was the one ....

3 I went to a school ....

4 I visited the theatre ....

5 Why don't you call again at a time ....

6 Mrs Jackson is the kind of teacher ....

7 Faraday was the man ....

8 Is there any reason ....

9 What was the name of that company ....

10 That's the woman ....

a Mozart performed many of his operas.

b flat I rent.

c every student wants to have.

d are classed as 'mature' because they are over 21.

e advised me to study law.

f I'm not as busy.

g invented the first electric motor.

h factory burned down yesterday?

i didn't have very good sports facilities.

j manufacturers like to keep demand above supply?

2 Rewrite the sentences below as single sentences using non-defining relative clauses.

1 My father lives in a small house full of ornaments. This makes it really difficult to clean.
My father lives in a small house full of ornaments, which makes it really difficult to clean.

2 Some students take a year out before university. This allows them to work or travel.
Some students ....

3 The Guggenheim Museum is in Bilbao. It only displays contemporary art.
The Guggenheim Museum, ...

4 My English teacher is leaving. His lectures are very interesting.
My English teacher, ...

5 The lecture was about current economic policy. It was not very easy to understand.
The lecture ....

6 In 1951 my parents arrived in New York. They stayed there for the rest of their lives.
My parents arrived in New York ....

7 I gave my assignment to the faculty secretary. She was not very friendly.
I gave my assignment ....

3 There is a mistake with relative clauses in each of the email extracts below. Find the mistakes and correct them.

1

I wonder if you can help me. I want to get in touch with the woman which we met at the meeting last week. Do you know the one I mean?

~~which~~ who

2

I'm sending this email to ask for more information about the language courses which I saw them advertised in *The Daily Star* yesterday.

....

3

How are you getting on with your new job? I'm finding my new job exhausting, that is not surprising considering I have to travel so much.

....

4

I really enjoyed the lecture which you gave it on Wednesday, and am thinking about doing my assignment on the same topic.

....

5

You left your notebook at my house. Do you need it? It's the one which in you have written your lecture notes.

....

6

I'm just emailing you to find out if you want to go to the cinema on Thursday. I've got today's newspaper which has a list of films. If you're free, let me know.

....

7

Can you pick up some shopping on your way home? I want some of those bread rolls what we had last week. Will you be able to stop at the shop?

....

8

You are clearly a person who life is full and busy and that is why we think you would like our *Ladies Personal Organiser*. For just £15.99 you ...

....

4 Read the description of how chocolate is made. Add the relative clauses (a–i) to the text in the gaps and write in the appropriate relative pronoun *where, which* or *that*.

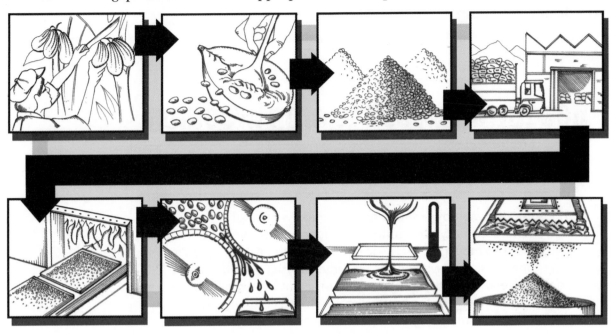

Chocolate's varied flavours, colours, shapes and textures result from different recipe traditions **1** ......g..... . The essential ingredient in all chocolate is cocoa, which is made from the cream-coloured beans **2** .... The cacao tree, **3** .... , produces a fruit about the size of a small pineapple, **4** ....

After harvesting, the cocoa beans are removed from the pods and piled in heaps **5** .... The dried beans are then transported to factories **6** .... The shells are then removed and the beans are ground into chocolate liquor – a thick brown liquid **7** .... This liquor contains a high percentage of fat (cocoa butter), **8** .... The solid block of cocoa that remains is then made into a powder **9** .... , or is mixed back with some of the cocoa butter, sugar and other flavour such as vanilla to make the different kinds of chocolate.

a .... is removed by using presses

b .... they are sorted and roasted

c .... are left for several days to dry

d .... can be used to make a hot chocolate drink

e .... grows in equatorial regions such as South America, Africa and Indonesia

f .... forms a solid at about room temperature

g ....which.... have evolved in different parts of the world

h inside .... are the tree's seeds

i .... grow in pods on the cacao tree

Academic Reading

*You should spend about 20 minutes on **Questions 1–12** which are based on the Reading Passage below.*

Robotic approach to crop breeding

Jennifer Manyweathers takes a look at a robot that is being used to identify drought-tolerant crop varieties

A The Australian sunflower industry is the major source of polyunsaturated fatty acids found in margarines and spreads. Recognised as the type of fatty acid most able to protect against heart disease, it is in everybody's best interest that Australia has a competitive and healthy sunflower industry, but in Australia there is a constant struggle with the harsh climate. However, thanks to one special robot, farmers may be able to win the battle against drought.

B Dr Chris Lambrides, a research fellow at the University of Queensland, is nearing the end of a project that aims to develop more drought-tolerant sunflowers by selecting flowers that use water more efficiently. He's done this with the help of a robot developed by the Australian National University's Research School of Biological Sciences.

C Plants undergo photosynthesis to produce energy in the form of sugar. This involves allowing carbon dioxide to enter the leaves through pores called stomata. Transpiration is the mechanism by which plants lose water through their leaves. This system is thought to facilitate the passage of minerals through the plant and is vital for healthy plants.

D However, in conditions of drought, the plants that can use the available water efficiently and lose less to the environment will be more likely to thrive and, in a commercial sense become more profitable. These plants are classified as having a high transpiration efficiency. When plants transpire, the leaves become cooler due to evaporation. Therefore, by measuring the temperature of the leaves, scientists can determine how much water is being lost through transpiration.

E   When the project first began, the researchers used hand-held infrared thermometers to measure the temperature difference between leaves of different varieties of sunflowers in an experimental plot. Wind can affect leaf temperature, and the research team discovered that its initial approach did not cater for changes in wind speed, which could not be controlled as an experimental variable. The team therefore needed a technique to measure temperature continuously that would allow it to examine the effects of other variables such as humidity. They needed a robot.

F   They designed a robot with two infrared thermometers set at 180° to each other. The robot runs on an oblong track around the experimental plot and the thermometers operate on each side of the track. In order to minimize any variables from the two thermometers, they are rotated 180° at the beginning of each run and the results are averaged. The infrared thermometers can be rotated on an angle to examine different parts of the foliage.

G   The robot is also able to detect light intensity. It has a garage on the track, where it waits until the light intensity is high enough to give useful results. If the skies darken due to rain, heavy cloud cover or sunset, the robot makes its way back to the garage to wait.

H   The main difficulty faced by the research group was to find an agronomist who could grow the perfect crop of sunflowers. The sunflower canopy had to be complete, with no visible soil, so that the thermometers would only measure the temperature of the plants and not the surrounding environment. Eight varieties of sunflower were examined. The data collected by the robot has been used by the research team to determine which variety has the highest transpiration efficiency.

I   This is not the first time such methods have been used to determine drought-resistance in plants. The team and their robot have already made a major breakthrough in the Australian wheat industry with Drysdale Wheat, which signalled the arrival of a new technique for selecting drought-resistant species.

Questions 1–4

Complete the sentences with words taken from the passage.

*Use **NO MORE THAN TWO WORDS** for each answer.*

Write your answers next to Questions 1–4.

1 In terms of our health, sunflowers are important in defending humans against

....

2 The research team wanted to find a sunflower that could cope well in ....
conditions.

3 The name of the process which is believed to help keep plants in good condition is

....

4 The research team had to rethink their initial approach when they realised they needed to
measure the impact of external conditions such as .... and ....

Questions 5–12

*The reading passage has nine paragraphs labelled **A–I**.*

Which paragraph contains the following information?

*Write the correct letter **A–I** next to Questions 5–12.*

5   the precise growing conditions required to allow the experiment to work
6   a description of the how the robot operates
7   an explanation of two important processes used by plants
8   a reference to a previous study using a different crop
9   details of what the robot does when conditions are poor
10 the name of the group responsible for making the robot
11 the number of different types of sunflower tested
12 the purpose of taking the temperature of the plants

Grammar focus task

Look at these extracts from the text. For each extract answer the following questions.

1 Do they contain defining or non-defining relative clauses?

2 Which words or ideas do the relative pronouns refer to?

3 Does the relative pronoun act as the subject or the object of the verb?

1 Dr Chris Lambrides, a research fellow at the University of Queensland, is nearing the end of a project that aims to develop more drought-tolerant sunflowers by selecting flowers that use water more efficiently.

2 ... the research team discovered that its initial approach did not cater for changes in wind speed, which could not be controlled as an experimental variable.

3 It has a garage on the track, where it waits until the light intensity is high enough to give useful results.

4 The main difficulty faced by the research group was to find an agronomist who could grow the perfect crop of sunflowers.

5 The team and their robot have already made a major breakthrough in the Australian wheat industry with Drysdale Wheat, which signalled the arrival of a new technique for selecting drought-resistant species.

21

Ways of organising texts

subject choice; introductory *it*; ellipsis;
organising information; *it*- and *what*-clauses

A Context listening

1 You are going to listen to a student interviewing a woman for a survey on shopping habits. Look at these questions. How would you answer them?

> Do you live alone?

> Do you always shop at the same place?

Super Market

> How many times a week do you do the shopping?

> Do you always shop on the same day?

2 🎧 **21** Listen and compare your answers with the woman in the interview.

3 **21◀◀** Listen again and fill in the gaps. <u>Underline</u> the subject of each verb.

1 'No, ... with my family – my husband and three children.'

2 'And how many times a week .... the food shopping?'

3 'Oh, ... it on my own. If .... with the others, ...
too many things in the trolley and .... me a fortune!'

4 '........................ the food shopping on Thursdays because .... Monday to
Wednesday and .... fewer people in the supermarket on Thursday than on
Friday.'

5 'Well, ... it once but .... it.'

'And .... you why not?'

'Well, what I like is being able to see the products and walking around the shop and
maybe buying things that aren't on my shopping list, you know. .... do
that on your computer, can you?'

4 Now read part of the student's written report. What is the difference between the kinds
of words that are used as subjects in the spoken text in Exercise 3 and the <u>underlined</u>
words that are used as subjects in the written report?

Nowadays <u>people</u> appear to do their shopping on a weekly basis at large supermarkets. <u>These supermarkets</u> seem to have largely replaced the smaller, individual shops. <u>Most people</u> tend to go to the same store on the same day of the week and, according to my survey results, it is still the women who do most of the shopping. In general, <u>the people who were interviewed</u> were not positive about online shopping. However, it is important to note that <u>the respondents</u> were interviewed at the supermarket and were not a random sample of the general public.

B Grammar

Ways of organising texts

1 The subject

We use different kinds of words as subjects depending on the context.

In informal contexts (e.g. conversation) subjects are very often personal pronouns such as *I*, *you*, *we*:
*'First **I** need to ask about your household. Do **you** live alone?'*
*'No, **I** live with my family.'*

In formal contexts (e.g. academic writing) subjects are often nouns or noun phrases, which makes the message sound factual rather than personal:
***Most people** tend to go to the same store on the same day of the week each time.*

The introductory *it*

We often use expressions beginning with *it* when the pronoun does not refer to any noun (e.g. *it is important, it is clear, it is useful, it is possible, it is difficult, it is likely, it seems, it appears*). We use this introductory *it* when the subject of the sentence is an infinitive, *-ing* or *that*-clause. This structure is more common in written English than in spoken:
***It is important to note** that these respondents were interviewed at the supermarket.* (**not** ~~To note that these respondents were interviewed at the supermarket is important.~~)
***It is clear that** women do most of the shopping.* (**not** ~~That women do most of the shopping is clear.~~)

2 Ellipsis: leaving words out

We can leave out the subject of a verb to avoid repetition, as well as any other repeated words such as auxiliaries or other verbs:
The respondents were interviewed at the supermarket and (they) were not a random sample of the general public.
The students were researching and (they were) planning their seminar presentations.

3 Organising information in a text

In formal writing we often start clauses or sentences with information that has been mentioned before. We usually place new information at the end of the clause or sentence. To develop our texts in an organised and logical way we can use the information at the end of one clause as the start of the next. This 'zigzag pattern' is common in academic writing where new ideas are taken up and developed:

new information

*People appear to do their shopping on a weekly basis at **large supermarkets**.*

***These supermarkets** seem to have largely replaced **the smaller, individual shops**.*

mentioned before   new information

The new information in the first sentence becomes known information in the second sentence.

4 Adding emphasis or contrast in a text

We can use *it*-clauses and *what*-clauses to emphasize or highlight the information that directly follows them.

It-clauses

It + *be* + main focus + relative clause	*It is* still **the women who** do most of the shopping.

Compare these sentences:
The women still do most of the household shopping at local supermarkets. (no emphasis)
***It is still the women who** do most of the household shopping at local supermarkets.* (emphasizes the women)

⚠ We cannot say: ~~They are still the women who do most of the shopping.~~

What-clauses

What + secondary focus + *be* + main focus	**What I like is** being able to see the products.

Compare these sentences:
I like seeing the products.
***What I like is** seeing the products.* (highlights being able to see products in contrast with online shopping where you can't see products)

We normally use a singular verb after a *what*-clause.

5 Repeating ideas in a text

We can link ideas in a text by using related words. These related words can be
* pronouns:
  ***Most people** tend to go to the same store on the same day of the week each time, and **they** spend between £100 and £200 a week on their household shopping.* (they = most people)

* synonyms or rewording:
  *These **supermarkets** seem to have largely replaced the smaller, individual shops. Most people tend to go to the same **store** on the same day of the week each time.* (supermarket = store)

(See Unit 9 for more information about avoiding repetition in texts.)

C Grammar exercises

1 Rewrite sentences 1–8 using *it-* or *what*-clauses to emphasize the underlined words.

1 I find <u>writing essays</u> really difficult.
   What ‌I find really difficult is writing essays.

2 The government needs <u>a lot more loyal supporters</u>.
   What ....

3 We don't want words. We want <u>action</u>.
   We don't want words. What ....

4 I really like reading novels. I don't enjoy <u>watching TV</u>.
   I really like reading novels. What ....

5 In my country <u>the bride</u> is the most important person at a wedding.
   In my country it ....

6 Governments should be dealing with <u>the causes of poverty</u>, not the results of it.
   It ....

7 I first decided to study medicine <u>when I was ill in hospital as a child</u>.
   It ....

8 When you are seriously ill <u>your family</u> suffer the most.
   When you are seriously ill it ....

2 Look at the sentences from the first paragraph of an essay answering this question.

   'The camera has changed the way we look at the world and the way that we celebrate special occasions.' To what extent do you agree with this statement?

The beginnings of the sentences are mixed up, but the endings are in the correct order. Match the beginnings (a–g) to the endings (1–7).

a Unfortunately, <u>this</u> can often interfere	..d..	1	has brought many changes to our lives.
b However, it is also true that the photographs record the event	....	2	the way we see and experience the world.
	....	3	and use <u>it</u> to create photographic records of their experiences.
c But has the photograph become			
ⓓ The invention of the camera	....	4	more important than the event or experience it is recording?
e On important occasions such as weddings,			
f One of <u>these</u> is	....	5	cameras often have a primary role.
g Most adults in this country have a camera these days	....	6	with the enjoyment of the occasion.
	....	7	so that in can be remembered in the future.

Look at the <u>underlined</u> words. What do they refer back to?

187

3 Fill in the gaps with a subject from the box.

A one kilowatt solar panel	a solar roof
~~Global energy consumption~~	Many countries
Solar panels, solar water heaters and wind generators	the government
These renewable energy systems	they
This rise	

The Future of Energy

A look at the challenge of providing the world with energy without damaging the environment.

1 _Global energy consumption_ is predicted to rise nearly sixty per cent in the next twenty years. 2 .... is due to factors such as population growth, urbanization, and economic and industrial expansion.

3 .... have set themselves renewable energy targets, hoping to be able to generate a proportion of the electricity by such renewable means as wind or solar power. On a cloudy day in Britain 4 .... can generate enough electricity for the household to play 140 hours of TV and make 35 cups of tea. 5 .... saves up to a ton of CO_2 emissions each year. 6 .... all help to provide alternative sources of energy for private homes and 7 .... are no longer prohibitively expensive. 8 .... can make savings for householders in the long run, and in Britain 9 .... is providing financial help with the cost of installing them.

4 Read the test task and the model answer. A teacher has <u>underlined</u> the problem areas and written comments. Write the corrections below.

> *Many health problems in adults such as obesity and heart disease can be linked to poor diet. Research shows that it is important to encourage healthy eating patterns at an early age in order to avoid ill-health as an adult.*
>
> *What action can be taken to encourage children to eat more healthily?*

1 <u>To educate our children about healthy eating and physical exercise is important</u>. Children need to learn what to eat and **2** <u>children need to experience</u> eating a wider variety of foods.	**1** grammar problem **2** avoid repetition
Packed lunches which are produced by the same person every day tend to contain the same food items every day too and also **3** <u>these foods tend not</u> to be the healthy option. Very often the contents of children's lunch boxes are crisps, sweets and biscuits.	**3** avoid repetition
In order to prevent the problems associated with poor diet, such as obesity and heart disease in adulthood, parents need to encourage their children to eat a greater variety of healthier foods. **4** <u>The lack of experience of eating different kinds of foods often</u> leads to poor diet in adults. Experiencing a wider variety of foods can lead to a more rounded and nutritious diet and **5** <u>experiencing a wider variety of foods can therefore lead</u> to better health.	**4** add emphasis **5** avoid repetition
6 <u>To provide support and help to parents is important</u>. One way to do this is to implement a system whereby all children get the same food. **7** <u>No child would feel ashamed or embarrassed by the contents of their lunch boxes with this system</u>. Although difficult to achieve, this would control the foods that all children ate, thereby ensuring a healthy diet. **8** <u>Eating a healthy diet</u> as a child undoubtedly has a huge influence on how healthy we are as adults.	**6** grammar problem **7** try starting with 'This system ...' **8** avoid repetition

1 It is important to educate our children about healthy eating and physical exercise.

2 ....

3 ....

4 ....

5 ....

6 ....

7 ....

8 ....

D Test practice

Academic Writing Task 2

You should spend about 40 minutes on this task.

Write about the following topic:

> *Children today play very violent games. This must be the reason for the increase in violence and crime in most major cities of the world.*
>
> *What are your opinions on this?*

Give reasons for your answer and include any relevant examples from your own knowledge or experience.

Write at least 250 words.

Grammar focus task

Put the sentences of the first paragraph of this model answer in the correct order. What is the new information in each sentence?

.... These games have become more violent over the past few years.

.... Some are concerned that playing violent games might encourage them to become aggressive in real life.

1
.... Nowadays most children regularly play games on a computer or on their television.

.... What we need to establish is whether or not this is actually true.

.... In fact, many parents worry about this and the effect these games are having on their children.

A Context listening

1 You are going to hear a student representative talking to new students and answering their questions. Before you listen, match the words (1–8) with the definitions (a–h).

1	union	a	deal with / handle documentation etc.
2	president	b	speak for
3	process (*verb*)	c	buildings, equipment or services
4	represent	d	leader
5	run (*verb*)	e	working group or board
6	election	f	organised group or association
7	committee	g	organise/manage
8	facilities	h	an organised vote

2 ∩ 22 Listen and answer the following questions.

1 What do new students need to do to get a library card?

....

2 What is the students' union?

....

3 What is the students' union responsible for?

....

3 22 ◀◀ Listen again and fill in the gaps.

Questions

1 '............................... applications quite quickly?'

2 'So, ... the student's union?'

3 'And how .... the executive committee?'

Answers

'Oh, yes. All applications ....
on the spot so they'll be able to issue you a
card straight away.'

'No, the union .... by students,
seven students to be precise.'

'Well, the executive committee ....
by the students through an election process.'

4 Look at the objects of the verbs in the questions in Exercise 3. What happens to them in the answers?

B Grammar

1 The passive: form

The active voice shows what something does. The passive voice shows what happens to something. We make the passive with a form of the verb *be* + past participle.

Tense	Passive form: *be* + past participle (+ *by* + agent)
present simple $\rightarrow$	*The union **is run** by 7 executive officers.*
present continuous $\rightarrow$	*The union **is being run** by 7 executive officers.*
past simple $\rightarrow$	*The union **was run** by 7 executive officers.*
past continuous $\rightarrow$	*The union **was being run** by 7 executive officers.*
present perfect $\rightarrow$	*The union **has been run** by 7 executive officers.*
past perfect $\rightarrow$	*The union **had been run** by 7 executive officers.*
going to $\rightarrow$	*The union **is going to be run** by 7 executive officers.*
will $\rightarrow$	*The union **will be run** by 7 executive officers.*
Other forms	
infinitive $\rightarrow$	*The union **is to be run** by 7 executive officers.*
-ing form $\rightarrow$	*The university insists on the union **being run** by 7 executive officers.*
used to $\rightarrow$	*The university **used to be run** by 7 executive officers.*
modals $\rightarrow$	*The university **should be run** by 7 executive officers.*
need to / have to $\rightarrow$	*The university **needs to/has to be run** by 7 executive officers.*
need + -ing $\rightarrow$	*The university **needs running** by 7 executive officers.*

⚠ We do not use the passive with intransitive verbs (verbs which cannot have an object): *he arrived* (**not** ~~he was arrived~~)

2 The passive: use

We use the passive

♦ when the object is more important than the subject and the agent is either obvious, not important, or unknown:
   All applications are processed *on the spot.* (it is obvious that it is the library staff who process the cards)

♦ in formal writing to make it less personal:
   You are advised *to return the application form within three days.* (impersonal)

   The active voice is more direct and personal:
   I advise you *to return the application form within three days.*

♦ when we describe a process:
   *The union **is run** by seven executive officers who **are elected** by students.*

   ⚠ We do not generally use the passive for natural (or biological) processes, where people are not involved (e.g. the carbon cycle):
   *Plants **take up** carbon dioxide from the air as part of photosynthesis.*

Notice how if we want to repeat the ending of the previous clause or sentence at the beginning of the next, we may need to use the passive:

Does the university run the union?

No, the union is run by seven executive officers

who are elected by students each year.

The executive officers are held accountable by the union council.

The council is also elected by the student population.

This pattern is typical of academic writing.

3 Reporting with passive verbs

With reporting verbs and verbs of thinking or feeling we can use
- *it* + passive verb + *that* (e.g. *agree, announce, argue, believe, claim, decide, disclose, expect, feel, hope, know, predict, recognize, report, say, suggest, think, understand*):
  It was felt that the facilities were in need of renovation.
- subject + passive verb + *to*-infinitive (e.g. *ask, believe, consider, estimate, expect, feel, know, mean, report, say, see, suppose, think, understand*):
  Our sports facilities are said to be among the best in the country. (= people say our sports facilities are among the best in the country)
  This building **is believed to be** the oldest in the town.

4 Have something done

To show that someone performs a paid service for us we use *have* + object + past participle:
You'll need to **have your photo taken**. (= someone else will take your photograph)

In informal English *get* + past participle can be used in the same way:
I **got my photo taken** *yesterday*.

5 Need + -ing

We can sometimes use *need* + *-ing* as an alternative to the passive to say that it is necessary to do something without stating who will do it:
Some facilities **need improving** *around the campus*. (= it is necessary to improve some facilities)

C Grammar exercises

1 Read the test task. Fill in the gaps in the model answer with the verbs in the box in the passive.

> **The flowchart below shows how banana chips are made.**
> **Summarise the information by selecting and reporting the main features and make comparisons where relevant.**

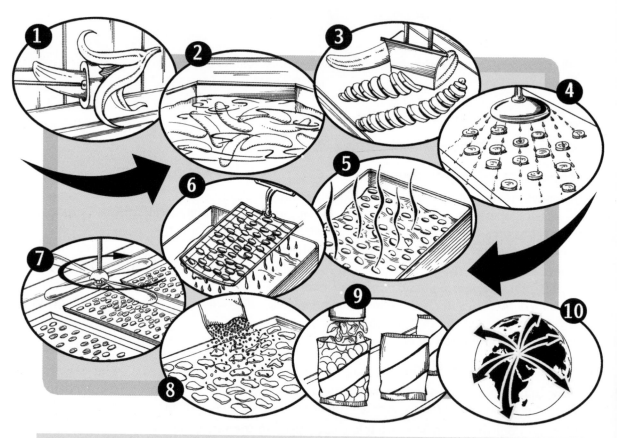

| add | distribute | fry | leave | ~~make~~ | peel | put | remove | rinse | sell | slice | soak |

The flowchart shows how banana chips **1** _____are made_____ . First, the bananas **2** _____
by a special machine and then they **3** _____ in water. Next the clean bananas
4 _____ into a chipping machine where they **5** _____ into thin chips. After this
they **6** _____ . Once they are dry, the banana chips **7** _____ in hot oil in large
deep fat fryers. The cooked banana chips **8** _____ from the fryers using a special sieve
which allows all of the oil to drain off. The banana chips **9** _____ (then) to cool. When they
have reached the right temperature, spices **10** _____ for extra taste. Finally the banana
chips are packaged ready to **11** _____ around the world and **12** _____ .

2 There are 12 mistakes with active or passive verbs in this conversation. Find and correct the mistakes.

Teacher: People <u>are said</u> that the increase in travel will lead to a loss of different cultures around the world. Do you agree?

Student: Well, yes, I suppose that is a possibility. I'm sure the way of life of many people around the world has changed by contact with tourists. But the change might have been happened anyway, I suppose.

Teacher: Yes, maybe. So, do you think we should try to stop the disappearance of native cultures?

Student: Oh, yes. I think it will be very sad if we lose different cultures. They enrich our world, don't they? But it is also argued that many people from poor countries have given opportunities that they wouldn't have had if there wasn't any tourism. Their cultures may have changed, but they have been benefited from improvements in education and health as well as their standard of living.

Teacher: So do you think that improvements like this inevitably bring about a loss of culture, as some people have been suggested?

Student: I suppose I do think that, yes. As we are continued to be provided with better and better education and we have more and more contact with the world outside our own countries, we are being become more and more the same!

Teacher: Can you give some examples of what you mean?

Student: Well, in my country we now have American restaurants and we watch American movies on TV. American culture feels to be too dominant by many people in my country. And English words have been come into my language too.

Teacher: Oh, that's interesting. And do you think that there will one day be only one language in the world?

Student: Well, the way we live has affected in a big way by things like the Internet, email and cheap travel. All countries are using English for these things, and so we all know a little bit of English already. But I am not sure it will use by all countries instead of their own language. That seems unlikely to me.

Teacher: You've made some very interesting points. Thank you.

1 ......say......	4	7	10 ....
2	5	8	11 ....
3	6	9	12 ....

3 **Fill in the gaps with an appropriate form of the verb in brackets.**

1 For a long time people ......thought..... (*think*) the giant panda was a type of raccoon.

2 At the beginning of the experiment, the chemicals .... (*place*) in the beaker.

3 In medieval times the earth .... (*believe*) to be flat.

4 Up until now students .... (*allow*) to wear what they want, but the new head-teacher has decided to introduce a uniform.

5 I can't drive you to the airport because my car .... (*service*) tomorrow.

6 Next year the new theatre .... (*open*) by some of Britain's biggest acting stars.

7 It .... (*expect*) that the President will resign due to the recent revelations.

8 Chocolate .... (*make*) from the bean of the cacao tree.

9 This report .... (*claim*) that there is corruption throughout the company.

10 Several students .... (*know*) to have cheated in their exams.

11 People need .... (*encourage*) to use public transport if we want to reduce our carbon emissions.

12 I went on holiday because I really needed .... (*take*) a break.

4 **Underline the correct words.**

> **Air pollution in cities is growing at an alarming rate. What measures could be taken to address this problem?**

Air pollution can **1** define / be defined as the addition of something harmful to the air at a faster rate than it can **2** absorb / be absorbed. Everyone should be concerned about air pollution. It **3** affects / is affected us all, and as it **4** continues / is continued to worsen, so the environmental impact increases.

One of the major causes of air pollution in cities is car use. Cars **5** use / are used for even the shortest of journeys, and all efforts by governments to encourage people **6** to use / to be used public transport seem to be failing. Industry is another major cause of pollution in our cities, but fortunately, new industrial sites **7** are building / are being built away from large urban centres.

It **8** says / is said that there are too many contributing factors for us to **9** to decide / to be decided exactly which one is the main problem, but I believe that one of the most serious problems that needs **10** to tackle / tackling is the use of the car. In some cities laws **11** have passed / have been passed concerning car use. Athens, for example, only **12** allows / is allowed a certain number of cars into the city centre each day. In my opinion, this is a good idea. With this kind of law, people have no choice and **13** force / are forced to use buses and trains. This ensures governments **14** know / is known that public transport **15** will use / will be used, and can therefore justify the investment and expense of ensuring the system works properly.

Another thing governments could do is to force people to **16** have their cars checked / check their cars for carbon emissions and fine people with cars that produce high levels of harmful gases.

D Test practice

Academic Writing Task 1

You should spend 20 minutes on this task.

The diagram shows how fruit is canned.
Summarise the information by selecting and reporting the main features, and make comparisons where relevant.

You should write at least 150 words.

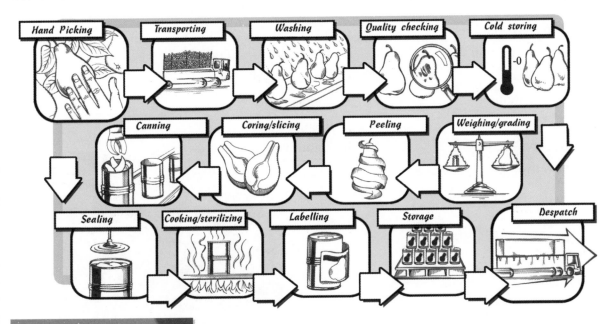

Grammar focus task

Look at these sentences describing the flowchart. Rewrite them using a passive verb. Then put the sentences in the correct order according to the flowchart.

1 They allow the cans to cool.

   Passive: ....

2 They sterilize the cans using a special heating process.

   Passive: ....

3 They take the fruit to the cannery in large trucks.

   Passive: ....

4 They check the fruit before storage and they reject any poor quality fruit.

   Passive: ....

Now write your own answer.

A Context listening

1 You are going to hear a student presenting a report on eating fish. Before you listen, match the words (1–9) to the definitions (a–i).

1	staple (*adj*)	a	advantages and disadvantages
2	controversy	b	be greater than
3	benefits and risks	c	main / basic
4	consumption	d	a heavy silver metal
5	mercury	e	harmful to the body
6	poisonous	f	contact with
7	dose	g	disagreement
8	exposure to	h	amount
9	outweigh	i	eating

2 🎧 **23** Listen and say whether these statements are true or false.

1 Eating fish might be bad for the heart.
2 Eating fish is good for the growth of the brain.
3 Some fish may contain a poison.
4 The Fisheries Scholarship funded this student's project.
5 The Fisheries Scholarship influenced the results of the study.
6 Comprehensive information is available about the pros and cons of eating fish.
7 The research noticed strong negative effects on the brain from the mercury contained in fish.
8 The student concludes that it is better for one's health to avoid eating fish.

3 Fill in the gaps in the extract from the talk with the words from the box.
23◀◀ Listen to the second half of the recording again and check your answers.

| although | despite | finally | firstly | however | in spite of |
| secondly | to sum up |

We discovered that, **1** .... the literature available on the risks and benefits of fish consumption, there are still important gaps in this information. **2** .... these gaps, **3** ...., decisions about how to advise people on fish consumption should be made based on what we know now.

4 ...., in terms of heart disease, it has been shown that consuming even small quantities of fish can lower your risk of heart disease by 17%. **5** ...., consuming fish is known to have a beneficial effect on brain development. **6** ...., **7** .... exposure to mercury through eating fish can have a negative effect on IQ levels, the effects that have been observed are relatively small.

8 ...., it would seem that the health benefits of eating fish outweigh the risks.

4 Which of the words in the box is used:

1 to show contrast? ....

2 to give one idea in a list of ideas? ....

3 to introduce the conclusion? ....

B Grammar

1 Ways of linking ideas

We use conjunctions (e.g. *but*, *because*) to join two clauses in one sentence:

clause 1   clause 2

Fish has long been a staple food in many cultures, **but** *there has been some controversy recently about the benefits and risks of fish consumption.*

clause 1   clause 2

Fish is known as a 'brain food' **because** *it is beneficial to the development of the brain.*

We can use adverbial expressions (e.g. *consequently*, *however*) to connect ideas in separate sentences. These usually go at the beginning of the sentence or clause:
Fish is known as a 'brain food' because of the benefits it has for brain development. **However,** *recent studies have shown that fish can also contain mercury.*

Some adverbial expressions (e.g. *therefore*, *however*, *also*) can be used in a variety of positions:
People **therefore** *are unsure of whether to eat fish.*
People are **therefore** *unsure of whether to eat fish.*
People are unsure **therefore** *of whether to eat fish.*

We can use prepositions (e.g. *in spite of*, *because of*) before a noun phrase or an *-ing* form:
The match was cancelled **because of the snow**. (**not** ~~because of it snowed~~)
In spite of *los****ing*** *the first game, the team went on to win the tournament.*

2 Linking expressions

Adding information

> **conjunctions:** *and, as well as*
> **adverbials:** *also, anyway, besides, furthermore, in addition, likewise, moreover, similarly*

We use these expressions to give additional information:
Fish supplies us with substances that might protect against heart disease. **Moreover,** *in many cultures fish is known as a 'brain food'.*

Sequencing

> **adverbials:** *first, next, after that, then; firstly, secondly, finally*

Firstly, secondly and *finally* are used to order points in an argument:
Firstly, *in terms of heart disease, it has been shown that consuming even small quantities of fish can lower your risk of heart disease by 17%.* **Secondly,** *consuming fish is known to have a beneficial effect on brain development.* **Finally,** *...*

First, next, after that and *then* describe the order of activities in a process:
First *the fruit is picked by hand.* **Then** *it is transported to the factory.*

Cause, reason, result

conjunctions: *because, so*
adverbials: *therefore, consequently, so, thus, as a result*
prepositions: *because of, due to, on account of, owing to*

Because introduces the reason for something, and *so* introduces the result:

reason
*I eat fish three times a week **because** it protects against heart disease.*

result
*Fish protects against heart disease **so** I eat it three times a week.*

Therefore, consequently, so, thus, and *as a result* introduce the result of a situation or action:
***As a result**, people are unsure whether to increase or decrease the amount of fish they eat.*

We use *because of, due to, on account of* and *owing to* to introduce the reason for something:
*The match was cancelled **because of** the snow.* (**not** ~~because of it was snowing~~)
*The buses were all running late **owing to** the bad weather.*

⚠ We can use *due to, on account of* and *owing to + the fact that* with a clause:
*The match was cancelled **due to the fact that** it was snowing.*

Contrasting

conjunctions: *but, although, though*
adverbials: *alternatively, however, in contrast, nevertheless, on the contrary, on the other hand, yet*
prepositions: *in spite of, despite*

We use *but* between two contrasting ideas:
*Fish has long been a staple food in many cultures, **but** there has been some controversy recently about the benefits and risks of fish consumption.*

Although can come at the beginning or in the middle of two contrasting ideas. We use a comma between the two clauses:
***Although** the work was supported by grants from the Fisheries Scholarship Fund, this did not affect the research findings.*
*The work was supported by grants from the Fisheries Scholarship Fund, **although** this did not affect the research findings.*

We use *in spite of* and *despite* + noun/-*ing* at the beginning or in the middle of two contrasting ideas:
***In spite of the considerable amount** of literature on the risks and benefits of fish consumption, there are still important gaps in this information.* (**not** ~~in spite of there is a considerable amount~~)
*I eat fish regularly for health reasons **despite not** liking it much.* (**not** ~~despite I don't like it~~)

⚠ We can use *despite* and *in spite of + the fact that* with a clause:
*I eat fish regularly for health reasons **despite the fact that** I don't like it much.*

Giving examples

> **adverbials:** *that is to say, in other words, that is (i.e.), for example*

We use these expressions to link two clauses that give the same information in a different way or to give examples:

*There has been some controversy recently about the benefits and risks of fish consumption. **For example**, we know that fish supplies us with polyunsaturated fatty acids, substances that might protect against heart disease.*

Grammar extra: Written and spoken English

Some linking expressions are more common in either written (formal) or spoken English:

Written: *thus, therefore, finally, furthermore, hence, moreover, nevertheless, in addition, firstly, secondly, finally*
*Regular comsumption of fish can lower your risk of heart disease by 17%. **Furthermore**, it can have a beneficial effect on brain development.*

Spoken: *so, then, anyway*
*Eating fish is good for you **so** I try to eat it regularly.*

C Grammar exercises

1 Choose the best endings for these sentences.

1 I hurt my knee quite badly so
   (a) I had to go to hospital.   **b** I didn't have the right running shoes.

2 One way to improve your health is to eat more fruit and vegetables. Alternatively,
   a you could increase your risk of heart disease.   **b** you could exercise more.

3 Humans like to form social groups. Likewise,
   a many other mammals live independently of each other.
   b many other mammals live together in small communities.

4 I didn't work hard at school. Consequently,
   a I did well at university.   **b** I failed most of my exams.

5 I believe travelling can help us to understand other cultures. Furthermore,
   a it can help you to become more independent.
   b it can be a lonely experience at times.

6 In spite of the fact that learning to speak a foreign language requires a lot of time and effort,
   a many people give up after a short time.   **b** many people manage it successfully.

7 In my experience, vegetarians tend to be quite healthy. In contrast,
   a many meat-eaters do not have a healthy diet.   **b** they look after their bodies well.

8 Fifty per cent of all newspaper readers in this country only read the sports section of the paper. In other words,
   a many people are not interested in news.
   b sports are reported very well in the newspaper.

9 Sydney is the biggest city in Australia, yet
   a it isn't the capital.   **b** it is the oldest city.

10 You wouldn't be allowed to drive in my country because
   a there is no point in getting a car.   **b** you need to be over 21.

11 Studies suggest that although sales of cookery books have increased significantly in the past five years,
   a we spend less time than ever in the kitchen.   **b** we enjoy experimenting.

12 There are delays on all trains due to the fact that
   a passengers should allow extra time.   **b** there is a shortage of drivers.

2 <u>Underline</u> the correct linking expressions.

> *It is generally accepted that smoking causes the deaths of large numbers of people. In order to address this problem governments should ban smoking in public places.*
>
> *To what extent do you agree or disagree with this statement?*

Many people think that the best way to reduce deaths from smoking is to ban smoking in public places. **1** <u>However,</u> / In addition, it is not as simple as that. There are several reasons why I do not consider this approach to be suitable.

2 Alternatively, / Firstly, banning activities often increases their popularity by making them seem more exciting. **3** Furthermore, /In contrast, most smoking takes place in the privacy of people's homes, and would **4** therefore / nevertheless not be affected by the ban. **5** Thirdly, / Similarly, a ban on smoking would make extra demands on the police.

6 Although / Despite the ideas behind banning smoking in public places are good, an alternative approach needs to be taken, in my opinion. Schools should lead the way in discussing the harmful effects of smoking not only on the smokers themselves but on others around them. **7** In addition, / Consequently, parents need to support these efforts by encouraging their children to understand the negative aspects of smoking.

If we adopted these measures, I believe fewer people would take up smoking **8** as a result. / moreover. To some extent these things are already happening. **9** And / Nevertheless, further efforts are needed.

3 Fill in the gaps with the linking expressions in the box.

as a result	because	but	firstly	for example	however	~~moreover~~	similarly

1. Regular exercise increases the blood flow to your heart and keeps your heart healthy.
   ......Moreover...... , it provides you with a general sense of well-being.

2. In times of recession people stop spending, which can have serious consequences for the economy. .... , poor sales can lead to closures of some businesses.

3. In this talk I will outline several possible reasons for melting polar ice caps.
   .... , it could be because of climate change. Another reason could be ...

4. These days many famous musicians are getting involved in political causes. .... , famous actors are often seen on television promoting some charity or other.

5. Pets can have a calming effect on their owners. .... , having a pet can increase stress due to the demands made on the owner to look after the pet properly.

6. Some people believe that we have too many public holidays, ... I believe they are a good idea .... it is important to find time to celebrate traditions.

7. In my city there are too many cars on the road and there are always traffic jams.
   .... , it is difficult for people to judge how long their journeys will take.

4 Write one or two sentences with a similar meaning to the sentences below, using the words in brackets and any other words you need.

1 Despite the rise in profits this year, our company is still losing money. (*although*)

Although there has been a rise in profits this year, our company is still losing money.

2 The head of my department called an emergency meeting so I had to cancel all of my afternoon appointments. (*because*)

3 It is now much cheaper to rent a DVD at home so fewer people are going to the cinema these days. (*due to*)

4 The cost of basic foods has risen because petrol prices increased last month. (*As a result*)

5 Although there are over 30 girls on this course, the boys still outnumber the girls by two to one. (*but*)

6 Although there are some advantages to the pace of modern life, it also has its disadvantages. (*However*)

7 The numbers of red deer in the wild increased slightly in the 1980s, although the increase was not sufficient to take them off the endangered species list. (*in spite of*)

D Test practice

Academic Reading

You should spend about 20 minutes on **Questions 1–12** which are based on the Reading Passage below.

Experience versus *speed*

Certain mental functions slow down with age, but the brain compensates in ways that can keep seniors as sharp as youngsters.

Jake, aged 16, has a terrific relationship with his grandmother Rita, who is 70. They live close by, and they even take a Spanish class together twice a week at a local college. After class they sometimes stop at a café for a snack. On one occasion Rita tells Jake, 'I think it's great how fast you pick up new grammar. It takes me a lot longer.' Jake replies, 'Yeah, but you don't seem to make as many silly mistakes on the quizzes as I do. How do you do that?'

In that moment, Rita and Jake stumbled across an interesting set of differences between older and younger minds. Popular psychology says that as people age their brains 'slow down'. The implication, of course, is that elderly men and women are not as mentally agile as middle-aged adults or even teenagers. However, although certain brain functions such as perception and reaction time do indeed take longer, that slowing down does not necessarily undermine mental sharpness. Indeed, evidence shows that older people are just as mentally fit as younger people because their brains compensate for some kinds of declines in creative ways that young minds do not exploit.

Just as people's bodies age at different rates, so do their minds. As adults advance in age, the perception of sights, sounds and smells takes a bit longer, and laying down new information into memory becomes more difficult. The ability to retrieve memories also quickly slides and it is sometimes harder to concentrate and maintain attention.

On the other hand, the ageing brain can create significant benefits by tapping into its extensive hoard of accumulated knowledge and experience. The biggest trick that older brains employ is to use both hemispheres simultaneously to handle tasks for which younger brains rely predominantly on one side. Electronic images taken by cognitive scientists at the University of Michigan, for example, have demonstrated that even when doing basic recognition or memorization exercises, seniors exploit the left and right side of the brain more extensively than men and women who are decades younger. Drawing on both sides of the brain gives them a tactical edge, even if the speed of each hemisphere's process is slower.

In another experiment, Michael Falkenstein of the University of Dortmund in Germany found that when elders were presented with new computer exercises they paused longer before reacting and took longer to complete the tasks, yet they made 50% fewer errors, probably because of their more deliberate pace.

One analogy for these results might be the question of who can type a paragraph 'better': a 16-year-old who glides along at 60 words per minute but has to double back to correct a number of mistakes or a 70-year-old who strikes keys at only 40 words per minute but spends less time fixing errors? In the end, if 'better' is defined as completing a clean paragraph, both people may end up taking the same amount of time.

Computerized tests support the notion that accuracy can offset speed. In one so-called distraction exercise, subjects were told to look at a screen, wait for an arrow that pointed in a certain direction to appear, and then use a mouse to click on the arrow as soon as it appeared on the screen. Just before the correct symbol appeared, however, the computer displayed numerous other arrows aimed in various other directions. Although younger subjects cut through the confusion faster when the correct arrow suddenly popped up, they more frequently clicked on incorrect arrows in their haste.

Older test takers are equally capable of other tasks that do not depend on speed, such as language comprehension and processing. In these cases, however, the elders utilize the brain's available resources in a different way. Neurologists at Northwest University came to this conclusion after analyzing 50 people ranging from age 23 to 78. The subjects had to lie down in a magnetic resonance imaging (MRI) machine and concentrate on two different lists of printed words posted side by side in front of them. By looking at the lists, they were to find pairs of words that were similar in either meaning or spelling.

The eldest participants did just as well on the tests as the youngest did, and yet the MRI scans indicated that in the elders' brains, the areas which are responsible for language recognition and interpretation were much less active. The researchers did find that the older people had more activity in brain regions responsible for attentiveness. Darren Gleitman, who headed the study, concluded that older brains solved the problems just as effectively but by different means.

Questions 1–3

*Choose the correct answer **A, B, C** or **D**.*

1 The conversation between Jake and Rita is used to give an example of

    A the way we learn languages.
    B the changes that occur in our brains over time.
    C the fact that it is easier to learn a language at a young age.
    D the importance of young and old people doing things together.

2 In paragraph six, what point is the analogy used to illustrate?

    A Working faster is better than working slower.
    B Accuracy is less important than speed.
    C Accuracy can improve over time.
    D Working faster does not always save time.

3 In the computerized distraction exercises, the subjects had to

    A react to a particular symbol on the screen.
    B type a text as quickly as possible.
    C move an arrow in different directions around the screen.
    D click on every arrow that appeared on the screen.

Questions 4–7

*Complete each sentence with the correct ending **A–F**.*

*Write the correct letter **A–F** next to Questions 4–7 below.*

4 According to popular psychology
5 Researchers at the University of Michigan showed that
6 Michael Falkenstein discovered that
7 Scientists at Northwest University concluded that

    A the older we get the harder it is to concentrate for any length of time.
    B seniors take longer to complete tasks but with greater accuracy.
    C old people use both parts of their brain more than young people.
    D older people use their brains differently but achieve the same result.
    E the speed of our brain decreases with age.
    F older people do not cope well with new technology.

Questions 8–12

Complete the summary below.

*Choose **NO MORE THAN ONE WORD** from the passage for each answer.*

Write your answers in spaces 8–12 below.

People's bodies and **8** .... grow older at varying stages. As we age our senses take longer to process information and our aptitude for recalling **9** .... also decreases.

However, older people's brains do have several advantages. Firstly, they can call upon both the **10** .... and **11** .... which is already stored in their brain. Secondly, although the **12** .... of each side of their brain is reduced, they are able to use both sides at once.

Grammar focus task

These extracts are from the text. Without looking back at the text, match the beginnings (1–7) and endings (a–g).

1 ... evidence shows that older people are just as mentally fit as younger people because
2 ... although certain brain functions such as perception and reaction time do indeed take longer,
3 Although younger subjects cut through the confusion faster when the correct arrow suddenly popped up,
4 Just before the correct symbol appeared, however,
5 The ability to retrieve memories also quickly slides and
6 Drawing on both sides of the brain gives them a tactical edge, even if
7 ... when elders were presented with new computer exercises they paused longer before reacting and took longer to complete the tasks, yet

a the speed of each hemisphere's process is slower.
b they more frequently clicked on incorrect arrows in their haste.
c the computer displayed numerous other arrows aimed in various other directions.
d they made 50% fewer errors.
e their brains compensate for some kinds of declines in creative ways that young minds do not exploit as well.
f it is sometimes harder to concentrate and maintain attention.
g that slowing down does not necessarily undermine mental sharpness.

24

Showing your position in a text
pronouns; adverbs; verbs; adjectives

1 You are going to hear two students, Nick and Tina, discussing a topic with their tutor. Look at the pictures below. What do you think the topic is?

2 🎧 24 **Listen and decide whether these statements are true or false.**

1 Tina believes that her time at school was good for her.

2 Nick had a bad experience at school.

3 Nick believes that the boy who was bullied probably feels bad about his school days.

4 Nick likes the idea of staying at home all day.

5 Tina's friend was able to meet new friends easily.

6 Tina believes that you receive a better standard of education in school.

3 24◄◄ **Listen again and fill in the gaps.**

1 Well, I'm a bit like you, Tina. I went to a normal school and, ... , I had a great experience there. Mind you, ... that being educated at home would be good for some children. There was a boy in my class who was bullied by some older boys, and .... he must look back at his school days and feel really bad.

2 Yes, I think that's a good point. But, ... , schools do seem to be more overcrowded and less well-funded these days and .... the advantages of home education in terms of the quality of education. That's .... the way my friend felt. Mind you, ... she finds it hard to interact in large groups of people. And, ... , she doesn't have a great relationship with her parents these days. .... she had enough of them as a child!

4 Look at your answers in Exercise 3 and find examples of:

1 two verbs that express the speaker's attitude or opinion ....

2 three adverbs that show how the speaker feels about the idea ....

3 two adverbs that show possibility ....

B Grammar

When speaking or writing we can choose language to indicate our feelings, attitudes, judgments and beliefs. Task 2 in the Writing section of the IELTS test generally asks you to discuss a topic. We have to decide where to position ourselves on the topic and demonstrate this through the language we use.

1 Pronouns

In formal writing, first person pronouns (e.g. *I*, *you*, *we*) are not very common, but we can use them to

♦ give our opinion of the topic being discussed with *I* or *we*:
I would argue that all children should attend school.

♦ show we are part of the group and identify with the reader, usually with *we* or *us*. Compare:
*Is it better for **us** to educate **our** children at home rather than send them to school?*
*Is it better for **parents** to educate **their** children at home rather than send them to school?*
The use of *us* in the first sentence changes the text from objective comment to a more subjective one.

2 Adverbs

To show our attitude, feelings or assessment of something we can use

♦ single adverbs (e.g. *actually, frankly, fortunately, unfortunately, personally, luckily, interestingly, naturally, surprisingly*):
***Frankly**, I'd be totally bored staying at home all day.*
*But, **unfortunately**, schools do seem to be more overcrowded and less well-funded these days.*

In speech we often use *actually* to correct someone or to show that we disagree with something that has been said:
***Actually**, she believes that she received a better education as a result.*

♦ adverbial phrases that express the speaker's view of a generalization (e.g. *broadly speaking, by and large, in general, overall, on the whole, to a great extent*):
*But, **in general**, I don't think it is a good idea.*

♦ adverbial phrases of opinion (e.g. *in my/our view, in my opinion*):
***In my opinion** that's a disadvantage.*

To soften the tone of an argument we can use adverbs of possibility (e.g. *certainly, definitely, maybe, perhaps, possibly, presumably, probably*):
*Well, that's **certainly** the way my friend felt.*
***Perhaps** she had enough of them as a child!*
*So, **maybe** that's a result of her education experience.*

To show that the information has come from somewhere/someone else, we can use adverbial phrases that report the views of other people (e.g. *apparently, according to (somebody), evidently*):
***According to my friend** they did fun things like going out for walks.*
***Apparently** there is a network of parents who teach at home.* (someone else told me this)

Position of adverbs

Comment adverbs often come at the beginning or the end of a clause (e.g. *according to, fortunately, interestingly, luckily, surprisingly, unfortunately*):

Interestingly, *she doesn't have a great relationship with her parents these days.*
She doesn't have a great relationship with her parents these days, **interestingly**.

Many adverbs can also come before the main verb or after *be*:
It is **probably** *best.*
He would **possibly** *feel quite differently.*

⚠ *Definitely* is not usually used at the beginning of a clause:
I am **definitely** *coming to the party.* (**not** *Definitely I am coming to the party.*)

3 Verbs

To show our opinion or feelings we can use verbs such as *think, suppose, believe, feel, guess, see*:
I **think** *that's a good point.*
I **can see** *that being educated at home would be good for some children.* (= I can understand)

When the subject is *I*, it is sometimes preceded by *personally*:
Personally, *I feel the teachers did a really good job.*

To show that we are expressing our ideas rather than facts or to sound more cautious we can use modal verbs of possibility (e.g. *may, might, could, must, can*) and verbs like *seem* or *appear*:
I think he **must** *look back at his school days and feel really bad.*
Schools **seem** *to be more overcrowded and less well-funded these days.*

4 Adjectives

We can use adjectives
- to show our feelings (e.g. *glad, delighted, overwhelmed*):
  Anyway, I'm **glad** *that my parents didn't educate me at home.*
- with *it* + *be* + adjective + *that* to show possibility and opinion (e.g. *clear, possible, probable, likely*):
  Yes, but **it is likely that** *those people will be very similar.*

C   Grammar exercises

1   <u>Underline</u> the correct word or phrase in the sentences below.

1   I'm very worried about the plans to build a new shopping centre here. <u>*According to*</u> / *Apparently* my friend they want to knock down some of the houses.

2   *Apparently,* / *Personally,* I believe that we will live longer in the future.

3   Joshua is working this weekend so *presumably* / *actually* he will have some time off at a later date.

4   We cannot say for sure but *definitely* / *perhaps* an advertising campaign would encourage people to recycle their waste more.

5   *Overall,* / *Luckily,* we can see that the experiments done by the early scientists have had a great effect on our lives today.

6   We should *probably* / *personally* all reflect on the way we live our lives and try to be more environmentally aware.

7   *Certainly,* / *Surprisingly,* John agreed to come when I invited him – I hadn't expected that!

8   *In my opinion* / *Unfortunately* the number of students leaving university without completing their degrees is rising.

2   Put the words in brackets into the sentences below in a suitable place. There may be more than one possible answer.

    certainly
1   I ∧ believe she is the right person for the job, but I feel she may need some further training. (*certainly*)

2   The start of the course has been delayed because the tutor is ill. (*apparently*)

3   I want to go to university when I leave school. (*definitely*)

4   I was late for the exam because my bus didn't come, but the exam hadn't started on time so I only missed a few minutes. (*luckily*)

5   The university has decided to close the music department. (*unfortunately*)

6   It is time to reorganise our company structure. (*perhaps*)

7   My tutor was impressed with the effort I had put into my assignment, but suggested a few changes. (*On the whole*)

8   It is true that people are living longer today than in the past. (*probably*)

3 Replace the underlined part of each sentence with an adverb from the box.

> actually _apparently_ evidently frankly
> on the whole possibly surprisingly unfortunately

1 <u>I've heard that</u> he is a teacher. ...Apparently...

2 <u>To be honest</u> I don't really like this kind of literature. ....

3 <u>I found it unexpected that</u> the survey revealed that university students today spend longer on their work than in the past. ....

4 <u>I'm not happy about it but</u> I can't come to your party because I'm working. ....

5 <u>To sum it up, it seems that</u> people prefer to spend festivals with their families or friends rather than alone. ....

6 <u>From what I have read in the journal, it seems that</u> scientists believe the new drug will work. ....

7 <u>I am not absolutely certain about this but</u> if we reduce the amount we consume, we will become happier. ....

8 <u>As a matter of fact</u> I think this is the best piece of work you've done so far. ....

4 Put the words or expressions in brackets into a suitable place in the model answer and make any other necessary changes.

> *Many people have changed from a mainly meat-based diet to a vegetarian one in recent years. What are the possible reasons for this and to what extent do you consider it a sensible option?*

There are many reasons why people follow a vegetarian diet. Firstly, it is because ∧ it is wrong to kill [they believe that] animals. This ∧ is due to religious beliefs or it is their own personal philosophy. (they believe that; may be; [may be] could be)

Another motivation for stopping eating meat is health. The high fibre content of a vegetarian diet reduces the likelihood of suffering from some bowel problems and heart disease. In addition, fewer vegetarians than meat-eaters are overweight. A further advantage is that a vegetarian diet is cheaper than eating meat. (it is possible that; according to research; seems to; can be)

Nevertheless, there are some disadvantages. Vegetarians lack a lot of the vitamins and minerals that are present in meat, such as iron or vitamin B12, or calcium if you do not include dairy products in your diet. There is also the social problem of not being able to eat food available at parties and restaurants. However, in terms of health a vegetarian is more likely to be healthy than a non-vegetarian and the advantages outweigh the disadvantages. (it is clear that; can; overall; personally I feel that)

D   Test practice

Academic Writing Task 2

You should spend about 40 minutes on this task.

Write about the following topic:

> *School children are becoming far too dependent on computers. This is having an alarming effect on reading and writing skills. Teachers need to avoid using computers in the classroom at all costs and go back to teaching basic study skills.*
>
> *Do you agree or disagree?*

Give reasons for your answer and include any relevant examples from your own knowledge or experience.

Write at least 250 words.

Grammar focus task

Look at the sentences from a model answer to the question above. Fill in the gaps using the words in the box.

| actually   definitely   frankly   I believe   in my opinion |

1 Modern technology does a lot of our thinking for us and as a result .... we are losing our ability to work things out for ourselves.

2 Rather than holding students back, I believe modern technology has .... improved standards of education considerably.

3 .... handwriting and spelling skills have .... deteriorated in recent years.

4 ...., I find some notes or texts which are handwritten impossible to read.

Now write your own answer.

25

Nominalisation in written English
forming nouns from other parts of speech (verbs, adjectives and linking words)

A Context listening

1 You are going to hear Julie describing what happened when she was stung by a bee. Which symptoms do you think she had?

> itching   pain   redness   shaking   sneezing   swelling

2 🎧 25 Listen and check if you were right.

3 25◀◀ Listen again and answer these questions.

1 What was unusual about what happened when Julie was stung by a bee? ....

2 Where did she get stung? ....

3 How did it feel? ....

4 What happened to her foot? ....

5 What other effects were there? ....

4 Read this written scientific account of the effects of bee stings.

> Following a bee sting the normal reaction is burning pain, redness, irritation and itching. After a person has been stung by a bee once, they may become allergic to the bee's venom. There is a 60% risk of a serious reaction upon re-sting. In this situation there may be swelling in the area around the bite, it may become red and sore, the victim may have breathing difficulties, a dry cough, abdominal pain and vomiting. In extremely serious cases, the throat may swell, blocking the airway and the heart may stop.

Look at the <u>underlined</u> words in the extracts from what Julie said. How are these words expressed in the written text?

1 I was really surprised by how much <u>it hurt</u>. ....

2 <u>It itched</u> a bit too. ....

3 My foot began to go red and <u>swell up</u>. ....

4 Then I began to find it <u>difficult to breathe</u> and <u>kept coughing</u>. ....

5 Compare the language in the written report with the spoken language.

1 What happens to the spoken verbs in the written report? ....

2 What are the most common verbs in the written text? ....

B Grammar

When we choose to give the main information in a clause as a noun phrase rather than as a verb this is called 'nominalisation'.

1 Nominalisation in written English

In spoken English we usually use a subject + verb to describe an event:

subject + verb
*I **reacted** badly.*

subject + verb   + verb
*Then really quickly **my foot began to go red** and **swell up**.*

In formal written language we use language that is less personal, so we often use a noun form instead of a verb. The written scientific account describes the same reaction like this:

noun   noun   noun   noun
*Following a bee sting the normal **reaction** is **redness**, **irritation** and **itching**.*

noun
*In this situation there may be **swelling** in the area around the bite.*

In the spoken example the events are expressed by verbs (*go red*, *swell up*). In the written examples the events have been changed into nouns (*redness*, *swelling*). Notice that the only verb in the written examples is the non-action verb *be*.

We can also change some adjectives to nouns. Compare:
*The cathedral is **tall** and can be seen from all over the town.*
*The cathedral's **height** makes it visible all over town.*

The common differences between spoken and written English are:

Spoken
- action or events are expressed as verbs:
  swell up

- events happen to people or are carried out by people:
  I reacted badly, my foot began to go red

- personal pronouns are used as subjects:
  I, she

- verbs are often action or event verbs:
  reacted, trod, itched

Written
- actions or events may be expressed as nouns or noun phrases:
  swelling

- events are expressed impersonally:
  the normal reaction is ...

- nouns used as subjects:
  a person, the throat

- verbs are often not action or event verbs:
  be, have

- sentences have a lot of vocabulary words

2 Reasons for using nominalisation

Making texts impersonal and authoritative

By turning actions into nouns we make the text sound less personal and more authoritative. We don't use personal pronouns (e.g. *I*, *you*, *he*) as much.

Compare:

*Following a bee sting **the normal reaction** is **burning pain**, **redness**, **irritation** and **itching**. In this situation there may be **swelling** in the area around the bite.*

*Then really quickly **my foot began to go red** and **swell up**. **It just got bigger** and bigger. **It itched** a bit too. **I** was really surprised by how much **it hurt**.*

The nominalisations have been underlined. The spoken account is much more personal and uses active verbs.

Adding information

Nominalisation is particularly useful for Academic Writing Task 1 because we can do several things to add information to nouns in English:

- count: *the **two** charts*
- describe: *the two **coloured** charts*
- classify: *the two coloured **bar** charts*

We cannot do the same with verbs. It is only by changing verbs into nouns that we can add information words to a text in such a concise way.

Avoiding repetition

We can use nominalisation to avoid repetition when we want to refer back to a previously mentioned idea (see Unit 21):

*The number of unemployed **increased** by 5% last month. The reason for **this increase** is still unclear.*

Nominalisation can also be used to paraphrase what has been said. In the IELTS Listening and Reading tests different words are used in the texts and the questions. Compare:

Listening text:

Then I began to find it difficult to breathe and kept coughing, although I didn't have a cold.

Question:

Which TWO of the following symptoms did Julie experience?

    A breathing problems
    B shaking
    C a cough
    D a high temperature
    E chills

Options A and C are nominalisations of the verbs used in the listening text.

C Grammar exercises

1 Write possible noun forms for the following verbs.

1 to research: _research, researcher_
2 to study: ....
3 to find: ....
4 to respond: ....
5 to measure: ....
6 to earn: ....
7 to advertise: ....
8 to examine: ....
9 to suggest: ....
10 to create: ....

2 Complete the sentences with the noun form of the adjectives in brackets.

1 The graphs show a significant _difference_ (*different*) between the ages at which men and women marry.
2 The .... (*strong*) of the government's argument for changing the law is that many car accidents happen whilst drivers are speaking on their mobile phones.
3 The .... (*deep*) of the lake means that no one has ever seen the bottom.
4 Some parts of the world are not only important in terms of their biodiversity, but they also have a special .... (*beautiful*) that must be conserved.
5 This is a good essay in parts, but you need to express yourself with more .... (*clear*) at times.
6 The discovery of a new species of monkey in Africa is of great .... (*interesting*) to both naturalists and the general public alike.
7 The .... (*difficult*) facing the scientists now is how to prove their theory.
8 The results of this research need to be treated with .... (*cautious*).
9 The .... (*significant*) of the findings surprised even the researchers.
10 Many older people are afraid to go out at night due to the increase in .... (*violent*) in our larger citites.
11 The current .... (*controversial*) over pensions is likely to continue for some time.
12 We apologise for any .... (*confusing*) caused by the last-minute change to the schedule.

3 Underline the best answers.

> *The two pie charts show the average spending by households in a country at two different points in its economic development.*
>
> *Summarise the information by selecting and reporting the main features, and make comparisons where relevant.*

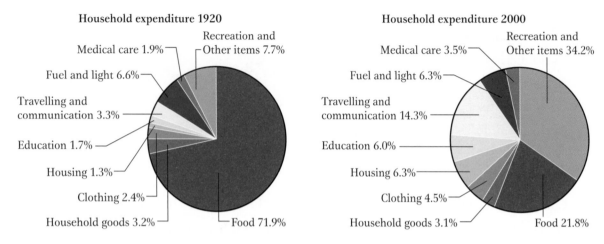

The two pie charts give information about **1** *what households spent their money on /*
household expenditure on goods and services in 1920 and 2000. It is immediately obvious
that **2** *there are some quite significant differences / some things are significantly different*
between the two charts.

In 2000 **3** *the largest proportion of expenditure was / most money was spent* on recreation
and other items whereas in 1920 it was on food, with recreation and other items
accounting for just 7.7%. There is a great difference in terms of **4** *the amount of money*
people spent on food / food expenditure between the two years. In 1920 nearly 72% of
5 *the total household budget / the total of what households spent* went towards food,
compared to only 22% in 2000.

6 *There has been a notable increase in / People have notably increased* the amount of money
spent on travelling and communications between the two dates. In addition, the charts
show **7** *a significant rise in the proportion of money spent on clothing / that people spent more*
on clothes in 2000 compared to 1920.

There are some similarities, however. For example, in both 1920 and 2000 **8** *people spent a*
similar proportion on fuel and lighting. / the proportion of fuel and lighting expenditure was
roughly the same.

4 Fill in the gaps in the second sentences with nouns so that they have a similar meaning to the first sentences.

1 a <u>She wrote books</u> that children enjoyed.

   b Children enjoyed ..<u>her writing</u>.. .

2 a Young girls <u>are spending increasing amounts</u> on make-up because they have been <u>influenced</u> by advertising.

   b .... on make-up amongst young girls is on the .... due to the .... of advertising.

3 a <u>I failed</u> to get good enough grades to get into university because <u>I was ill</u> on the day of the exam.

   b The reason for my .... to get good enough grades to get into university was my .... on the day of the exam.

4 a If you <u>eat</u> healthily you can <u>reduce</u> the chances of getting ill.

   b A healthy .... can lead to a .... in the chances of getting ill.

5 a If you <u>use</u> the Internet you <u>risk</u> getting viruses and <u>losing</u> important information.

   b .... of the Internet increases the .... of getting viruses which may cause the .... of important information.

6 a When people <u>are content</u> because their lives are <u>successful</u> they tend to be easier to <u>communicate</u> with.

   b .... due to personal .... tends to lead to improved .... with other people.

7 a In the thirteenth century engineers <u>developed</u> new ways to <u>construct</u> buildings which made it possible to build the soaring arches of Salisbury Cathedral.

   b .... in .... in the thirteenth century made it possible to build the soaring arches of Salisbury Cathedral.

8 a The IELTS reading module is <u>difficult</u> because it has long articles with lots of new vocabulary in them.

   b The .... of the IELTS reading module is due to its long articles containing a lot of new vocabulary.

D   Test practice

Academic Writing Task 1

You should spend 20 minutes on this task.

> *The graph below shows the population figures of different types of wild birds in the United Kingdom between 1970 and 2004.*
>
> *Summarise the information by selecting and reporting the main features, and make comparisons where relevant.*

Write at least 150 words.

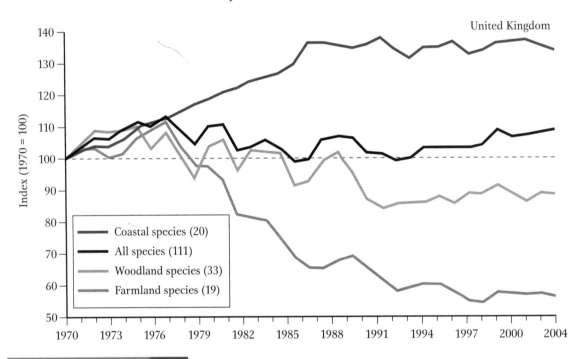

Population of wild birds: 1970–2004

Look at the extracts from a model answer and <u>underline</u> all examples of nominalisation.

1   Since 1994 there has been an improvement in numbers of all species, although the graph shows a slight decrease in 2000.

2   There was also a fall in the number of woodland birds of around 30% between 1974 and 1998.

3   It is only the coastal birds that have seen a steady increase in population over this period.

46 A (➢ Unit 23)
47 C (➢ Unit 23)
48 B (➢ Unit 24)
49 C (➢ Unit 24)
50 A (➢ Unit 25)

Entry test

If you have the wrong answer, see the units indicated for more information.

1 B (➢ Unit 1)
2 C (➢ Unit 1)
3 B (➢ Unit 2)
4 B (➢ Unit 2)
5 C (➢ Unit 2)
6 B (➢ Unit 3)
7 A (➢ Unit 3)
8 B (➢ Unit 4)
9 C (➢ Unit 4)
10 A (➢ Unit 5)
11 A (➢ Unit 5)
12 C (➢ Unit 6)
13 B (➢ Unit 6)
14 C (➢ Unit 7)
15 B (➢ Unit 7)
16 A (➢ Unit 8)
17 C (➢ Unit 8)
18 A (➢ Unit 8)
19 B (➢ Unit 9)
20 C (➢ Unit 10)
21 A (➢ Unit 10)
22 C (➢ Unit 10)
23 B (➢ Unit 11)
24 C (➢ Unit 11)
25 A (➢ Unit 12)
26 B (➢ Unit 12)
27 A (➢ Unit 13)
28 B (➢ Unit 13)
29 A (➢ Unit 14)
30 A (➢ Unit 14)
31 C (➢ Unit 15)
32 B (➢ Unit 15)
33 A (➢ Unit 16)
34 A (➢ Unit 17)
35 C (➢ Unit 17)
36 A (➢ Unit 18)
37 C (➢ Unit 18)
38 B (➢ Unit 19)
39 A (➢ Unit 19)
40 B (➢ Unit 20)
41 B (➢ Unit 20)
42 C (➢ Unit 21)
43 C (➢ Unit 21)
44 A (➢ Unit 22)
45 B (➢ Unit 22)

Unit 1

A: Context listening

2 1 playing and watching football; playing the guitar in a band
3 1 T   2 F He is studying really hard for his exams this month.
   3 F His parents own a restaurant.   4 F He practises the piano most mornings.   5 T   6 F His cousin is living in Thailand.   7 F He supports his local team.
4 1 sentences 3 and 7   2 sentences 4 and 5   3 sentence 1
   4 sentences 2 and 6

C: Grammar exercises

1 2 b   3 a   4 b   5 a   6 b   7 a   8 b (➢ B1 and B2)
2 2 sees   3 isn't studying; don't think   4 's he doing; 's trying
   5 breathe in; give out   6 want   7 drive   8 are travelling
   9 runs   10 are falling (➢ B1–B3)
3 2 have (state verb)   3 is going up (*year by year* tells us this is a gradual change over time)   4 is catching up   5 know
   6 is causing   7 think   8 agree (➢ B2 and B3)
4 2 ~~are increasing~~ is increasing   3 ~~decreases~~ is decreasing
   4 ~~is warming~~ warms   5 ~~is rising~~ rises   6 ~~change~~ changes
   (be careful of verb/subject agreement) (➢ B1 and B2)

D: Test practice

Listening

Questions 1–3: multiple choice
Test tip: Read all the questions carefully before you listen. Underline or highlight any key information or words that you need to listen for (e.g. *How long is the heated swimming pool?*) Use the questions to help you find your way through the listening text. If you miss an answer, just move on to the next one.

1 A (*a heated indoor pool, which is just 15 metres long*)   2 A (*We even offer complimentary classes for beginners*)   3 C (*we can only have a maximum of seven people in the sauna at any one time, so you do need to put your name on the list for that*)

Questions 4–10: notes completion
Test tip: Read through the notes carefully before you listen and try to predict what type of information you need to hear (e.g. for question 4 you will need to write down two days of the week, or for question 5 you will need to write a time). Pay careful attention to the word limit and check your spelling at the end.

4 Tuesday; Friday (*There are classes on Monday, Tuesday and Friday in the morning*)   5 6.00/six (pm); 7.30/seven thirty (pm)
(*There are classes ... every Saturday and Sunday in the evening. Those classes are a bit longer, starting at 6.00 and finishing at 7.30.*)
6 one day/1 day/once (*each day is a different level, so you only come once a week*)   7 level(s)/class(es) (*Most people start at the*

lower level, and then you can talk to the instructor about changing if you think it's too easy.)   8 Doherty (*My name is John Doherty, that's DOHERTY*)   9 11.00/eleven (am) (*I have appointments from 9.00 to 10.30, so could you make it 11.00?*)   10 0117 965 478 (*my number's 0117 965 478*)

Grammar focus task
1 want   2 are always looking   3 Do members have to
4 don't actually allow   5 suits   6 think

Unit 2

A: Context listening
1   A CDs   B a laptop computer   C a roast chicken   D a purse
E a handbag   F a TV
2   1 CDs; a roast chicken; a purse   2 B (*So you see, you do need to be careful to lock your door at all times of the day*)
3   1 called   2 happened; was watching   3 used to keep
4 would leave   5 walked   6 didn't hear; was listening
7 went; opened; took
4   1 sentences 2 and 6   2 sentences 1 and 5   3 sentence 7
4 sentences 3 and 4   5 past simple; past continuous; *would*; *used to*

C: Grammar exercises
1   2 was   3 took   4 was   5 received   6 meant   7 invented
8 laid   9 allowed   10 replaced   11 increased   12 did not
own   13 walked   14 rode (> B1 and Appendix 1)
2   2 made   3 were studying   4 was describing   5 picked up
6 noticed   7 was crying   8 apologised   9 said   10 didn't
know   11 made   12 happened   13 was showing
14 was examining   15 was smiling   16 got   17 said
18 laughed   19 wasn't looking   20 inspired   21 started
(> B1 and B2)
Used to is possible in 1 and 2: *used to have* and *used to make*
3   2 would/used to follow   3 moved   4 visited
5 would/used to give   6 Did you use to have (*would* is not used with state verbs or in questions)   7 really used to like/used to really like (*would* is not used with state verbs)
8 used to/would go   9 used to/would spend   10 took
11 did you use to have to (*would* is not used in questions)
12 used to have to (*would* is not used with state verbs)
13 didn't use to look forward to (*would* is not generally used with negatives) (> B1 and B3)
4   3 used to go   4 ✓   5 noticed   6 ✓   7 realised
8 was snowing   9 skidded   10 ✓   11 phoned   12 ✓
(background scene)   13 stopped (event)   14 ✓   15 came
16 ✓ (> B1–B3)

D: Test practice
Reading
Questions 1–9: locating information
Test tip: Scan the passage for relevant information, and then check that it matches the question exactly (e.g. for question 2 the experiment is mentioned several times but only paragraph D describes how it was done). Remember that the words in the passage may paraphrase the words in the questions.
1 E (*prey spiders did not respond to them in any way*)   2 D (*The researchers allowed various prey spiders to spin webs in the*

laboratory and then introduced Portia spiders.*)   3 F (*lions hunting at night, for example*)   4 D (*To simulate the shaking effect of a breeze the zoologists used either a model aircraft propeller or attached a tiny magnet to the centre of the web*)   5 B (*They will attack something about twice their own size*)   6 A (*for jumping spiders that sneak onto other spiders' webs to prey on their owners, it can be the difference between having lunch and becoming it*)   7 B (*Portia spiders live mostly in tropical forests, where the climate is hot and humid.*)   8 B (*The fifteen known species of Portia jumping spiders*)
9 F (*Portia spiders are clearly intelligent and they often learn from their prey as they are trying to capture it. They do this by ...*)

Questions 10–13: multiple choice
Test tip: Read all the questions and options and underline or highlight any important information or key words that you need to find in the passage. Use the questions to locate the relevant part of the reading passage. If you cannot find an answer, just move on to the next one and come back to this one later.
10 A (*Portia spiders moved more when the webs were shaking* (vibrating) *than when they were still* (motionless) so B is incorrect; C is incorrect: *they were more likely to capture their prey during tests in which the webs were periodically shaken than in those where the webs were undisturbed*; D is incorrect: *If the spiders were placed onto unoccupied webs, they would make no attempt to change their movements*)   11 A (*They'd make a big pluck with one of their hind legs* = make strong vibrations with one leg; B and C are incorrect: *the spiders would ... then creep forwards up to five millimetres before the vibrations died down*; D is incorrect: *the violent twanging produces a pattern of vibrations that match those caused by a twig falling onto the web*)   12 C (*this is the first example of an animal making its own smokescreen that we know of*; A is incorrect: lions also do this; B is incorrect: Portia spiders mimic trapped insects not other prey-eating animals; D is incorrect: we are not told that spiders are the only animal that uses 'trial and error')
13 B (*Sometimes they will even take an indirect route to reach a prey spider ... When it does this, the Portia spider is actually solving problems and thinking ahead about its actions.*)

Grammar focus task
1 a   2 c   3 b

Unit 3

A: Context listening
1   A logical order would be: 1 F   2 C   3 A   4 D   5 E   6 B
2   1 C   2 A   3 D   4 E   5 B
3   1 've collected   2 read   3 've been feeling   4 've just got up
4   a sentence 4 (present perfect simple)   b sentence 1 (present perfect simple)   c sentence 3 (present perfect continuous)
d sentence 2 (past simple)

C: Grammar exercises
1   3 have already seen   4 have just received   5 were   6 ✓
7 represented   8 have played   9 ✓   10 have not travelled
11 went   12 ✓ (> B1)
2   2 has increased (*since*)   3 rose (*in 2005*)
4 has risen (*each year*)   5 was (*from 1995 to 2005*)
6 have overtaken (*since 2005*)   7 has grown (*each year*);
occurred (*between 1995 and 2000*) (> B1)

3 2 've been working 3 have now finished 4 've made
5 said (*at last week's lecture*) 6 haven't found 7 've done
8 used 9 went 10 learnt 11 've been wondering
12 've given (➤ B1 and B2)

4 2 've been living (*for the past three years*) 3 've been studying
(focus on activity) 4 Have you done 5 've been (state verb)
6 've travelled 7 've done 8 've started 9 've been having
('*ve been taking* is also possible – focus on activity and
duration) 10 've just passed (recent activity) 11 've taken
(*it's the first time*) 12 've never felt ('*ve never been* is also
possible) 13 've been doing ('*ve been taking* is also possible –
focus on activity) 14 've always wanted 15 've always been
16 've already worked (➤ B1 and B2, Grammar extra)

Answers will vary. Suggestions: 17 I've been studying English
since I was six years old. 18 I haven't studied any other
languages. / I have studied … / I studied French at school but
I've forgotten almost everything now. 19 I've been to …
20 I've been reading a lot and taking lots of practice tests.
21 My life has changed a great deal. I've finished university …
(➤ B1 and B2)

D: Test practice
General Training Writing Task 1

Test tip: Read the question carefully. Make sure you include all
the information required in your letter and make sure you stick
to the time limit so that you leave enough time to answer Task 2.
Do not write any addresses.

See model answer in unit.

Grammar focus task

1 I have lived in this town all my life 2 I have been working as
a receptionist at a local hotel 3 I have read many guidebooks

Unit 4

A: Context listening

1 1 d 2 a 3 f 4 c 5 h 6 b 7 g 8 j 9 e 10 i

2 1 January 27, 1756 / 27 January 1756 / January 27th, 1756 /
27th January 1756 2 one/1 3 (a) composer 4 six/6
5 (the) violin

3 1 was born; had already died 2 was; had also been
3 mastered; had copied 4 was; had written
5 hurried; spread 6 were; had ever been

4 1 past simple 2 past perfect

C: Grammar exercises

1 2 had entered 3 had made 4 had not discovered
5 had also turned up 6 had multiplied (➤ B1)

2 2 had doubled 3 remained 4 began 5 had tripled
6 was 7 increased 8 had reached 9 had peaked
10 had managed (➤ B1)

3 2 'd always been 3 'd heard 4 arrived 5 'd been feeling
6 had come 7 'd walked 8 'd learnt 9 had prepared
10 'd been expecting ('d expected) 11 took off
12 didn't feel 13 approached 14 had done 15 stepped
16 hadn't burnt 17 'd been hoping ('d hoped)
18 managed 19 'd done (➤ B1 and B2, Grammar extra)

4 2 had started 3 bought 4 'd never taken 5 stayed; visited;
'd been; 'd liked (liked); 'd decided 6 'd been developing 7 'd
already discussed; 'd made; 'd phoned; felt; hadn't waited 8 'd
been running (➤ B1 and B2)

D: Test practice
Reading
Questions 1–6: choosing paragraph headings

Test tip: Try to get the general idea of what each paragraph is
about. Make sure that the heading you choose reflects the overall
message in the paragraph and not just one fact.

1 vii (Paragraph A tells us about an advertisement for pens that
brought 5,000 people into a shop.) 2 ix (Paragraph B tells us
about earlier pens and their problems; there were 350 patents for
pens in fifty years. A patent is a formal application to
manufacture something so that no one else can copy it.) 3 vi
(Paragraph C tells us that one of the Biro brothers was annoyed
at problems he had with fountain pens, so he decided to invent a
new one.) 4 iv (Paragraph D tells us about the problem with
the first design and how this was solved with a second design
which worked better. We also learn that the brothers moved to
Argentina.) 5 viii (Paragraph E tells us that the United States
Department of War requested the pens be made in the U.S., so an
American company bought the rights from the Biro brothers.)
6 iii (Paragraph F tells us that an American man on holiday in
Argentina saw the pens and copied them back in the U.S.)

The following headings are incorrect: i (Although fountain pens
are mentioned in the text none of the paragraphs tells us that
they are no longer used = *are history*.) ii (The Biro brothers were
never very famous.) v (Paragraph E tells us that the United
States Department of War actually helped the progress of the
Biro pen.)

Questions 7–9: multiple choice

Test tip: Read all the questions and options and underline or
highlight any important information or key words that you need
to find in the passage. Use the questions to locate the relevant
part of the reading passage. If you cannot find an answer, just
move on to the next one and come back to this one later.

7 D (*Depending on the climate or air temperature, sometimes the
pens would do both* i.e. leak and clog. A is incorrect: the pens were
never manufactured; B is incorrect: there is no mention of the
manufacturing technology; C is incorrect: the first pen was
designed for use on leather – we are not told that it could not
write on paper.) 8 A (*The first Biro pen, like the designs that had
gone before it, relied on gravity for the ink to flow to the ball bearing
at the tip.* B is incorrect: the second pen was based on capillary
action, not the first; C is incorrect: the pen did not work with
heavy ink; D is incorrect: the pen only worked when held
upright.) 9 C (*The Biro brothers had failed to secure a U.S. patent
on their invention.* A is incorrect: it was Loud's patent that had
expired, not the Biro brothers' patent; B is incorrect: we know
that a patent gave the sole rights to manufacture; D is incorrect:
there is no mention of Reynolds having any contact with the Biro
brothers, and they sold the permission to Eversharp.)

Questions 10–12: short-answer questions

Test tip: Scan the text for the information you need. It is
important to write only the key words and take note of the word
limit (here you are told to write no more than two words and/or a
number).

10 leather 11 (in) Argentina (**not** ~~it was in Argentina~~)
12 (in) 1945 (**not** ~~it was in 1945~~)

Grammar focus task

1 had taken out; had sold   2 had patented; soon became
3 had observed   4 bought; returned; discovered; had long since
expired   5 challenged; lost; had failed

A: Context listening

1   hockey; Scotland and Greece
2   1 Scotland   2 four/4   3 3/three   4 mountain lodge
    5 Greece   6 three/3   7 four/4   8 (a) (small) hotel   9 islands
3   1 A   2 B   3 A   4 C   5 A
4   1 present continuous   2 *will*   3 *going to*   4 sentences 1 and 5
    5 sentences 2–4

C: Grammar exercises

1   2 will be   3 are predicted to work   4 are going to feel
    5 will certainly have   6 is likely to become
    7 are going to happen   8 will undoubtedly continue
    9 will probably result   10 will find   11 are likely to lead to
    12 will develop (➢ B2 and B3, Grammar extra)
2   2 we'll take   3 we're going to visit   4 they're holding
    5 they aren't staying   6 we'll probably do   7 we're going to do
    8 we're also going to try   9 You'll love   10 you'll probably
    end up   11 we'll see (➢ B1–B3)
3   2 'm taking   3 'll tell   4 'll pick   5 'm seeing
    6 will probably finish   7 'll need   8 'm meeting
    9 'll probably want   10 won't go on   11 will be
    12 'll see (➢ B1 and B2)
4   Answers will vary. Suggestions: 1 I'm going to visit my
    grandmother. (*I will visit my grandmother at the weekend*
    sounds like a promise rather than a planned visit.)
    2 I'm travelling to America next week.
    3 I think we will stop using fax machines. (➢ B1–B3)

D: Test practice

Reading

Questions 1–5: sentence completion

Test tip: Sentence completion with a box of possible answers is
similar to matching questions. Scan the passage for the key words
in the questions and underline or highlight them. Then carefully
read the information close to those words and try to match it to the
ideas in the options (A–F). Remember there are more options than
you need to use. Some of the extra options may not be mentioned
at all, or may be the opposite of the information in the passage.

1 F (*For some careers like medicine and law, it's essential you have
specific qualifications.*)   2 D (*Mature entrants don't always need
formal qualifications*)   3 E (*If you are interested in self-development
and meeting people, you should find out who else will be on the
course.*)   4 B (*You might prefer an open or distance learning course
if ... you're at home looking after pre-school children.*)   5 C (*... and
want to be a journalist, you could write for the student newspaper or
work on the radio*)

Questions 6–9: classification

Test tip: Underline or highlight the key words in the reading passage
(e.g. *academic, vocational*). Carefully read the information nearby and
try to match the information in the passage to the facts in the
questions (6–9). Remember the words in the questions will not always
match the words in the passage exactly. Here you need to decide
whether these questions apply to only one type of course or to both.

6 C (*Further education colleges offer academic courses and work-
related courses*)   7 B (*For a career in plumbing, a vocational course
is essential.*)   8 A (*You might prefer an academic course if you like
researching, analysing and presenting arguments.*)   9 B (*A
vocational course is better if you like doing things with your hands
and working manually.*)

Grammar focus task

1 will help   2 'll need   3 'll ensure   4 am I going to do
5 will help

The future forms used are: *will, going to*

Will is used to give suggestions and advice ➢ B2

Going to is used to talk about future intentions ➢ B3

A: Context listening

2   Phil advises Janet to practise in front of the mirror.
3   1 will be working   2 will have given   3 will be feeling
    4 will have rehearsed   5 leaves
4   1 sentences 2 and 4   2 sentences 1 and 3   3 sentence 5

C: Grammar exercises

1   2 won't (will not) be reading   3 will be playing computer games
    4 will be doing sport; studying   5 will be resting
    6 will be seeing friends (➢ B3)
2   2 will have peaked – a   3 will have risen – d
    4 will have grown – f   5 will have gone up – b
    6 will have increased – e (➢ B4)
3   2 ✓   3 ~~they won't ask~~ they don't ask
    4 ~~is your meeting about to start~~ does your meeting start
    5 ~~after I'll get~~ after I get   6 ✓   7 ✓
    8 ~~We're about to fly~~ We fly
    9 ~~I'll receive~~ I receive (➢ B1)
4   2 'll be travelling   3 'll hopefully have saved up
    4 get (*when* + present simple)   5 'll probably have been
    travelling (*for a few months* = duration)   6 'll have visited (*by
    then*)   7 was going to do   8 'll be starting/'m about to start
    9 won't have finished   10 find out (*as soon as*) (➢ B1–B5,
    Grammar extra)

D: Test practice

Academic Writing Task 2

Test tip: Make sure that you read all parts of the question
carefully and address each point made. Organize your thoughts
and ideas well. Do not try to memorize essays. Make sure you
have at least 40 minutes to spend on this task and try to leave
time to check you spelling at the end.

Model answer

Nowadays, most people worry about over-population and living in
crowded cities. However, it is predicted that we will have the
opposite problem by the year 2030 when one third of the
population will be aged 65 or over and birth rates are predicted
to decline. What effect will this have on our society?

By 2030 the percentage of the population aged 65 or older will
have risen significantly, to more than 30%. This means that fewer
people will be working, and therefore fewer people will be paying
income tax. In the future it may be necessary for governments to
increase the official retirement age to 70 or even older. When

today's 30-year-olds are in their sixties it is unlikely that they will enjoy the relaxed lifestyle that today's older generation can expect when they give up work. Governments will therefore need to make sure that this older generation is healthy and fit enough to continue working.

However, I believe the biggest impact will be on the younger generation. In 2030 the younger generation will need to work much harder to support the large number of older people. If this trend continues then it is possible that our entire culture will change. For example, most marketing companies today try to target the younger generation with their products and advertisements. If the majority of the population is older then this will change and companies will begin to target the older generation instead.

So, what can be done now to prevent these problems? Firstly, I believe that governments of developed countries should find ways to encourage people to have larger families and increase the birth rate. Secondly, I believe that they should encourage migration from developing countries so that the problems of over-crowding can be solved.

Grammar focus task

1 will have risen   2 will be working   3 will be paying   4 are

Unit 7

A: Context listening

2   1 A, C, G   2 B
3   1 room   2 garden   3 transport   4 60   5 week
6 electricity
4   Group 1 nouns are countable; group 2 nouns are uncountable.
Other countable nouns: bed, bedside table, bills, desk, garden, lamp, location, mirror, wardrobe, rent, room, types, view, week
Other uncountable nouns: furniture, transport, electricity

C: Grammar exercises

1   2 advice   3 information   4 cakes   5 sizes   6 situations
7 electricity (➢ B1, B2 and Grammar extra)
2   2 has come   3 were   4 shows (*data* is uncountable)
5 is included   6 were   7 is   8 was (➢ B1 and Grammar extra)
3   2 many   3 amount   4 few   5 little (*sleep* is uncountable)/
few (*hours* are countable)   6 much/many   7 little
8 number   9 many   10 many   11 much (➢ B3)
4   2 something (positive statement)   3 ✓   4 Few (*places* is countable)   5 some/many (positive statement)   6 a few (a small quantity)   7 plenty of / a lot of / lots of (*much* is not usually used in positive sentences)   8 ✓   9 any (= it does not matter which time)   10 ✓ (*places* is countable)
11 No (➢ B2 and B3)

D: Test practice

Reading

Questions 1–6: matching

Test tip: Underline or highlight each of the company names listed (1–6) in the passage. Then read the relevant information for each company carefully and match it to one of the ideas in the box. Remember there will be more ideas in the box than you need and that the words in the box will not match the words in the passage exactly.

1 D (*Corpe Nove ... has made a prototype shirt that shortens its sleeves when room temperature rises*)   2 G (*Nexia Biotechnologies ... scientists have caused a stir by manufacturing spider silk from the milk of genetically engineered goats*)   3 C (*Nano-Tex ... can make fabrics more durable, comfortable, wrinkle-free and stain-resistant*)
4 A (*Schoeller Textil ... uses nanotechnology to create fabrics that can store or release heat*)   5 B (*Created in 2003 by Quest International ... and Woolmark ... SPT is a new technique of embedding chemicals into fabric...Designers could incorporate signature scents into their collections ... Hay fever sufferers might find relief by pulling on a T-shirt* = hay fever sufferers would find relief if their medication was put into the material)   6 F (*Developed by Cargill Dow, it is the first man-made fibre derived from a 100% annually renewable resource* = environmentally-friendly)

Options E and H are not used; E refers to a material that no one has made yet (see paragraph 6) and H refers to materials made by companies not on this list (see paragraphs 7–9).

Questions 7–14: summary completion

Test tip: Read through the summary carefully and try to predict what type of information you need to find in the passage (e.g. for question 7 you will need to find the name of a company). Pay careful attention to the word limit you are given and make sure you copy the words correctly.

7 Ingeo (*Ingeo's impact on fashion will derive instead from its emphasis on using natural sustainable resources.*)   8 soya bean (*Soya bean fibre ... is a better absorber and ventilator than silk, and retains heat better than wool.*)   9 weaving (*Clunky earlier attempts involved attaching electronic components after the normal weaving process.*)   10 electronic components   11 battery (*powered by a small battery, Luminex ...*)   12 costumes (*Costumes made of the fabric wowed audiences at Verdi's Aida in Washington, DC, last year.*)   13 fragile (*this ultimate of ambitions has remained elusive in daily fashion, largely because electronic textiles capable of such wizardry are still too fragile to wear*)   14 accessories / handbags (*Accessories with this chameleon-like capacity – for instance, a handbag that alters its colour*)

Grammar focus task

2 C   3 U   4 C   5 U   6 C   7 C   8 C *Choice* can also be uncountable: *I don't have much choice.*

Unit 8

A: Context listening

1   environment: climate, global warming, ozone depletion
satellites: fully-equipped, observation, launch, monitoring, outer space, instrument, operational costs, precise
2   1 in 2002   2 ten/10   3 ERS 1   4 ERS 2
5 fifteen/15 years   6 two/2 cups
3   1 a   2 The   3 the; –   4 this   5 None
4   1 Sentence 1 = the first time it is mentioned; sentence 2 = the same satellite we have just mentioned.   2 We use *the* with superlatives; we mean scientists in general, not a specific group.
3 2.3 billion euros   4 There are more than two countries.

C: Grammar exercises

1   3 The sun   4 the piano   5 the United Arab Emirates   6 ✓
7 by ~~the~~ bus   8 a doctor   9 the (my) car   10 the river Nile
11 ✓   12 ~~the~~ antiques (➢ B1)

2 2 ✗ (no article with countries)   3 the (referring back to Borneo which has just been mentioned)   4 a   5 the (there is only one sultan of Borneo)   6 the (there is only one eighteenth century)   7 ✗ (no article necessary when the name of the university comes first)   8 The (the findings of this study)/their (the scientists' findings)   9 the (the specific differences between this DNA)   10 the (the elephant populations already mentioned)   11 the (the scientists mentioned earlier = biologists)   12 the (the island of Borneo)   13 a (not mentioned before and only one of many which have occurred)   14 an (used to classify this group of elephants) (➢ B1)

3 2 people's (people in general)   3 interviews (not referred to before and plural)   4 questionnaires (not referred to before and plural)   5 our (data for our survey)   6 Both (only two methods)   7 these (referring to something just mentioned)   8 neither (only two are mentioned)   9 Our findings (not findings in general but the ones we got from our survey)   10 This (the idea just referred to: *people like to take holidays in the summer*)   11 the people   12 the survey (the one previously mentioned)   13 Beach holidays (in general not specific ones)   14 Spain (no article with countries)   15 France   16 Most (more than two were surveyed)   17 Each (*person* is singular; it would need to say *all of the people*)   18 every (*all* here means 'the whole year')   19 The price of the holiday (*holiday* = thing, not person or animal) (➢ B1–B4)

4 2 Both   3 neither   4 Every (Each)   5 this (that)   6 that (this)   7 my   8 their   9 That   10 none   11 those /these (➢ B2–B4)

D: Test practice

Listening

Questions 1–5: multiple choice (one and multiple answers)

Test tip: Read all the questions carefully before you listen. Underline or highlight any key information or words that you need to listen for (e.g. for question 1 you need to listen for information about Europe). Make sure you read the instructions carefully (e.g. for questions 3 and 4 you need to write two letters). Use the questions to help you find your way through the listening text. If you miss an answer, just move on to the next one.

1 C (*health-club membership has doubled there as well*)   2 A (*even if people today ate no more than the previous generation, they would still be getting fatter*)   3 & 4 B, C (*So what exactly has brought about this change in fitness levels? ... We can blame the car and other such machines ... On top of this, the changes in how and where we work have reduced the amount of daily calories people actually need.*)   5 B (*an exercise machine that did not even exist a decade ago – the elliptical cross trainer ... delivers an elliptical or swinging motion, with both the hands and feet tracing semi-circular patterns – the feet on two moving platforms rather than bicycle pedals, and the hands gripping handles that move but are not meant to support any weight, which is important as there is no seat*)

Questions 6–10: classification

Test tip: Listen carefully for the key words (e.g. *treadmill, elliptical trainer, running/road*) and match what you hear to the ideas in the questions. Remember the words in the questions will not match the words in the recording exactly.

6 C (*Running on a treadmill results in forces that are roughly two and a half times the subject's body weight*)   7 A (*But using an elliptical machine gives forces that are roughly equal to the subject's weight*)   8 A (*This is much kinder on the body and makes the impact comparable to that of walking*)   9 B (*when reaching speeds above 14 kilometres per hour or so, running on firm ground uses up substantially more calories, and therefore leads to a greater reduction in weight, than running on a treadmill – or using an elliptical machine.*)   10 B (*running on firm ground creates a greater force on the body's joints than using machines*)

Grammar focus task

1 the parents of the current generation of people
2 relying on cars and other machines and eating fast food
3 the fact that people have poor health so are looking for answers
4 45 million Americans   5 elliptical cross trainer
6 in respect of the impact on the body   7 running to gym

Unit 9

A: Context listening

2 1 A   2 B   3 A   4 B   5 C   6 A   7 C

3 1 you; mine   2 she; herself   3 me   4 I; we; they   5 myself   6 you; yourself   7 themselves   8 yours

4 I, you, she, we, they; me, you; myself, yourself, herself, themselves; mine, yours

C: Grammar exercises

1 2 themselves (*these bats*)   3 their   4 they   5 their   6 their   7 its (*the bat*)   8 its   9 it   10 itself   11 their (*all bats*)   12 they   13 their   14 themselves (➢ B1 and B2)

2 Dear Liz

I'm sorry I haven't emailed you for a while. I'm really busy with my studies at the moment. My course is going well and I'm enjoying ~~my course~~ it a lot. The trouble is that ~~my course~~ it takes up all my time. How is ~~your course~~ yours going?
I hope you will be able to visit me soon. I'd like you to meet my friends. My best friend here is Paul. ~~Paul~~ He lives in the flat next to ~~my flat~~ mine, and I usually eat most of my meals with ~~Paul~~ him. At the moment I'm doing most of the cooking though, because ~~Paul~~ he had an accident last week. One of the reasons for the accident is connected to some changes at the university recently. ~~The university authorities~~ They have decided that students shouldn't be allowed to bring cars up to the campus, so more and more of ~~the students~~ us are cycling. Because of this new rule, Paul was riding his bicycle to the university. While he was cycling along a car driver drove into the back of his bike. ~~The car driver~~ He didn't stop to check if Paul was okay. Luckily ~~Paul~~ he was not badly hurt and managed to pick up his bike and get to the doctor's surgery. The doctor said his finger was probably broken and strapped ~~his finger~~ it up, so he can't hold anything in his right hand at the moment and ~~Paul~~ he can't really cook for ~~Paul~~ himself.
Anyway, he'd like to meet you, so we must arrange a time for you to come here.
Get in touch soon. Love Sandy (➢ B1 and B2)

3 2 they   3 they   4 It   5 it   6 it (= to understand this is difficult)   7 its   8 themselves   9 they   10 There (➢ B1–B3)

4 **2** it is   **3** it (= for people to recycle their waste)
4 their (*households* = plural)   **5** it (= the government making a new law)   **6** you (= everyone in general)   **7** It is not practical to do this.   **8** themselves (people in general)   **9** it (to avoid repeating *something*)   **10** the ones   **11** they (to avoid repeating *the government*)   **12** There   **13** it easier for people to recycle   **14** they (⩾ B1–B3)

D: Test practice
Academic Writing Task 2

Test tip: Make sure that you read all parts of the question carefully and address each point made. Organize your thoughts and ideas well. Do not try to memorize essays. Make sure you have at least 40 minutes to spend on this task and try to leave time at the end to check your spelling.

Model answer

There is always going to be a discussion about the amount of money that is spent on space exploration. Scientific studies of the moon and the planets may provide information that is useful for us on earth. However, some people believe this cannot justify the huge amount of money spent on space research when there is a greater need for it here.

In the past, different countries used space exploration to compete with each other. For example, the US and the USSR raced each other to see who could put a man on the moon first. It would have been much easier and cheaper if they had pooled resources and information, and made a joint expedition into space. Fortunately, nowadays this is happening more and more, and thus less money overall is being wasted.

Nevertheless, some critics believe that all money given to space exploration is wasted. They argue that if the millions of dollars spent on space research were put into health and education programmes around the world, many lives would be significantly improved. It is certainly likely that if this money were invested in crop development in different parts of the world, we could save many more lives in countries where people do not have enough food. It is very difficult to argue against these criticisms.

In my opinion, we need a balance between how much money is spent on space exploration and how much money is invested into solving problems here on earth. With continued co-operation between nations over space travel more will be achieved for less money. This should leave more money to be spent on problems at home.

Grammar focus task

1 C   **2** A   **3** B   **4** E   **5** D

Unit 10

A: Context listening

2 The man visited Morocco, Turkey and India.

3 **1** Morocco   **2** historical buildings   **3** Turkey   **4** boat
5 local crafts   **6** Turkish carpet   **7** India   **8** Museum
9 Indian silk   **10** (more) remote   **11** colourful   **12** spiders

4 historical; beautiful; good; local; Turkish; Gujarati; great; Indian; silk; remote; incredible; colourful; poisonous

C: Grammar exercises

1 **3** tall old trees   **4** interesting wild animals   **5** blue and yellow stripes   **6** dark wooden floor   **7** ✓   **8** a beautiful ancient ruined castle   **9** ✓   **10** narrow and winding (*and* is needed because the adjectives come after the noun)
11 busy and noisy   **12** happy childhood memories (⩾ B1)

2 impressively; slightly; steadily; sharply; steep (⩾ B2)
2a impressive **b** impressively
3a dramatically **b** dramatic
4a steadily **b** steady   **5a** steeply; sharply **b** steep; sharp
(⩾ B1 and B2)

3 **2** surprising – b   **3** frightened – g   **4** satisfying – e
5 interested – h   **6** relaxing – d   **7** exciting – a   **8** tired – f
(⩾ B1)

4 **2** work hard   **3** often say   **4** take action immediately
5 really important   **6** act responsibly   **7** can install easily
8 work well   **9** safely inside   **10** absolutely essential (⩾ B2)

D: Test practice
Reading

Questions 1–8: multiple matching

Test tip: Read the questions (1–8) carefully to identify the kind of information you need to find; simply scanning the text for a key word is not enough. Remember the words in the questions will not always match the words in the passage exactly.

1 A (*and an outdoor theatre hosts dance and drama performances on weekends*)   **2** B (*displays rare specimens of animals, ores, and species of insects ... shellfish, insects, butterflies and birds*)
3 E (*This is the sole museum in Korea dedicated to sports* = the only one)   **4** C (*Audio guides, touch screens, and video rooms all help to bring the ancient world alive here*)   **5** D (*this museum is located on the former site of Kyonghee-gung palace*)   **6** A (*Recently, a time capsule containing 600 items representing the lifestyle of modern-day people of Seoul was buried to celebrate the city's 600th anniversary. In 2394, it will be opened!*)   **7** C (*housing art and archaeological relics from Korean prehistory*)   **8** D (*the museum offers art courses every Friday*)

Question 9–14: identification of writer's views (Yes / No / Not Given)

Test tip: *Yes* means the ideas or opinions in the statement match the ideas or opinions in the passage. *No* means that the ideas or opinions in the statement are incorrect and do not match the ideas or opinions in the passage. *Not Given* means that these ideas are not mentioned in the passage.

9 No (*... 49 companies that sell or make rucksacks; few* has a negative meaning)   **10** Yes (*consider what you want your rucksack for*)   **11** Not given (We are only told that the writer has a backpack and that it is big enough: *My current backpack is a Craghopper AD30 (30 litres) which is just big enough*. There is no information about how comfortable it is.)   **12** No (*Today you can get quite technically advanced backpacks boasting excellent features: ... clever ventilation systems to keep your back cool*)   **13** Yes (*choose a backpack that fits the length of your back. Being six feet I need a long, thin rucksack rather than a short, wider one.*)   **14** Yes (*Last, and probably least, we have the look of the sack to consider*)

Grammar focus task

a frequency b manner c time d intensity e place

A: Context listening

3 1 T 2 F Runners aged 50 and over are actually speeding up more rapidly that younger people. 3 F Women aged 60–68 running the New York marathon run on average four minutes faster each year. 4 F They are just as likely to achieve their peak fitness as younger athletes. 5 T

4 faster and fitter; less rapidly than; two minutes faster; less likely than; weaker; less active than 1 sentence 1 (*fitter, faster*) sentence 4 (*likely, younger*) sentence 5 (*weaker, active, younger*) 2 sentence 2 (*rapidly*) sentence 3 (*faster*) 3 *Faster* is both an adjective and an adverb.

C: Grammar exercises

1 2 the smallest 3 better (best) 4 more effective 5 the most exciting 6 braver 7 happier 8 most expensive 9 heavier (➢ B1)

2 3 friendlier / more friendly 4 hotter 5 colder (and colder) 6 not as good as 7 spicier 8 more delicious 9 the best 10 not as expensive 11 earlier 12 more quickly 13 The longer 14 the faster (➢ B1 and B2)

3 2 fewer 3 most 4 twice 5 more 6 less 7 lowest/smallest 8 highest/biggest/largest/greatest 9 significantly/considerably (much/far) 10 as 11 slightly/even (➢ B1, B3 and B4)

4 2 more silver medals ~~as~~ than gold 3 ✓ 4 the second ~~high~~ highest 5 ~~less~~ fewer silver medals than gold medals 6 ~~more good~~ better than 7 as well as 8 ~~more~~ (much) lower 9 significantly more successful 10 two more gold medals ~~that~~ than 11 ✓ 12 the ~~worse~~ worst (➢ B1–B4)

D: Test practice
Academic Writing Task 1

Test tip: Make sure you read all of the information provided very carefully. Look at the statistical information you are given and choose the most important features. Look for data which is the same or similar and features which show important differences or changes.

Model answer

The chart provides a summary of the average number of hours married men and women work every day both inside and outside of the home. In both age groups shown, the total number of hours worked by married women is greater than the total number of hours worked by men. Whilst women aged 45 to 64 may work fewer hours inside the home, they work the greatest number of hours per day due to the extra hours of paid work that they do.

Men aged 25 to 44 spend only slightly more time working outside of the home than men aged 45 to 64, but this figure is significantly higher than the number of hours of paid work that women of the same age do.

Women in the 25 to 44 age group work almost as many hours inside the home as outside, and there is only a slight difference in the 45 to 64 age group. However, men work on average three times longer outside of the home than inside.

Grammar focus task

1 greater than 2 fewer; the greatest 3 slightly more; significantly higher than 4 as many 5 three times longer

A: Context listening

2 The study showed that there were more fish in areas with rubbish. The team decided to put rubbish back into some areas of the harbour.

3 1 h 2 c 3 g 4 f 5 a 6 e 7 b 8 d

4 noun + preposition: sea tulips with bright red bodies; the rubble of the past; other possible sites with submerged rubbish
noun + past participle: the areas cleared of rubbish
noun + -*ing*: other debris lying on the sea floor
noun + *to*-infinitive: a decision to expand our study

C: Grammar exercises

1 2 of 3 in 4 of 5 for 6 of 7 to 8 on 9 in 10 with (➢ B1)

2 1 working; moving 2 buying; produced; grown 3 concerning; made; manufactured; resulting (➢ B2 and B3)

3 2 The number of people buying their own home is increasing. 3 The proposal made by the education department was rejected by the government. 4 We have computer software to predict (for predicting) earthquakes. 5 A new dictionary containing more words than ever before is about to be published. 6 My favourite novel is a story based on the author's own experience. (➢ B1–B3)

4 I recently had a wonderful holiday in Crete with my friends. When we arrived we saw a bus waiting to take us to our hotel. The hotel was nice with good views of the sea. The location was also very good with lots to do nearby. There are lots of Minoan sites to visit. It's a lovely island with beautiful beaches. We spent our time sightseeing, lying on the beach and walking. Actually, it was the walking that I liked best. We did one amazing walk through the Samarian Gorge. It took all day, but was well worth it. We saw a snake curled up on a rock. And lots of lizards and birds. We got really hot and were very tired when we arrived at the beach at the end of the long walk. It was great to see the sea sparkling in the sun. We ran into the water to cool down. It was the best holiday ever. (➢ B1–B3)

D: Test practice
Reading

Questions 1–5: multiple choice

Test tip: Read all the questions and options and underline or highlight any important information or key words that you need to find in the passage. Use the questions to locate the relevant part of the reading passage. If you cannot find an answer, just move on to the next one and come back to this one later.

1 D (*the more paper qualifications you hold and the higher your grades, the less able you are to cope with problems of everyday life and the lower your score in practical intelligence*) 2 C (*Deficit refers back to the final idea mentioned in paragraph 3: some high*

scorers failed to achieve in real life what was predicted by their tests)
3 D (*Instead of asking what intelligence was and investigating whether it predicted success in life, Professor Sternberg asked what distinguished people who were thriving from those that were not.*)
4 C (*high achievers are often unable to articulate or define what they know*) **5** A (*Training new or less capable employees to become more practically intelligent will involve learning from the genuinely practically intelligent rather than from training manuals or courses*)

Questions 6–12: classification

Test tip: Underline or highlight the key words in the reading passage (e.g. *IQ, EQ, practical intelligence*). Carefully read the information nearby and try to match the information in the passage to the facts in the questions (6–12). Remember the words in the questions will not always match the words in the passage exactly.

6 C (*most older adults contend that their ability to solve practical problems increases over the years*) **7** B (*EQ includes the abilities to … understand and empathize with others*) **8** C (*practical intelligence is scored by answers to real-life dilemmas*) **9** A (*IQ as a concept is more than 100 years old*; the text also tells us that the EQ and practical intelligence tests were devised after the IQ test) **10** C (*the best way to reach practical intelligence is to ask successful people to relate examples of crucial incidents at work where they solved problems demonstrating skills they had learnt while doing their jobs*) **11** B (*EQ includes the abilities to … regulate moods and keep distress from swamping the ability to think*) **12** C (*in practical intelligence tests – as in real life – there are several different solutions to the problem*)

Grammar focus task

1 record numbers of high school students; top grades in their final exams; expert on intelligence; the existence of a totally new variety **2** the only explanation offered; a study just published **3** the basic skills to succeed

Unit 13

A: Context listening

2 The newspaper headline refers to a patient with amnesia that the doctors are discussing.
3 **1** F He couldn't remember his personal details.
2 F He could have come from Yorkshire. **3** T **4** T
5 F Joe thinks he could have been married. **6** F He's been able to find his parents. **7** F She thinks that he must have hit his head. **8** F She thinks he could make a total recovery.
4 Ability: could; couldn't; be able to
Certainty and impossibility: will; must; can't
Possibility: could; might

C: Grammar exercises

1 **2** was able to / could (*could* is more natural) **3** managed to (*could* is not used to talk about a specific occasion) **4** didn't manage to / couldn't **5** can/ will be able to (*can* is being used to give permission) **6** can (it sometimes happens) **7** managed to **8** will be able to / will manage to **9** was able to (➢ B1–B2)

2 **2** a **3** a **4** b **5** b **6** a **7** b **8** b (we do not use *could not* for possibility) (➢ B2–B3)

3 **2** Their jobs at the temple may/might/could have provided **3** they may/might/could have grown **4** she may/might/could have been **5** she must have worried **6** she could not (cannot) have imagined (➢ B3)

4 Almost every family has a television these days, and many children watch a whole range of programmes every day. Some people believe that television ~~is~~ can be harmful to children, saying that it ~~influences~~ may/can influence behaviour in a negative way.

There are a lot of programmes on television that are not educational and that contain violence and bad language. However, watching violence on television ~~encourages~~ can/may encourage violent behaviour in children. This ~~is~~ may be true in cases of children who have already exhibited violent tendencies, but it ~~isn't~~ can't be true of all children, otherwise we would have an epidemic of child crime. It is also argued that bad language on television ~~encourages~~ can/may encourage the same in children.

However, overall I believe that restricting the viewing of children to mainly educational programmes shown at a time of day when there is no violence or bad language ~~will overcome~~ may overcome any risks of television being a bad influence. (➢ B1–B4)

D: Test practice

Listening

Questions 1–10: summary completion

Test tip: Read through the information in the summary carefully before you listen and try to predict what type of information you need to hear. Pay careful attention to the word limit and check your spelling at the end.

1 clothing (*initially, it was only ever used on clothing*) **2** modern (*the use of soap for personal hygiene was unheard of until fairly recently and this is considered to be a relatively modern notion*) **3** practical skills (*what these people lacked in technology they certainly made up for in practical skills*) **4** wealthy (*soap would most likely have only been available in the wealthy communities*) **5** Iron Age (*there is no real evidence that the British colonies of the Iron Age had access to such a product*) **6** written texts (*we have had to rely almost entirely on written texts for our discoveries*) **7** wool (*The first known written mention of soap was on Sumerian clay tablets dating from about 2500 BC. The tablets spoke of the use of soap in the washing of wool.*) **8** vegetables (*Egyptians … made soap by combining alkaline salts and oil which they extracted from vegetables*) **9** metal blade (*they reached a steamy room where dirt was sweated out and scraped away with a metal blade*) **10** soap factory (*During the excavation of Pompeii, a city that was buried under the eruption of Vesuvius in 79 AD, an entire soap factory was revealed*)

Grammar focus task

1 may be able to find (possibility) **2** must have provided (possibility) **3** could have discovered (ability) **4** might have observed (possibility) **5** have been able to make (ability)

Unit 14

A: Context listening

1 They discuss transport, langue lessons, work permits and accommodation.

3 1 'll need to allow 2 should try to use 3 'll have to learn
4 should always carry 5 'll need 6 have to get
7 mustn't dress 8 needn't buy 9 ought to take

4 strong obligation or necessity: mustn't, have to, need
advice or suggestions: should, ought to
no obligation or necessity: needn't, don't need to

C: Grammar exercises

1 2 must not 3 have to (a fixed appointment = external obligation) 4 didn't need to go (I did not go) 5 must (formal notice) 6 mustn't (*don't have to* = it is not necessary)
7 had to (past tense) 8 have to / must (*must* is more natural if this is a written instruction) 9 'll have to 10 needn't have worried (I did worry) (➤ B1 & B2)

2 1 won't have to / needn't / don't need to 2 has to / must / needs to 3 Do you have to; didn't have to; had to
4 didn't have to / didn't need to; will have to 5 mustn't; have to; do you really have to 6 have to; have to; should / must (➤ B1–B3)

3 3 must ~~to~~ encourage 4 ✓ 5 ~~also should~~ should also reduce 6 ✓ 7 ✓ 8 ought to try 9 ~~must~~ had to walk (past tense) 10 should ~~trying~~ try 11 will ~~must~~ have to make / must make 12 ~~mustn't~~ don't have to make / needn't make / don't need to make (➤ B1–B4)

4 2 have to consider (ought to consider) 3 have to have
4 ought to work 5 don't have to travel 6 ought to learn
7 mustn't shout 8 must always walk 9 ought to find out
10 do you have to arrange 11 have to have 12 ought to organise (have to organise) (➤ B1–B4)

D: Test practice

Reading

Questions 1–6: multiple matching

Test tip: Read the questions (1–6) carefully to identify the kind of information you need to find; simply scanning the text for a key word is not enough (e.g. bicycles are mentioned several times in the passage but question 3 asks you to find information about keeping a bicycle secure). Remember the words in the questions will not always match the words in the passage exactly.

1 D (*In the case of a pupil being absent from school, please telephone on the first day in all instances*) 2 F (*If a pupil appears to be doing too little work, parents should contact the form teacher at once.*) 3 J (*Any bicycles brought onto school grounds should be clearly labelled with the owner's name and must be left locked in the bicycle sheds provided.*) 4 C (*The school stongly disapproves of pupils taking paid employment.*) 5 G (*Homework can be excused only after the receipt and approval by the teacher concerned of a letter from a parent setting out the reasons.*) 6 H (*During the holidays the school and its grounds are out-of-bounds for all pupils, unless accompanied by a teacher.*)

Questions 7–13: identification of information in the text (True / False / Not Given)

Test tip: *True* means the ideas or opinions in the statement match the ideas or opinions in the passage. *False* means that the ideas or opinions in the statement are incorrect and do not match the ideas or opinions in the passage. *Not Given* means that these ideas are not mentioned in the passage.

7 False (*the material you cover is the same as in the courses offered on campus*) 8 Not given (There is no information about how study materials will be delivered. Although there is a *shipping and handling fee*, we do not know if this relates to posting course materials, and some materials may be delivered online.) 9 False (*All Independent Study students must purchase a Study Guide*) 10 False (*This fee entitles a student to free replacement copies of end-of-course documentation for life.*) 11 False (*A course can be finished in a minimum of two weeks per module*) 12 True (*... and must be finished in a maximum of four weeks*) 13 True (*Modules cannot always be completed in the minimum amount of time.*)

Grammar focus task

1 must (obligation) 2 must (obligation) 3 need to (necessity)
4 should (advice) 5 need to (necessity)

Unit 15

A: Context listening

2 He mentions voluntary redundancy and good business sense.

3 1 'll be offering 2 hope 3 Are these cuts 4 hasn't been doing 5 has 6 are you saying 7 are not
8 decided to change

4 1 announced 2 hoped 3 asked 4 denied 5 said
6 claimed 7 assured 8 promised

5 Reporting verbs are used to indicate the way in which things were said in Exercise 4. There are changes in tense, word order and pronouns.

C: Grammar exercises

1 2 (that) I was doing it the following 3 (me) if I felt
4 that her classes had been 5 me (that) I'd made
6 (that) I was feeling 7 me not to 8 (that) I'd worked
9 (that) I thought I'd be 10 was doing (➤ B1, B3 and B4)

2 2 urge 3 reminded 4 complained 5 suggested
6 insisted 7 refused 8 apologised 9 advised
10 warned (➤ B2)

3 2 encouraged students ~~to~~ take out 3 ~~did I want~~ if/whether I wanted 4 ~~that they should~~ to vote
5 ~~making~~ to make 6 promised ~~to~~ mark 7 ~~going~~ to go
8 ~~were my hobbies~~ my hobbies were 9 complained about the quality 10 announced ~~about~~ the changes
11 ~~to pay~~ on paying 12 ~~would I~~ I would (➤ B2 & B4)

4 2 encouraged me to apply for the job. 3 refused to help me.
4 agreed to go to the meeting. 5 denied causing (having caused) the accident. / that he had caused the accident.
6 apologised for losing my application form. 7 asked why there aren't (weren't) many poisonous snakes in Britain.
8 asked if (whether) I was going to the lecture the next day. / if I'm going to the lecture tomorrow. 9 she suggested (that) I have (had) a day off. 10 persuaded Dan to go (come) to the theatre with her. (➤ B1–B4)

D: Test practice

Listening

Questions 1–3: sentence completion

Test tip: Try to identify the type of information you need before you listen (e.g. for question 2 you need to listen for a date, or for question 3 you need to listen for a place). Pay careful attention to the word limit and check your spelling at the end.

1 (columns of) (hot) air (*They actually work by using the sun to make columns of hot air that rise upwards through the centre of the tower.*)   **2** seventeenth/17th century (*The first time solar energy was produced was in the seventeenth century*)
3 Spain (*he chose Spain to build the first tower*)

Questions 4–8: flowchart completion

Test tip: Completing a flowchart is similar to completing notes. Read through the flowchart carefully before you listen and try to predict what type of information you need to hear (e.g. for questions 4 and 5 you need to listen for a type of material). Pay careful attention to the word limit and check your spelling at the end.

4 concrete (*They're constructed out of high-strength concrete*)
5 plastic (*a sunlight collector which is basically a large sheet of plastic*)
6 greenhouse (*it acts like a greenhouse*)   **7** rises (*this hot air rises up the chimney or the tower and drives the turbines at the top*)
8 two hundred / 200 (*it can generate 200 megawatts of power*)

Questions 9–10: multiple choice (multiple answers)

Test tip: Read all the questions carefully before you listen. Underline or highlight any key information or words that you need to listen for. Some of the options may not be mentioned at all; others will be incorrect. Pay attention to how many choices you need to make (here you need to choose two letters).

9 and 10 B, E in any order (*One problem they do have is that a lot of the energy in the sunlight is lost in the form of heat from the collector ... keeping them stable is another drawback*)

Grammar focus task

Suggested answers: **1** asked   **2** explained   **3** denied
4 admitted   **5** insisted

Unit 16

A: Context listening

1 She wants to work in a zoo or a safari park.
2 1 She is doing a diploma course in animal management.
2 She enjoys feeding the animals most.   3 She has overcome a fear of snakes.
3 1 to do   2 to study   3 working   4 taking   5 cleaning
6 treat   7 handle   8 feeling   9 to do   10 bark; to be
11 to work
4 1 decide, choose, remember, tell, would like   2 start, prefer, not mind, remember   3 let, make, hear,
Remember can be followed by either the *to*-infinitive or *-ing*.

C: Grammar exercises

1 2 to add   3 to have   4 to do   5 to finish   6 working / to work   7 writing / to write   8 to complete   9 to get
10 to show   11 putting   12 to be   13 to email
14 to remember (➤ B1 and B3)
2 2 looking   3 to become   4 cleaning   5 falling
6 not to worry   7 to take   8 to renew   9 rising
10 to bring (➤ B3)

3 3 ✓   4 tried very hard to please   5 have made me feel
6 made me want   7 ✓   8 will stop making   9 ✓
10 don't mind working   11 ✓   12 doesn't force them to
teach   13 ✓   14 let their students decide (➤ B1–B4)
4 2 did not feel like waiting   3 finished (had finished) talking
4 tried to find   5 failed to do   6 saw me standing
7 needed (had needed) to send   8 carried on looking
9 have bothered to write   10 started eating / to eat
11 considered leaving   12 expected him to get
13 hope to receive   14 advise you to give (➤ B1–B4)

D: Test practice

Reading

Questions 1–6: identification of information in the text (True / False / Not Given)

Test tip: *True* means the ideas or opinions in the statement match the ideas or opinions in the passage. *False* means that the ideas or opinions in the statement are incorrect and do not match the ideas or opinions in the passage. *Not Given* means that these ideas are not mentioned in the passage.

1 True (*understanding how consumers make decisions and the crucial role of packaging in this process, has been a neglected area of research so far*)   **2** True (*'heuristic processing' ... is based on very simple rules: ... choose what a trusted source suggests*)   **3** False (*'heuristic processing' ... requires comparatively little effort ... 'systematic processing' involves much deeper levels of thought ... This form of thinking, which is both analytical and conscious, involves much more mental effort.*)   **4** Not given (the text does not give us any information about who developed this concept)   **5** True (*'systematic processing' involves ... taking account of the product information, including its price, its perceived quality and so on*)
6 False (*Under heuristic processing, for example, consumers may simply need to be able to distinguish the pack from those of competitors.*)

Questions 7–8: multiple choice

Test tip: Read all the questions and options and underline or highlight any important information or key words that you need to find in the passage. Use the questions to locate the relevant part of the reading passage. If you cannot find an answer, just move on to the next one and come back to this one later.

7 D (*testing the effectiveness of your packaging can be ineffective if the methods you are employing concern one form of thinking ... but your consumers are purchasing in the other mode*)   **8** A (*getting consumers to change brands may involve developing packaging that includes information that does stimulate systematic processing*)

Questions 9–13: summary completion

Test tip: Notice that the summary has a title; this helps you to locate the part of the text being summarized. Read through the information in the summary carefully and try to predict what type of information you need to find in the passage. Pay careful attention to the word limit and make sure you copy the words correctly.

9 advantages / characteristics (*A crucial role of packaging in this situation is to communicate the <u>characteristics</u> of the product, highlighting its <u>advantages</u> over possible competitors.*)   **10** situation (*people only engage in effort-demanding systematic processing when the <u>situation</u> justifies it*)   **11** information (*people have an upper limit to the amount of <u>information</u> they can absorb. If we present too much, therefore, they will become confused. This, in turn, is likely to lead them* to disengage and choose something else.) **12** ingredients (*will not be able to deal with things they do not already understand, the ingredients of food products, for example*) **13** simple (*Our research has differentiated between people with a high need for thinking – who routinely engage in analytical thinking – and those low in the need for cognition, who prefer to use very simple forms of thinking.*)

Grammar focus task

1 developing **2** looking at; thinking about **3** to be able to **4** to be able to **5** to be **6** thinking **7** making **8** to change; developing; to challenge

Unit 17

A: Context listening

2 They talk about a car, travelling and investing the money.

3 1 c 2 h 3 f 4 a 5 g 6 b 7 d 8 e

4 provided that; unless; as long as
None of the sentences refer to events in the past.

C: Grammar exercises

1 2 e 3 b 4 d 5 f 6 h 7 a 8 g (➤ B1 and B2)

2 **1** became; were (was); 'd hate **2** didn't have; wouldn't know; don't find (can't find); 'll find; will save; do **3** will surprise; are used to **4** kept; 'd take; don't have; 'll have to (➤ B2 and B3)

3 **2** don't have **3** ✓ **4** will probably **5** start **6** have **7** isn't **8** ✓ **9** wouldn't be able **10** ✓ **11** met **12** might not happen (may not happen) **13** need **14** help (➤ B1–B3)

4 **2** As long as **3** unless **4** unless **5** in case **6** as long as **7** Provided that **8** When **9** if **10** unless (➤ B4)

D: Test practice

Reading

Questions 1–3: multiple choice

Test tip: Read all the questions and options and underline or highlight any important information or key words that you need to find in the passage. Use the questions to locate the relevant part of the reading passage. If you cannot find an answer, just move on to the next one and come back to this one later.

1 C (*its sweet white buds hang from the trunk and along a few fat branches*) **2** B (*using temporary plantings of banana to shade the cacao while it's young*) **3** A (*In the United States, for example, imported cacao is the linchpin of an $8.6 billion domestic chocolate industry that in turn supports the nation's dairy and nut industries.*)

Questions 4–9: locating information

Test tip: Scan the passage for relevant information, and then check that it matches the question exactly (e.g. for question 4 you need to find a list of countries or places, not just one). Remember that the words in the passage may paraphrase the words in the questions.

4 E (*from South America and the Caribbean to West Africa, east Asia, and New Guinea and Vanuatu in the Pacific*) **5** H (*One such disease, witches broom, devastated the cacao plantations in the Bahia region of Brazil*) **6** C (*which they frothed up with water and spices to make bracing concoctions*) **7** D (*In the last 200 years the bean has been thoroughly democratized – transformed from an elite drink into ubiquitous candy bars, cocoa powders and confections. Today chocolate is becoming popular with new markets opening up in Eastern Europe and Asia.*) **8** F (*groves like this may produce*

annual yields of 50 to 60 pods per tree for 25 to 30 years*) **9** C (*In 1753, the Swedish botanist Carolus Linnaeus gave the cacao tree genus the name* Theobroma)

Questions 10–13: notes completion

Test tip: Read through the notes carefully and try to predict what type of information you need to find in the passage (e.g. for question 12 you need to identify a farming method). Pay careful attention to the word limit and make sure you copy the words correctly.

10 disease (*try to address this problem by establishing disease resistant plants*) **11** (local) middlemen (*Most are at the mercy of local middlemen who buy the beans then sell them for a much higher price to the chocolate manufacturers. If the situation is to improve for farmers, these people need to be removed from the process.*) **12** sustainable (*ensure that sustainable farming practices are used*) **13** profits (*Typically, farmers who grow cacao get a pittance for their beans compared with the profits reaped by the rest of the chocolate business … They also need to empower the farmers by guaranteeing them a higher price for their beans so that they will be encouraged to grow beans and can maintain their way of life.*)

Grammar focus task

1 scoop **2** let **3** dry **4** roast **5** happens **6** become **7** grind **8** press **9** will obtain

Unit 18

A: Context listening

1 Simon regrets buying a new car because it has cost him a lot of money.

2 1 F 2 T 3 T 4 F 5 F

3 **1** 'd bought; wouldn't have needed **2** wouldn't be; hadn't almost doubled **3** 'd waited; 'd have managed **4** 'd listened; would have happened **5** 'd taken; 'd own

4 **1** past perfect; past time **2** sentences 1, 3 and 4; *would have* + past participle **3** sentences 2 and 5; *would* + infinitive without *to*

C: Grammar exercises

1 **2** would (might) have got **3** would (might) have received **4** 'd made **5** would (might) have been **6** 'd planned **7** 'd prepared **8** would (might) have restricted **9** 'd started **10** wouldn't have been **11** hadn't left **12** would (might) have been able **13** 'd come **14** would (could) have helped (➤ B1)

2 **2** had been any germs **3** wouldn't have abandoned his research **4** hadn't seen Fleming's research papers **5** hadn't worked with RAF **6** wouldn't have decided **7** wouldn't have failed **8** hadn't opposed (➤ B1)

3 **2** ~~would you done~~ would you have done **3** ~~am starting~~ would be starting **4** ~~would have kept~~ had kept **5** ~~didn't have~~ hadn't had **6** ~~was very excited~~ 'd be very excited **7** ~~might make~~ might have made **8** ~~will be~~ would be **9** ~~didn't make~~ wouldn't have made **10** ~~didn't go~~ hadn't gone (➤ B1 and B2)

4 **2** wish you'd asked **3** wish I hadn't chosen (shouldn't have chosen); should have chosen **4** wish I'd studied **5** wish he'd stop **6** should have let **7** wish I had **8** wish it would stop **9** wish I hadn't done (shouldn't have done) **10** shouldn't have told (➤ B3 and B4)

D: Test practice

Reading

Questions 1–8: classification

Test tip: Underline or highlight the key words in the reading passage (e.g. *giant panda, spectacled bear*). Carefully read the information nearby and try to match the information in the passage to the facts in the questions (1–8). Remember the words in the questions will not always match the words in the passage exactly. Here you need to decide whether these facts apply to only one animal or to both.

1 A (*the giant panda has evolved a sixth digit*) **2** B (*The spectacled bear is a more frequent climber ... They also construct tree nests to act as a bed.*) **3** C (*Both are survivors of an ancient lineage dating back 18 million years*) **4** B (*Spectacled bears are highly adaptable and are found in a wide range of habitats including rainforest, dry forest and coastal scrub desert.*) **5** A (*They* (giant pandas) *also both have a distinctive cry which they use to communicate with others in their group.* Here the giant panda is being compared to the red panda.) **6** C (*They* (giant pandas) *feed mainly on the ground but are capable of climbing trees as well. The spectacled bear is a more frequent climber*) **7** C (*the giant panda supplements its diet with meat which it scavenges. Spectacled bears eat carrion, too, and some have been known to kill small calves*) **8** A (*the red panda, a member of the raccoon family ... The giant panda shares many physical characteristics with the red panda*)

Questions 9–13: sentence completion

Test tip: First identify the type of information you need to find (e.g. for question 1 you need to find out why a giant panda eats constantly). It may help to turn the sentences into questions (e.g. what do spectacled bears build to help them reach their food?) Make sure you stick to the word limit.

9 carnivore (*This is rather strange given that its physiology is typical of a carnivore*) **10** digest (*A panda manages to digest only about 17% of the bamboo it eats*) **11** hibernate (*Unable to store fat effectively, it continues eating in the bitterly cold winter, at a time when many other bears hibernate.*) **12** (tree) nests / platforms / a (tree) nest / a platform (*They also construct tree nests to act as a bed as well as a platform to feed from fruit-laden branches.*) **13** eye patches ('*In pandas, a stare is a threat,' Schaller says. 'The eye patches enlarge the panda's small, dark eyes tenfold, making the stare more powerful.'*)

Grammar focus task

1 had had; would/might have been able to **2** had not dissected; might/would not have thought **3** did not resemble; might/would not have been **4** had not contradicted; might/could/would have been

A: Context listening

2 She is worried about: finding maths difficult, being unprepared to teach, controlling the class and pupils being rude to her.

3 **1** interested in **2** share **3** with **4** impressed by **5** learning about **6** warned **7** about **8** good at **9** experience of **10** worried about **11** shout at

4 **1** warn; learn **2** worried **3** good **4** shout **5** interested **6** experience **7** share **8** impressed

C: Grammar exercises

1 **2** A **3** C **4** C **5** B **6** B **7** A **8** B (➤

2 **2** ~~amongst~~ between **3** ~~about~~ for **4** ✓ **5** ~~to~~ **7** ~~about~~ of **8** ~~in~~ by **9** ~~at~~ with **10** ✓ **11** ~~in~~ **12** ~~in~~ at (➤ B1, B3 & B4)

3 **2** bad for **3** effect on **4** depend on (rely on) **5** obsessed with **6** true for **7** worried about **8** choose between/from **9** rely on (depend on) (➤ B1–B3)

4 **2** for **3** by **4** for **5** about **6** for/of **7** for **8** at **9** of **10** with **11** by **12** of **13** for **14** of (➤ B1–B4)

D: Test practice

Listening

Questions 1–2: multiple choice

Test tip: Read all the questions carefully before you listen. Underline or highlight any key information or words that you need to listen for (e.g. *How far away is the nearest big town to Greenville?*) Use the questions to help you find your way through the listening text. If you miss an answer, just move on to the next one.

1 C (*but emergency services have to drive 500 kilometres to reach us from the closest large town*) **2** B (*thanks to the arrival of Doctor Jones earlier this year, we no longer have to drive so far if anyone gets sick*)

Questions 3–10: notes completion

Test tip: Read through the notes carefully before you listen and try to predict what type of information you need to hear (e.g. for question 6 you will need to listen for a measurement, or for question 10 you will need to listen for a month or date). Pay careful attention to the word limit and check your spelling at the end.

3 contact / call / telephone (*Well, immediately after the storm has passed, the first thing you need to do is call the national weather station.*) **4** report card (*After that you simply have to complete what they call a report card*) **5** (local) (news)paper (*keep an eye out for any reports in the local newspaper of storms or storm damage. You need to cut these out and send them in as well.*) **6** two centimetres / 2cm (*report any that is two centimetres in diameter or bigger*) **7** large/big trees (*They also need to know about damage caused by high winds, especially if it uproots large trees. ... restrict it to those big enough to cause a problem, especially on our roads.*) **8** training (*... we'll be conducting training next month. This will only take up a day so don't worry too much about it.*) **9** police (*If you do have the time and would like to come along then you'll need to talk to the police who are coordinating the event*) **10** October (*you'll need to put your name down by the end of October at the very latest*)

Grammar focus task

1 about **2** about **3** at **4** about **5** about **6** about **7** to

A: Context listening

2 The problems mentioned are: the ladder left out, the letters in the letterbox, the open window, overhanging branches.

3 **1** where there are **2** that could become **3** that can check **4** which have **5** who can collect

4 **1** *Where* refers to a place. **2** *That* and *who* are used to refer to people. **3** *That* and *which* are used to refer to things.

C: Grammar exercises

1   2 who/that; e   3 which/that; i   4 where; a   5 when/that; f
6 who/that; c   7 who/that; g   8 why; j   9 whose; h
10 whose; b   The relative pronoun can be left out in
sentences 6 and 8 (➤ B1 & B2)

2   2 Some students take a year out before university, which allows
them to work or travel.   3 The Guggenheim Museum, which is
in Bilbao, only displays contemporary art. / The Guggenheim
Museum, which only displays contemporary art, is in Bilbao.
4 My English teacher, whose lectures are very interesting, is
leaving.   5 The lecture, which was about current economic
policy, was not very easy to understand. / The lecture, which
was not very easy to understand, was about current economic
policy.   6 My parents arrived in New York in 1951, where they
stayed for the rest of their lives.   7 I gave my assignment to
the faculty secretary, who was not very friendly. (➤ B3)

3   2 which I saw ~~them~~ advertised   3 exhausting, ~~that~~ which is
not   4 the lecture which you gave ~~it~~ on Wednesday
5 It's the one which ~~in~~ you have written your lecture notes in.
6 today's newspaper, which has   7 those bread rolls ~~what~~
(which/that) we had   8 a pers~~on~~ ~~who~~ whose life is full
(➤ B1–B4)

4   2 which/that; i   3 which/that; e   4 which; h
5 which/that; c   6 where; b   7 which/that; f   8 which; a
9 which/that; d   (➤ B1–B4)

D: Test practice
Reading
Questions 1–4: sentence completion

Test tip: First identify the type of information you need to find
(e.g. for question 1 you need to find a disease or health problem).
It may help to turn the sentences into questions (e.g. what is the
name of the process that helps keep plants in good condition?)
Make sure you stick to the word limit.

1 heart disease (*Recognised as the type of fatty acid most able to
protect against* heart disease)   2 drought (*a project that aims to
develop more* drought*-tolerant sunflowers*)   3 transpiration
(Transpiration *is the mechanism by which plants lose water through
their leaves. This system is thought to facilitate the passage of minerals
through the plant and is vital for healthy plants.*)   4 wind (speed),
humidity (*the research team discovered that its initial approach did not
cater for changes in* wind speed *... The team therefore needed a
technique to measure temperature continuously that would allow it to
examine the effects of other variables such as* humidity)

Questions 5–12: locating information

Test tip: Scan the passage for relevant information, and then
check that it matches the question exactly (e.g. for question 7 you
need to find a mention of two processes used by plants, or for
question 11 you need to look for a number). Remember that the
words in the passage may paraphrase the words in the questions.

5 H (*The sunflower canopy had to be complete, with no visible soil, so
that the thermometers would only measure the temperature of the plants
and not the surrounding environment.*)   6 F (*The robot runs on an
oblong track around the experimental plot and the thermometers
operate on each side of the track.*)   7 C (*Plants undergo photosynthesis
to produce energy in the form of sugar. This involves allowing carbon
dioxide to enter the leaves through pores called stomata. Transpiration
is the mechanism by which plants lose water through their leaves.*)

8 I (*The team and their robot have already made a major breakthrough
in the Australian wheat industry with Drysdale Wheat*)   9 G (*If the
skies darken due to rain, heavy cloud cover or sunset, the robot makes its
way back to the garage to wait.*)   10 B (*a robot developed by the
Australian National University's Research School of Biological Sciences*)
11 H (*Eight varieties of sunflower were examined.*)   12 D (*by
measuring the temperature of the leaves, scientists can determine how
much water is being lost through transpiration.*)

Grammar focus task

1 defining relative clause; *that* refers to *a project* and acts as the
subject of *aims*   2 non-defining relative clause; *which* refers to
wind speed and acts as the subject of *could*   3 non-defining relative
clause; *where* refers to *a garage* and acts as the object of *waits*
4 defining relative clause; *who* refers to *an agronomist* and acts as
the subject of *could*   5 non-defining relative clause; *which* refers
to *Drysdale Wheat* and acts as the subject of *signalled*

Unit 21

A: Context listening

3   1 I live   2 do you do   3 I always do; I go; they always put;
it costs   4 I always do; I work; there are   5 I did try; I didn't
like; can I ask; You can't

4   In the conversation the subjects are mostly personal
pronouns: *I, you*
In the written report the subjects are mostly noun phrases:
*These supermarkets; The people who were interviewed; the
respondents.*

C: Grammar exercises

1   2 the government needs is a lot more loyal supporters
3 we want is action   4 I don't enjoy is watching TV
5 is the bride who is the most important person at a wedding
6 is the causes of poverty (that) governments should be
dealing with, not the results of it   7 was when I was ill in
hospital as a child that I first decided to study medicine
8 is your family that suffer the most (➤ B4)

2   2 f *These* refers to *changes.*   3 g *It* refers to *a camera.*   4 c
5 e   6 a *This* refers to the *primary role* of the camera.
7 b (➤ B3)

3   2 This rise   3 Many countries   4 a solar roof   5 A one
kilowatt solar panel   6 Solar panels , solar water heaters and
wind generators   7 they   8 These renewable energy systems
9 the government (➤ B1, B3 and B5)

4   2 ~~children need to~~ experience   3 ~~these foods~~ tend not
4 It is often the lack of experience of eating different kinds of
foods that   5 ~~experiencing a wider variety of foods~~ can
therefore lead   6 ~~To provide support and help to parents is
important.~~ It is important to provide support and help to
parents.   7 ~~No child would feel ashamed or embarrassed by
the contents of their lunch boxes with this system.~~ This
system would ensure that no child felt ashamed or
embarrassed by the contents of their lunch boxes.
8 Eating ~~a healthy diet~~ healthily (➤ B1–B4)

D: Test practice
Academic Writing Task 2

Test tip: Make sure that you read all parts of the question
carefully and address each point made. Organize your thoughts

and ideas well. Do not try to memorize essays. Make sure you have at least 40 minutes to spend on this task and try to leave time at the end to check your spelling.

Model answer

Nowadays most children regularly play games on a computer or on their television. These games have become more violent over the past few years. In fact, many parents worry about this and the effect these games are having on their children. Some are concerned that playing violent games might encourage them to become aggressive in real life. What we need to establish is whether or not this is actually true.

First, it may help to look back at the games that children used to play many years ago before the invention of computers. In those days children would probably have played popular board games such as Monopoly or chess, or they may have played card games or some type of outdoor sport. These sports or games would probably only have encouraged children to become more competitive rather than violent.

However, throughout history children have always played fighting games with toy or pretend weapons. Even now many parents will buy a toy gun or sword for their child. Why do we never read reports in the media about the impact plastic weapons could have on children? Perhaps this is because the link between play fighting and actual fighting is not very strong.

In conclusion, the way children play games has changed with the times but the ideas behind those games have actually changed very little. Just as playing at soldiers did not increase violence in the past, I believe that playing computer games will not lead to an increase in violence in the future. I think that if we looked more closely at life in our major cities then we would find there are many other possible causes for the increase in crime and violence.

Grammar focus task

The new information is underlined.

Nowadays most children regularly <u>play games on a computer or on their television</u>. These games <u>have become more violent</u> over the past few years. In fact many parents worry about this and <u>the effect these games are having on their children</u>. Some are concerned that playing violent games <u>might encourage them to become aggressive in real life</u>. What we need to establish is <u>whether or not this is actually true</u>.

Unit 22

A: Context listening

1   1 f   2 d   3 a   4 b   5 g   6 h   7 e   8 c

2   1 They need to go to the library and fill in a form and have their photo taken.   2 It is a group which represents students' views to the university.   3 It is responsible for extra facilities around the campus that are not related to study e.g. restaurants, entertainment and sports facilities.

3   1 Do they process; are processed   2 does the university run; is run   3 do you choose; is chosen

4   They become the subject of the passive verb.

C: Grammar exercises

1   2 are peeled   3 are soaked   4 are put   5 are sliced   6 are rinsed   7 are fried   8 are removed   9 are then left   10 are added   11 be distributed   12 sold (➢ B1 and B2)

2   2 <s>has changed</s> has been changed   3 <s>might have been happened</s> might have happened   4 <s>have given</s> have been given   5 <s>have been benefited</s> have benefited   6 <s>have been suggested</s> have suggested   7 <s>are continued</s> continue   8 <s>are being become</s> are becoming   9 <s>feels</s> is felt   10 <s>have been come</s> have come   11 <s>has affected</s> has been affected   12 <s>will use</s> will be used (➢ B1–B3)

3   2 are (were) placed   3 was believed   4 have been allowed   5 is being serviced   6 will be opened   7 is expected   8 is made   9 claims   10 are known   11 encouraging (to be encouraged)   12 to take (➢ B1–B4)

4   2 be absorbed   3 affects   4 continues   5 are used   6 to use   7 are being built   8 is said   9 to decide   10 tackling   11 have been passed   12 allows   13 are forced   14 know   15 will be used   16 have their cars checked (➢ B1–B5)

D: Test practice

Academic Writing Task 1

Test tip: Study the diagram carefully to identify all of the key stages and make sure that you don't miss any important information out of your description. You may need to change the words on the diagram (e.g. to change verbs to nouns) to make them fit grammatically into your sentences.

Model answer

The diagram shows how fresh fruit is canned. First the fruit is picked from trees by hand. It is then transported to the cannery by large trucks. At the cannery the fruit is washed and quality checked, and any poor quality fruit is rejected. The good quality fruit is put into cold storage. When it is ready for canning the fruit is weighed and graded. The grading ensures that fruit of a similar size is kept together. After this the fruit is peeled and the cores are removed. It is then sliced into the required sizes and put into cans. Juice or syrup is also added to the cans. Once the cans have been filled they are sealed and cooked over heat to ensure that the cans are sterilized. When the cans are cool, a label is attached and they are placed into storage. The canned fruit is now ready to be despatched to supermarkets and sold.

Grammar focus task

1 The cans are allowed to cool.   2 The cans are sterilized using a special heating process.   3 The fruit is taken to the cannery in large trucks.   4 The fruit is checked before storage and any poor quality fruit is rejected.
The correct order is: 3, 4, 2, 1

Unit 23

A: Context listening

1   1 c   2 g   3 a   4 i   5 d   6 e   7 h   8 f   9 b

2   1 F   2 T   3 T   4 T   5 F   6 F   7 F   8 F

3   1 in spite of   2 Despite   3 however   4 Firstly   5 Secondly   6 Finally   7 although   8 To sum up

4   1 in spite of; however; despite; although   2 firstly; secondly; finally   3 to sum up

C: Grammar exercises

1   2 b   3 b   4 b (result)   5 a   6 b (contrasting idea)   7 a (contrasting idea)   8 a (restates the previous idea)   9 a (contrasting idea)   10 b (reason)   11 a   12 b (reason) (➢ B1 and B2)

2 2 Firstly (the first idea in a list) 3 Furthermore (adds to the previous idea) 4 therefore (this idea is a result of the previous one) 5 Thirdly (introduces a third important point) 6 Although (introduces a contrasting idea: *despite* cannot be followed by a subject + verb) 7 In addition (adds further information) 8 as a result (this idea is the result of the previous one) 9 Nevertheless (gives contrasting information) (➤ B1 and B2)

3 2 For example 3 Firstly 4 Similarly 5 However 6 but; because 7 As a result (➤ B1 and B2)

4 2 I had to cancel all of my afternoon appointments because the head of my department called an emergency meeting. 3 Fewer people are going to the cinema these days due to the fact that it is now much cheaper to rent a DVD at home. 4 Petrol prices increased last month. As a result, the cost of basic foods has risen. 5 There are over 30 girls on this course but the boys still outnumber the girls by two to one. 6 There are some advantages to the pace of modern life. However, it also has its disadvantages. 7 In spite of the fact that the number of red deer in the wild increased slightly in the 1980s, it (the increase) was not sufficient to take them off the endangered species list. / In spite of the slight increase in the number of red deer in the wild in the 1980s, this was not sufficient to take them off the endangered species list. / Red deer were not taken off the endangered species list in spite of the fact that their numbers in the wild increased slightly in the 1980s. (➤ B1 and B2)

D: Test practice

Reading

Questions 1–3: multiple choice

Test tip: Read all the questions and options and underline or highlight any important information or key words that you need to find in the passage. Use the questions to locate the relevant part of the reading passage. If you cannot find an answer, just move on to the next one and come back to this one later.

1 B (*In that moment, Rita and Jake stumbled across an interesting set of differences between older and younger minds.*) 2 D (*In the end, if 'better' is defined as completing a clean paragraph, both people may end up taking the same amount of time.*) 3 A (*subjects were told to look at a screen, wait for an arrow that pointed in a certain direction to appear, and then use a mouse to click on the arrow as soon as it appeared on the screen. The other arrows were used to distract the subjects.*)

Questions 4–7: sentence completion

Test tip: Sentence completion with a box of possible answers is similar to matching questions. Scan the passage for the key names or words in the questions and underline or highlight them. Then carefully read the information close to those words and try to match it to the ideas in the options (A–F). Remember there are more options than you need to use. Some of the extra options may not be mentioned at all, or may be the opposite of the information in the passage.

4 E (*Popular psychology says that as people age their brains 'slow down'.*) 5 C (*scientists at the University of Michigan for example, have shown that ... seniors exploit the left and right side of the brain more extensively than men and women who are decades younger*) 6 B (*Michael Falkenstein ... found that when elders were presented with new computer exercises they paused longer before reacting and took longer to complete the tasks, yet they made 50% fewer errors*)

7 D (*Neurologists at Northwest University came to this conclusion after analyzing 50 people ... Darren Gleitman, who headed the study, concluded that older brains solved the problems just as effectively but by different means.*)

Questions 8–12: summary completion

Test tip: Read through the information in the summary carefully and try to predict what type of information you need to find in the passage. Pay careful attention to the word limit and make sure you copy the words correctly.

8 minds (*Just as people's bodies age at different rates, so do their minds.*) 9 memories (*As adults advance in age, the perception of sights, sounds and smells takes a bit longer, and ... The ability to retrieve memories also quickly slides.*) 10 & 11 IN EITHER ORDER: knowledge, experience (*On the other hand, the ageing brain can create significant benefits by tapping into its extensive hoard of accumulated knowledge and experience.*) 12 speed (*Drawing on both sides of the brain gives them a tactical edge, even if the speed of each hemisphere's process is slower*)

Grammar focus task

1 e 2 g 3 b 4 c 5 f 6 a 7 d

Unit 24

A: Context listening

1 The topic is whether children should be educated at home or at school.

2 1 T 2 F 3 T 4 F 5 T 6 F

3 1 fortunately; I can see; I think 2 unfortunately; I can see; certainly; I think; interestingly; Perhaps

4 1 see; think 2 fortunately; unfortunately; interestingly 3 certainly; perhaps

C: Grammar exercises

1 2 Personally, 3 presumably 4 perhaps 5 Overall, 6 probably 7 Surprisingly, 8 Unfortunately (➤ B2)

2 2 Apparently, the start of the course has been delayed because the tutor is ill. / The start of the course has been delayed because, apparently, the tutor is ill. / The start of the course has been delayed because the tutor is ill, apparently. 3 I definitely want to go to university when I leave school. 4 I was late for the exam because my bus didn't come, but luckily the exam hadn't started on time so I only missed a few minutes. / I was late for the exam because my bus didn't come, but the exam hadn't started on time, so luckily I only missed a few minutes. 5 Unfortunately, the university has decided to close the music department. / The university has decided to close the music department, unfortunately. / The university has unfortunately decided to close the music department. 6 Perhaps it is time to reorganise our company structure. 7 On the whole, my tutor was impressed with the effort I had put into my assignment, but suggested a few changes. / My tutor was impressed with the effort I had put into my assignment on the whole, but suggested a few changes. 8 It is probably true that people are living longer today than in the past. (➤ B2)

3 2 Frankly, 3 Surprisingly, 4 Unfortunately, 5 On the whole, 6 Evidently 7 Possibly 8 Actually, (➤ B2)

4 There are many reasons why people follow a vegetarian diet. Firstly, it is because they believe that it is wrong to kill animals. This may be is due to religious beliefs, or it could be is their own personal philosophy.

It is possible that another motivation for stopping eating meat is health. According to research, the high fibre content of a vegetarian diet seems to reduces the likelihood of suffering from some bowel problems and heart disease. In addition, fewer vegetarians than meat-eaters are overweight. A further advantage is that a vegetarian diet can be is cheaper than eating meat.

Nevertheless, it is clear that there are some disadvantages. Vegetarians can lack a lot of the vitamins and minerals that are present in meat, such as iron or vitamin B12, or calcium if you do not include dairy products in your diet. There is also the social problem of not being able to eat food available at parties and restaurants.

Overall, however in terms of health a vegetarian is more likely to be healthy than a non-vegetarian and personally I feel that the advantages outweigh the disadvantages. (➤ B1–B4)

D: Test practice
Academic Writing Task 2

Test tip: Make sure that you read all parts of the question carefully and address each point made. Organize your thoughts and ideas well. Do not try to memorize essays. Make sure you have at least 40 minutes to spend on this task and try to leave time at the end to check your spelling.

Model answer

Nowadays, modern technology has totally changed our approach to study. In many countries students no longer have to copy notes by hand from the blackboard; instead the teacher gives them a photocopy. Rather than messy ink and pen, students present a typed-up copy of their assignments. Their computer even checks their spelling as they go. In fact, some people believe that modern technology does a lot of our thinking for us and, as a result, we are losing our ability to think for ourselves.

In my opinion, spelling skills have definitely deteriorated in recent years. So many young people use mobile phones to send text messages where speed and conciseness are more important than spelling or grammar. Some teachers complain that these students take the same attitude towards their written assignments.

On the other hand, typed assignments are much easier to read and are much neater. Frankly, I find some notes or texts which are handwritten almost impossible to read. Doctors, for example, have often had a reputation for illegible handwriting, which could lead to disastrous medical mistakes. Perhaps it is time we focused not on handwriting but on presenting information as accurately as possible.

One advantage of computers is that access to the Internet has opened up a world of learning to us. We no longer have to wait for a book that has already been borrowed from the library before we can do our research. In fact, the Internet can clearly be used to research information in the same way as a library but more conveniently.

On the whole, rather than holding students back, I believe modern technology has actually improved standards of education considerably.

Grammar focus task

1 I believe (in my opinion)   2 actually
3 In my opinion (I believe); definitely   4 Frankly

Unit 25

A: Context listening

2 She experienced itching, pain, swelling and redness.

3 1 She had a very bad reaction and had to go to hospital.
2 On her foot.   3 It hurt. / It was very painful.   4 It went red and swelled up.   5 Her foot itched, it was difficult for her to breathe and she kept coughing.

4 1 burning pain   2 itching   3 swelling
4 breathing difficulties; a dry cough

5 1 The verbs are changed to nouns.   2 be, become (non-action verbs)

C: Grammar exercises

1 2 study; studies; student   3 findings; find   4 response; respondent   5 measurement; measure   6 earnings; earner
7 advertisement; advertiser; advertising   8 examination; examiner
9 suggestion   10 creation; creator; creativity (➤ B1)

2 2 strength   3 depth   4 beauty   5 clarity   6 interest
7 difficulty   8 caution   9 significance   10 violence
11 controversy   12 confusion (➤ B1)

3 2 there are some quite significant differences   3 the largest proportion of expenditure was   4 food expenditure   5 total household budget   6 There has been a notable increase in
7 a significant rise in the proportion of money spent on clothing
8 the proportion of fuel and lighting expenditure was roughly the same. (➤ B1 and B2)

4 2 Spending (expenditure); increase; influence   3 failure; illness
4 diet; reduction   5 Use; risk; loss   6 Contentment; success; communication   7 Developments; construction   8 difficulty
(➤ B1 and B2)

D: Test practice
Academic Writing Task 1

Test tip: Spend time studying the information first. The title given may help you with your first sentence, but try to use different words and don't just copy words from the question paper. Try to identify key areas in the data (e.g. where the data changes considerably or where there is no change over a period of time). Do not miss out any important details in your description and make sure you stick to the time limit so that you leave enough time to answer Task 2.

Model answer

The total number of all species of wild birds in the UK has been relatively stable over the last two decades, although there were significant drops in numbers between 1977 and 1979 and again in 1982 and 1986. Since 1994 there has been an improvement in numbers of all species, although the graph shows a slight decrease in 2000.

In contrast, the population of farmland birds has suffered a severe decline, particularly in 1978 when numbers fell dramatically. The rate of decline in the population appears to have slowed and it has remained relatively stable since 2000.

There was also a fall in the number of woodland birds of around 30% between 1974 and 1992. The population increased slightly in 2000 but it had dropped again by 2004.

It is only coastal species that have seen a steady increase in population over this period. Their numbers dropped slightly in 1995 and again in 2003 but the overall trend has been a positive one.

Grammar focus task

1 an improvement in numbers; a slight decrease   2 a fall in the number of woodland birds   3 a steady increase in population

Recording scripts

Recording 1a

Interviewer: Excuse me. I'm conducting a survey on how people spend their free time. Do you mind if I ask you a few questions?

Pete: Oh, er, OK. I'm just waiting for my friends – they're always late, so I should have a few minutes!

Interviewer: Right, now, can I have your name?

Pete: It's Peter, Peter Harley – H A R L E Y.

Interviewer: And do you work or are you a student, Peter?

Pete: Well, both actually. I'm studying really hard for my exams this month – I'm doing maths at university – but I also help my parents out. They own a restaurant and I work there as a waiter in the evenings, so I don't get a lot of free time during the week.

Interviewer: It sounds as if you're very busy.

Pete: Yes, I am, and my mum's always saying I don't help enough in the restaurant! But I do manage to find some free time most days.

Interviewer: Great. Now, can you have a look at this list and tell me whether you do any of these things and if so, how often?

Pete: Sure. OK, well, I love music and I'm learning to play the piano. I get up really early and practise for an hour or so just about every day. I also play the guitar in a band with some other friends. We used to practise together at least three times a week but these days we only manage to meet about once every two weeks.

Interviewer: What about the next thing on the list: computer games? I assume you're too busy to play them.

Pete: Well, I used to play them all the time but now I'm too busy studying and I don't miss them at all!

Interviewer: And do you use a computer for other things?

Pete: I use the Internet just about every day for my studies, and I also use it to keep in touch with my friends and family. My cousin is living in Thailand at the moment and he sends me regular emails to let me know how much fun he's having! He's always visiting exciting places.

Interviewer: Yes, the Internet is making it much easier for people to stay in touch with each other. Now, how about team sport?

Pete: Actually, I joined the local football team when I was at school and I still play once a month provided I can get to training. I much prefer playing football to watching it on TV, though I do occasionally watch a match if there's a big final or something.

Interviewer: What about going to watch live matches?

Pete: I'd love to be able to afford to go every week because I support my local team, but students don't generally have much money, you know! I can't remember the last time I went to a live match. Oh, sorry, I can see my friends – I have to go now.

Interviewer: Thank you for your time.

Recording 1b

Man: Westfield Sports Centre, can I help you?

Woman: Yes, I hope so. I've recently moved to the area and I want to do some sports activities.

Man: Well, we have excellent facilities, including a new gymnasium and several tennis courts. Our tennis team are always looking for new people.

Woman: Oh, I was never any good at gymnastics and I don't think I've got the time to put into learning tennis. No, I'm more interested in swimming, and I'd also like to take a few yoga classes if I can.

Man: OK, well, we have three swimming pools: an Olympic size 50 metre pool and a 25 metre pool, which are both outdoors, and a heated indoor pool, which is just 15 metres long but is very popular with our members in the winter!

Woman: I bet it is! Do members have to pay to use the pools?

Man: Well, members don't pay for the pools if they just want to swim laps on their own. We even offer complimentary classes for beginners, but we do charge a small fee if you want to take part in the advanced training sessions, and there's also a fee for our water-based keep-fit class.

Woman: Right. And would I need to book any of the facilities or can I just come whenever I want?

Man: We don't actually allow anyone to book the swimming lanes or the gym equipment, but for safety reasons we can only have a maximum of seven people in the sauna at any one time, so you do need to put your name on the list for that.

Woman:	Fine. Now, I'd also really like to take a yoga class. Do you have any?
Man:	Yes. There are classes on Monday, Tuesday and Friday in the morning from ten till eleven, and then every Saturday and Sunday in the evening. Those classes are a bit longer, starting at six and finishing at seven thirty.
Woman:	Right, I'll just make a note of that. So, does that mean that if I enrol I can come on each of those days?
Man:	No, each day is a different level, so you only come once a week.
Woman:	Oh, I see. Well, I've been doing yoga for a little while now, but I am still finding it quite difficult. Which level do you think I should choose?
Man:	Most people start at the lowest level, and then you can talk to the instructor about changing if you think it's too easy.
Woman:	OK. How much are the classes?
Man:	They're £1.50 an hour for members.
Woman:	Great. Now, I'd like to come in and look at the facilities. Would someone be able to show me around?
Man:	Yes, no problem.
Woman:	Who should I ask for?
Man:	Ask for me. My name is John Doherty – that's D O H E R T Y.
Woman:	And should I just ask for you at the reception?
Man:	Actually, my office is on a different level. Take the lift up to level one and you'll see my name on the door right in front of you.
Woman:	Great. I'd like to come tomorrow if that's OK. What time suits you?
Man:	Well, I have appointments from nine to ten thirty, so could you make it eleven?
Woman:	I'm sure that will be fine, but can I just take your direct number in case something else crops up?
Man:	That's a good idea – my number's 0117 965 478.
Woman:	Great. I think that's everything, so I'll see you tomorrow. Oh, my name's Alison Martin, by the way.
Man:	Thanks, Alison. See you tomorrow.

Recording 2

Presenter:	Today's guest is Bill Murphy, who worked for the police force for over 17 years until his retirement last week. Welcome to the show, Bill. You're going to tell us how to protect our homes, is that right?
Bill Murphy:	Thank you, yes, that's right. As you say, I used to work for the police force and I must have seen hundreds of burglaries during that time. Unfortunately, burglary seems to be on the increase; the number of burglaries in our area rose by 25% last year. What's so frustrating is that it's possible to prevent many burglaries. For example, a few weeks ago a woman called to report a robbery at her house. It happened at five in the afternoon while she was watching the news on TV in a room at the back of the house. Her son was also at home; he was doing his homework in his bedroom when the burglar came into the house.
Presenter:	So, how did the burglar break in without anybody hearing him?
Bill Murphy:	Well, this woman used to keep the front door locked at all times, but when her son got older he often went out to visit his friends after school, so she would leave the door unlocked whenever she was at home so he could come and go easily. The burglar simply walked in through the front door, which was unlocked, and no one heard a thing. So you see, you do need to be careful to lock your door at all times of the day.
Presenter:	Absolutely. And what did the burglar steal?
Bill Murphy:	On this occasion, the burglar came in through the front door, picked up the woman's handbag and while she was watching the TV, he emptied it out and stole her purse. The son didn't hear anything because he was listening to music and working on his computer upstairs. Then the burglar went into the front room, opened all the cupboards and took a valuable collection of CDs. But the surprising thing is that after that he went into the kitchen and stole the roast chicken the woman had cooked for dinner! So you see, it really is important to ...

Recording 3

Sue:	Hi Carl. Have you written your assignment yet?
Carl:	Hi Sue. No, I haven't, but I've been trying to get some ideas together.
Sue:	What sorts of things have you been doing?
Carl:	Well, I've worked really hard for the last two weeks and I've nearly finished all the books on the reading list. I've made quite a lot of notes but they're not very structured. What about you?

Sue:	I did the reading a few weeks ago, and I made notes on the most important things. I've written a rough plan this morning, and I was going to make a start on writing the assignment today but I've decided I need to read the most important parts of the books again before I do that. I'm actually finding it quite hard. It's the first time I've ever had to write such a long essay so I'm a bit nervous about it.
Carl:	Yes, it's the longest essay I've ever had to write as well. I find all the reading so difficult. I read five books last week, and they all said different things!
(Pause)	
Sue:	I find the best approach is to read only the sections that you need in order to answer the question. You don't usually have to read the whole book. I've collected plenty of information for the assignment that way.
Carl:	That's good advice. I've been trying to read the whole of each book, and the more I read, the more confused I get. I probably wasted a lot of time last week.
Sue:	Oh, I'll tell you what other things I found really helpful. When I was in the library last week, I read those leaflets called 'How to get the best out of the library' and 'How to write assignments'. They really helped. Have you read them?
Carl:	No, I haven't even seen them. I'll have to get hold of a copy; they sound very useful. I really need some direction. I find I'm so tired at the moment. I've read six articles this week but I can barely remember what they said! In fact, I've been feeling tired since I started this course!
Sue:	Hmm, I know what you mean. I felt like that as well at the start until one of my tutors told me it was far more important to get enough rest than to stay up late studying. I've gone to bed early every night since then and I manage to concentrate for longer during the day, so in the end I do actually get more done. I went to bed at ten thirty last night and I feel great.
Carl:	Well, I've just got up and I'm already tired. I must try going to bed earlier – at least till I've done this assignment.
Sue:	Yeah, it should help.

Recording 4

Good morning and welcome to today's talk on famous composers. Today we're going to look at the remarkable career of Wolfgang Amadeus Mozart. Mozart was born in Salzburg on January 27, 1756, the last of seven children. However, when Mozart was born, five of his siblings had already died in infancy or early childhood. His only surviving sibling was his sister, Nannerl, who was five years older. Mozart's father, Leopold, was a composer and his grandfather had also been a musician. Times were hard and the family had been struggling for some time.

When she was eight, Nannerl began keyboard lessons with her father. Mozart's sister was extremely gifted at the keyboard and she had been making excellent progress when her brother, then aged three, demanded to be taught as well. In just 30 minutes Mozart mastered the piece of music, which his father had copied into Nannerl's notebook. Wolfgang's achievement was followed in rapid succession by others. By the time he was six, the little boy had written a composition of his own into the notebook. And by age seven, he had taught himself how to play the violin without ever having received a lesson.

When Leopold Mozart saw how extraordinary his son was, he decided not to waste Wolfgang's precocious talents and took him on a tour across Europe with his sister. At Linz, Wolfgang gave his first public concert. Among the audience were some important statesmen who were astonished and hurried on to Vienna to spread sensational reports of what they had seen. By the time he was 17, Mozart's reputation had already begun to spread through Europe and his family were richer than they had ever been before.

Recording 5

Amanda:	Hi Tim, just ringing to see if you've got the details of the hockey team's trip for next month.
Tim:	Hi Amanda. Yes, I went to the travel agency this morning. I've got the details right here in front of me.
Amanda:	Oh, great. Well, why don't you tell me all about it and I'll pass on the information to the rest of the team.
Tim:	Good, well, first of all we're flying to Scotland. We'll have to get up really early because our flight leaves at six thirty in the morning. We're playing four matches there, which I know sounds like a lot but we'll also have three days free. So, we're going to hire a bus and then drive through the mountains and we'll probably stay in some sort of mountain lodge there.
Amanda:	Sounds wonderful. I hope the weather's good.
Tim:	Me too, but it'll probably rain every day.

Amanda:	Still, not to worry – I'm sure we'll enjoy it whatever the weather. Where to after that?
Tim:	From there we fly to Greece. We were supposed to be playing five matches there but two have been cancelled, so it's only three now. Still, that means there's a bit of free time to do some tourist things as well, as we now have four days free altogether.
Amanda:	Great. What about accommodation over there?
Tim:	Well, it's more luxurious than last year's camping trip, so I think everyone will be happy with it. This time we're staying in a small hotel near the centre of Athens for a few days, and then we're going to get a boat to a couple of the islands, although we haven't decided which ones yet.
Amanda:	I'm sure we'll have good weather there, anyway, so lots of time for sunbathing on the beach.
Tim:	Yes, I think it'll be extremely hot there.
Amanda:	You're right – we'll probably end up wishing we were back in Scotland! Well, we're certainly going to have a varied trip.
Tim:	Yes. In Scotland we're probably going to do lots of walking and in Greece we're going to be lying on the beach. I imagine we'll even get a bit of a tan.
Amanda:	I think it's going to be a great trip!
Tim:	Ha! Just don't forget to concentrate on your game! Oh, and one more thing, don't forget that the manager is having a party just after we get back to celebrate the team's great results last season, and the best player on the tour will get a special trophy.
Amanda:	Wow! Don't worry, I'll let everyone know.

Recording 6

Phil:	Hey Janet, have you finished the report yet? Sarah was asking about it.
Janet:	I'm afraid not. I'm about to go to Rome for a conference and I won't be able to finish the report before I go.
Phil:	Oh. When do you think it will be ready?
Janet:	The conference only lasts three days, so I'm not in Rome for long – just the weekend. Then I'll be working on the report all next week.
Phil:	Can you do it before we have the departmental meeting at the end of the month?
Janet:	Oh, I'll easily have finished it by next Friday. I've got it in my diary.
Phil:	That's great. I'll be seeing Sarah at lunch, so I'll tell her.
Janet:	Thanks.
Phil:	Are you giving a talk at the conference?

Janet:	Yes, the same one I gave last month on plant diversity and environmental changes. By the end of the year I will have given the same talk at six conferences! Luckily it's a different audience each time, but I'll soon be getting polite requests to do something different! The funny thing is I still get nervous every time before I give it.
Phil:	Oh come on, I don't believe that.
Janet:	No, it's true. I'll be feeling really nervous when I get to Rome. I won't be able to relax until I'm actually giving my talk. Don't you get nervous when you give talks at conferences?
Phil:	Not really, although I always make sure I prepare well. I always practise in front of a mirror. I look a bit of an idiot, but no one can see so I don't mind. I'm giving a talk in London next month and by the time I give the talk I'll have rehearsed it at least ten times. Practising like that makes me feel confident – you should try it.
Janet:	That's a good idea. But even practice doesn't seem to help me.
Phil:	Well, good luck, I'll be thinking of you in Rome. When are you leaving?
Janet:	Well, I was going to leave this morning but they cancelled my flight, so I'm on the evening flight. Actually, I'd better get a move on, as the train to the airport leaves in 20 minutes.

Recording 7

Sara:	Alan! Will you help me write this advertisement for the spare room?
Alan:	Yes, we've got so much space. It would be great to get some money to help with the rent.
Sara:	Now, we need to make it sound inviting.
Alan:	Well, the room might be on the small side but the windows are very big so the natural light is really nice. Few rooms have such good natural light.
Sara:	Yeah, it's a great room for working in during the day, and it's also got a great view of the garden.
Alan:	Exactly. What shall we say about the furniture?
Sara:	Well, it's not luxurious but it is very comfortable. The room has everything you need. Oh, except they will need to bring their own lamp; both of the lights in the ceiling are really old and not very bright.
Alan:	That's true. But it has got a nice bed.
Sara:	Yes, and it's got a great wardrobe, which has even got a few shelves for clothes as well. They will need to bring their own mirror if they want one, though.

Alan:	Yes – there isn't one in the room at the moment. Now, there's no room for a bedside table but there is a good study desk in there.
Sara:	Yes, I wouldn't mind a desk like that myself, actually. It's better than mine. It's got three drawers – mine hasn't got any at all.
Alan:	Why don't you put it in your study then?
Sara:	It's too big. There isn't much room in there.
Alan:	I suppose not, because the desk has got shelves on top as well. They're really handy for putting books on. Now, what else?
Sara:	What about the location? We could say it's close to transport. We're really lucky because we've got the bus and the train nearby.
Alan:	That's true. And what shall we say about the rent? Shall we ask for £50 a week or is that too little?
Sara:	Well, let's say it includes electricity and any other household bills and make it £60. Our expenses are bound to go up with an extra person in the house.
Alan:	Yes, you're right, I hadn't thought of that! Now, pass me the newspaper.
Sara:	I thought you'd already read the news today?
Alan:	Yes, I have, but there are lots of advertisements for accommodation and I want to look at them before we finish ours.

Recording 8a

Good morning everyone. As part of the conference on environmental awareness I'd like to talk to you this morning about an exciting development in monitoring climate change: Europe's technological showpiece, Envisat. Envisat is a fully-equipped observation satellite and it is the largest, most technologically advanced, and most powerful one that the European Space Agency (the ESA) has ever created.

The satellite was launched in 2002 and is on the trail of climate change, delivering up-to-the-minute information about our changing environment. Seeing the earth from outer space highlights how tiny and fragile this planet of ours is. Envisat helps people to understand that and encourages us to protect our blue planet as our place of birth, and as the ancestral home where our children and grandchildren will live after us.

With its ten instrument systems Envisat is equipped with the best eyes possible and offers everything that scientists could wish for. This unique flying environment station follows in the footsteps of the successful remote sensing satellites ERS1 and ERS2, which were both launched in the 1990s.

Climate protection is a challenge for our entire society. The ESA contributes to such endeavours and has provided impressive scientific results in the field of atmosphere, ozone and climate monitoring, and more. The total cost of the Envisat programme is 2.3 billion euros over 15 years. Included in this sum is the development and construction of the instrument systems as well as the cost of the satellites, the launch and the operational costs. Each European citizen has therefore invested seven euros in the environment or about the cost of two cups of coffee per year. For that, every citizen will have access to precise information about changes in the environment including global warming, ozone depletion and climate change. This information is absolutely essential and long overdue as the basis for political decisions. The gas envelope around the earth is not determined by political boundaries and none of our countries is able to ignore the implications of global warming.

Recording 8b

Hello everyone and welcome to today's talk about the current trends in health and fitness. Nowadays, it seems as though everyone in the wealthiest parts of the world is battling with their weight and as a consequence, more and more people are joining local gyms or buying home-exercise machines.

In fact, according to the International Health, Racquet and Sportsclub Association, membership in health clubs in America doubled from a little over 17 million in 1987 to more than 36 million in 2005. While the figures for Europe are harder to come by, evidence over the past decade suggests that health club membership has doubled there as well.

What few people nowadays realize is that the average person in the developed world is now burning 800 fewer calories a day than a generation ago. This means that even if people today ate no more than the previous generation, they would still be getting fatter. Unfortunately, instead of eating less than their parents did, as they should, many people consume a lot more.

So what exactly has brought about this change in fitness levels? Well, people in developed countries are not only eating more but are also doing less exercise. Increased technology has not helped. The car and other such machines designed to help reduce our work load are as much to blame as deep-fried fast food. On top of this, the changes in how and where we work have reduced the amount of daily calories people actually need. Such factors are taking their toll on our health, with health costs soaring.

And this is where exercise machines come in. Walking machines or treadmills and the like may not be the most efficient way of burning off those excess calories and boosting cardiovascular fitness but they are certainly the most common. According to the Sporting Goods Manufacturing Association International, some 45 million Americans used a treadmill in 2003. That's an amazing number of people and an awful lot of treadmills.

Having said that, an exercise machine that did not even exist a decade ago – the elliptical cross trainer – is fast replacing the traditional treadmill. As its name implies, the machine delivers an elliptical or swinging motion, with both the hands and feet tracing semi-circular patterns – the feet on two moving platforms rather than bicycle pedals, and the hands gripping handles that move but are not meant to support any weight, which is important as there is no seat. Since the machine was introduced there, the number of people using elliptical machines in America has tripled to more than 11 million a year.

We have been doing some tests to find out if these machines are actually any better than the previous machines or if they are just another passing trend. Dr John Porcari, a professor of exercise and sport science, believes that ellipticals are at least better than the previous exercisers, but no better than treadmills in terms of increasing cardiovascular fitness. In one set of tests, Dr Porcari measured the oxygen consumption, heart rate and calorific expenditure of 16 volunteers, and found that there was virtually no difference between elliptical machines and treadmills. But elliptical machines have a lower impact on the user than running, claim their manufacturers. True, says Dr Porcari, who measured the 'ground reaction forces' of the test subjects on the various machines. Running on a treadmill results in forces that are roughly two and a half times the subject's body weight. But using an elliptical machine gives forces that are roughly equal to the subject's weight. This is much kinder on the body and makes the impact comparable to that of walking. In that respect, ellipticals are superior.

However, those who do not want to shell out for fancy exercise machines will be heartened by the results of a seminal study in 1969 by Lewis Pugh, a British physiologist, which has been confirmed many times since. Dr Pugh found that, when reaching speeds above 14 kilometres per hour or so, running on firm ground uses up substantially more calories, and therefore leads to a greater reduction in weight, than running on a treadmill or using an elliptical machine. Dr Pugh attributed the difference to air resistance. Manufacturers of exercise machines point out, correctly, that running on firm ground creates a greater force on the body's joints than using machines, in particular the knees and ankles. But, what they don't say is that modern running shoes go a long way to reducing the impact of such forces. So, perhaps the best exercise of all is simply to leave the car at home, and run to the gym – and then right past it. After that, just keep going and going and going ...

Recording 9

Mrs Smith:	Hello, you must be Chi Wen. I'm Mrs Smith, but my homestay students all call me Lucy.
Chi Wen:	Oh, hello, Lucy. I'm very pleased to meet you.
Mrs Smith:	So, how long have you been in Australia, Chi Wen?
Chi Wen:	Well, I only arrived last month and I'm still finding it all a bit strange, actually.
Mrs Smith:	Oh, don't worry. I'm sure it won't take long to settle in. If you like, I can introduce you to a friend of mine, Yi Ling. She's a student from China who stayed with me last year. I know she's really enjoying herself here in Australia.
Chi Wen:	Oh, that would be nice.
Mrs Smith:	Now, I have had a lot of students staying with me over the years and I do have a few rules.
Chi Wen:	Oh, of course.
Mrs Smith:	First of all, my husband and I want everyone to feel at home so we treat everyone as if they were a member of our own family.
Chi Wen:	That sounds lovely.
Mrs Smith:	I cook and serve dinner for everyone at six. We also make everyone speak English at dinner; it's really important to practise your English as often as you can.
Chi Wen:	I see, that's a very good idea. And what about other meals? Can I cook for myself?
Mrs Smith:	Yes, everyone makes their own breakfast. I do the shopping, and I always make sure there is plenty of food in the fridge so you can prepare yourself a packed lunch to take to college if you like.
Chi Wen:	Yes, I've noticed that in Australia you often eat sandwiches for lunch.
Mrs Smith:	Well, we often eat lunch in a bit of a hurry, so sandwiches are very convenient. Now, do you have any other questions about the house rules?
Chi Wen:	What about laundry? Can I use the washing machine?
Mrs Smith:	Oh, yes. I expect everyone to wash and iron for themselves, although I can put a load of washing on if you need me to. I will give you clean bed sheets every week. I clean the kitchen and the living areas myself but I expect all my students to help out and clean their own rooms.
Chi Wen:	I have one other question. I don't have a mobile phone here yet. Can I use yours to make a couple of local calls?
Mrs Smith:	That shouldn't be a problem. Just let me know when you want to use it.

Recording 10

Good evening, everyone. As many of you know I often travel for my job as a rug buyer and this evening I've been asked to give a talk about travelling in Europe and Asia. I'll try to pass on some useful advice for those of you who are planning to travel there yourselves. At the end of my talk, I'll be happy to answer questions.

My first piece of advice is to work hard on your research before you go if you want to make your trip enjoyable and rewarding. I plan my trips very carefully for at least three months before I leave, reading about the places I am going to visit on the Internet and in books.

I had a very memorable trip recently, starting out in Morocco. The city of Marrakech is an absolutely amazing place to visit and well worth adding to your itinerary. Try to stay near the old part of the city. There are so many historical buildings and so much to see. The mosques in particular are very beautiful.

After leaving Morocco I took a long tiring boat ride to Turkey. It was well worth the trip, especially if you like local crafts. I bought a beautiful Turkish carpet in one of the villages while I was there. The man that sold it to me spoke very good English and he told me all about the different styles of carpet. I was fascinated to see the extraordinary range of patterns.

I left the small mountain villages of Turkey to travel to the huge, crowded cities of India. India is a fascinating country, and I have always enjoyed my visits there. Everywhere you go the people are very welcoming and friendly towards visitors. They always seem pleased to see you. It's easy to see why India is such a popular destination for travellers.

One of the highlights for me on this visit was the Gujarati Textile Museum. It was the first time I had been there. If you are interested in textiles, this museum is really impressive, with lots of information and some absolutely stunning examples of Indian silk embroidery, and other fabrics.

If you're interested in seeing wildlife I recommend travelling in the more remote areas of the country. I was amazed at the variety of wonderful animals which I saw on my trip and the most incredible colourful birds with vivid blue and green feathers. I also saw several poisonous spiders, although I have to say that I found the insects rather frightening!

Recording 11

The Olympics is probably the most exciting event in the sports calendar. It's one of the few opportunities we get to see some of the best athletes in the world competing against each other. And amazingly, each year they seem to be getting better and better. So, you might imagine that the Masters Games, which is for athletes aged 30 and over, would be less exciting to watch. Well, this may not be true for long because recent studies have shown that older athletes are getter faster and fitter.

Now, it's true they're not as fast as their younger counterparts, and probably younger runners will always be faster than older runners. However, runners aged 50 and over are actually speeding up more rapidly than younger people. The researchers analysed the finishing times of 415,000 runners in the New York marathon between 1983 and 1999 and discovered that finishers from the older group showed the greatest increases in speed. Interestingly, women aged 60 to 68 improved the most markedly, running on average four minutes faster each year. Men of the same age ran just over one minute faster than previously.

Not only that, a second study proved that older athletes can achieve the same degree of physical improvement as those in their twenties and thirties. In other words, they are just as likely to achieve their peak fitness as younger athletes.

25 years ago few 60-year-old men and even fewer women would have considered it possible to complete a marathon let alone set record running times. The researchers concluded that people grow weaker not simply because of age, but because they don't keep as active as they did when they were younger. It would seem that the longer athletes keep competing, the greater their chances of setting new records are.

Recording 12

Good morning, everyone. What you can see on the screen behind me is Sydney Harbour and it may surprise you to learn that this horrible rubbish lying at the bottom of the harbour was actually put there intentionally as part of a conservation project! Now, the idea of putting rubbish into the harbour instead of cleaning it out may seem absurd to you, but allow me to explain. Two years ago I was involved in a study with the University of Sydney. We were asked to try to calculate the number of fish and different species living in Sydney harbour. During this study, the divers noticed that in the areas cleared of rubbish very little life remained, whereas the old cars and other debris lying on the sea floor actually provided a rich habitat for an abundance of creatures including up to twenty species of fish, crabs and seahorses and amazing plants such as sea tulips with bright red bodies.

We realized that if you remove all of the rubbish contained in the harbour then you also take away the homes of the creatures living there. Earlier this year, with the help of the Sydney Harbour Federation Trust, we reached a decision to expand our study and start putting rubbish back into particular areas of the harbour.

So far we have used things like old car tyres and rope, but we have a plan to carry out a more detailed study to test out a variety of artificial structures and see whether the sea creatures in the harbour find these as attractive a home as the rubble of the past. We'll also catalogue the creatures living there and the data collected from the sites will be analysed to establish whether these artificial reefs have in fact helped to increase the volume of fish in the harbour.

In the meantime, if you have any suggestions of other possible sites with submerged rubbish that would be suitable for our research, please speak to me after the lecture.

Recording 13a

Deborah:	Hi Joe.
Joe:	Hello Deborah. Listen, have you had much experience dealing with amnesia?
Deborah:	Actually, yes I have. It was a patient I had last year when I was working in a hospital in Canada.
Joe:	Can you remember much about it?
Deborah:	Well, a man was brought to us with some facial and head injuries and he couldn't remember who he was, where he lived or how he came to be in Canada.
Joe:	Were there any clues at all?
Deborah:	Well, he spoke with a strong British accent so the police realized he couldn't be Canadian. They took him to a language expert who said that he could have come from Yorkshire, in England. The police also managed to find out that he could speak French and Italian. But he couldn't remember his name, address, age, or anything. Can you imagine what it must be like to have your whole life lost like that?
Joe:	Yes, it must be awful. But do you think he was genuine? He might have been trying to run away from his past or something. People can do funny things when they've experienced something terrible.
Deborah:	Well, if he was, it certainly wasn't the best way to go about it, because his picture was in all the papers and on the news. He wouldn't have been able to fool everybody for so long if it wasn't true, I'm sure. At some point he was bound to have said something to give it away. No, I think he really had genuinely lost his memory and couldn't remember anything.

Joe:	He could have had a wife and children waiting for him somewhere wondering what had happened. Do you know if he was married?
Deborah:	Well, he can't have been, because if he'd been married, his wife would have reported him missing.
Joe:	Do you know what happened to him afterwards?
Deborah:	Well, apparently he's been able to find his parents and now he's back in England living with them.
Joe:	That's amazing. Did you ever work out how he had lost his memory?
Deborah:	Well, when he arrived at the hospital he had a head injury and no personal effects – no wallet or phone or anything. We assumed that he had probably been attacked and robbed, and he must have hit his head, resulting in the loss of memory.
Joe:	It can't be easy for his parents, living with someone who doesn't remember their past. They must be having a difficult time adjusting to it all.
Deborah:	Well, in my experience of these cases pieces of memory do gradually come back. He may remember some things already, and over a few years he'll probably be able to remember quite a lot. He could make a total recovery one day.

Recording 13b

Good afternoon, everyone. Today I am going to tell you about the research I have been conducting into the history of soap. While you may be able to find some information on the origins of soap, it is not a substance which has excited a great deal of study so far. What we do know is that even as long ago as 2500 BC soap was being used. Of course, initially it was only ever used on clothing rather than the body itself. In fact, although soap has existed for so many years, the use of soap for personal hygiene was unheard of until fairly recently and is considered to be a relatively modern notion. So we can only assume that other activities must have provided the basis from which this key concept arose.

To make soap you need to combine three materials in relatively exact proportions. So, how is it that these primitive people from over two thousand years ago could have discovered soap? Well, what these people lacked in technology they certainly made up for in practical skills. I carried out some experiments using basic techniques to try to find out what people without any chemical knowledge might have observed. And I was able to demonstrate that they would indeed have been able to make a soap-like substance that is not dissimilar to the one we know today.

However, it is fair to assume that, as the process requires a certain amount of time and specialization, soap would most likely have only been available in the wealthy communities. Although there are claims that the British Celts and their European counterparts used soap, there is no real evidence that the British colonies of the Iron Age had access to such a product.

Now, the history of soap is not easy to discover. As soap is an organic substance no traces of it remain in archaeological sites, so we have had to rely almost entirely on written texts for our discoveries. Fortunately there are many of these. The first known written mention of soap was on Sumerian clay tablets dating from about 2500 BC. The tablets spoke of the use of soap in the washing of wool. In another incidence, a medical document from about 1500 BC mentions that Egyptians bathed regularly. It also describes how they made soap by combining alkaline salts and oil which they extracted from vegetables.

We also know that the Romans used a mixture of earth, soda and wine to clean their clothes and pots. For the Romans bathing was not just a matter of hygiene; it was a form of relaxation, a social activity. The bather moved from room to room, getting progressively hotter, until they reached a steamy room where dirt was sweated out and scraped away with a metal blade. The Romans used scented bath oils but these were used to moisturize the skin rather than to cleanse it and there is no evidence that they used soap in this way. This is not to say that the Romans did not have soap. During the excavation of Pompeii, a city that was buried under the eruption of Mount Vesuvius in 79 AD, an entire soap factory was revealed, showing that they did in fact have access to soap but that they simply did not use it for personal hygiene.

Recording 14

Claire: Hello Jack. How much longer before you leave for Hong Kong?

Jack: Hi Claire, it's about a month now. Actually I could use a bit of advice. You used to live there, didn't you?

Claire: That's right. What sorts of things do you need to know?

Jack: Well, I've got to find somewhere to live quite quickly. The company are only paying for me to stay in a hotel for one week. Will that be enough?

Claire: Yes, you should be able to find something by then, but you'll need to allow a bit of extra time to get over the jet lag; there's a big time difference between there and the UK.

Jack: Oh, I hadn't thought of that. What's the accommodation like?

Claire: Well, the rooms tend to be smaller than here but you can get bigger places on one of the other islands. A friend of mine rented a lovely place on Lamma Island. The only problem was he had to get up really early to catch the ferry to work.

Jack: What's the transport like generally?

Claire: Fantastic! The underground system is called the MTR and there are trains every couple of minutes, so you don't have to wait for ages like we do here. You should try to use it whenever you can. The bus system is a bit more complicated because there are normal double decker buses but there are also smaller buses called 'public light buses'. They only stop when you ask them to so you'll have to learn some Cantonese if you want to take one of those. The Star Ferry is amazing. It's so cheap and you get the best view of the harbour – you really have to see it to believe it. You should always carry plenty of loose change though for the buses and the ferries.

Jack: The company has offered us Cantonese lessons when I get there. Do you think I should take them?

Claire: Oh, definitely, you must have lessons if you want to be able to pronounce things correctly. You don't need to speak Cantonese in the bigger shops but you'll need some basic phrases when you go shopping in the local market.

Jack: Is there anything else I need to know?

Claire: Well, nowadays you have to get a work permit before you go. We didn't have to worry about those when I was there.

Jack: Yes, that's already taken care of.

Claire: And you mustn't dress too casually for work. Everyone dresses really well in Hong Kong.

Jack: I'll remember that.

Claire: Oh, and you needn't buy lots of guide books before you go. You can get great ones there for a fraction of the price. Also, you ought to take lots of passport photos with you. You'll find you need lots to fill in any application forms.

Jack: Great! I'm getting pretty excited now.

Claire: I'm not surprised. Oh, one last thing …

Jack: What's that?

Claire: You must invite me to visit you!

Recording 15a

Interviewer: So, Mr West, what does the future hold for Angleside?

Mr West: Well, we've just announced our future plans for the company.

Interviewer: And how many jobs will have to go?

Mr West: We'll be losing 100 jobs here in Swindon, and another 50 jobs will go from our Birmingham branch. However, we'll be offering voluntary redundancy and early retirement and hope to cover most of the job losses this way.

Interviewer: And what has led to this situation? Are these cuts a result of Angleside's poor performance over the past five years?

Mr West: No, the company hasn't been doing badly. This has nothing to do with the figures; it just makes good business sense.

Interviewer: So are you saying that your figures are not the basis for this decision to cut jobs?

Mr West: Absolutely. We decided to change the way we operate our business two years ago.

Interviewer: So are you confident that the company will continue to operate into the future?

Mr West: Yes, of course. We are completely confident about this.

Interviewer: And how are you going to deal with the discontent of your workforce over this announcement?

Mr West: We will do our very best to make things as easy as possible for our employees.

Interviewer: Well, we're out of time. Thank you very much for answering my questions.

Mr West: Thank you.

Recording 15b

At local company Angleside, up to 150 employees will lose their jobs. Christopher West, the Managing Director, announced they would be offering voluntary redundancy and early retirement and hoped to cover the job losses in this way. I asked Mr West if these cuts were a result of Angleside's poor performance over the past five years but he denied that the company had not been doing well and said that the job losses have nothing to do with the figures. West claimed that they decided to make changes two years ago. He assured me that the company would continue to operate in the future and promised to do his best for the employees.

Recording 15c

Tutor: OK, so it's Millie's turn to give her tutorial today, isn't it?

Millie: That's right. I'm going to talk about renewable energy sources, and specifically solar towers. I'm not sure how much you already know about solar towers, so I thought I'd start with a few questions. First of all, does anyone know how solar towers work?

Tanya: Don't they somehow use the sun's energy to create electricity?

Millie: Yes, in a way. They actually work by using the sun to make columns of hot air that rise upwards through the centre of the tower. Now, do you know how old this idea is?

Luke: I would have thought it was a twentieth-century idea. That's when we've had to start thinking about how to solve energy problems, isn't it?

Tanya: No, I read something about this last week. The first time solar energy was produced was in the seventeenth century, wasn't it?

Millie: That's right, so it's not a modern idea at all. And Leonardo Da Vinci also made sketches of a solar tower, though he never actually built one. Their recent history starts really with a man called Jorg Schlaich.

Tanya: Yes, I read about him. He's a professor from Germany and he needed a country with plenty of sunshine and land for his research so he chose Spain to build the first tower.

Millie: Correct! Well, everyone seems to know something about these towers.

Luke: Yes, but I still don't really understand how they work.

Millie: Well, I've made a flowchart to help you. Firstly, you have to realize that they are very tall towers. They're constructed out of high-strength concrete and they can be as high as 1,000 feet; there's one being built in Australia that's one kilometre high. Now, all around the base of the tower they have a sunlight collector which is basically a large sheet of plastic. It extends out for as much as seven kilometres, and it is raised off the ground slightly so it heats up the air underneath it.

Luke: So it acts like a greenhouse then?

Millie: That's exactly right. In fact, they plan to try and grow plants underneath it as well.

Tanya: So what happens to the air?

Millie:	Well, the sunlight collector heats it to 65°C – that's on average 35° greater than the outside temperature – and the laws of physics mean that this hot air rises up the chimney or the tower and drives the turbines at the top. As the turbines revolve, they generate electricity. In fact, they can generate 200 megawatts of power or enough for 200,000 houses.
Tanya:	Wow, that sounds impressive. But it can't all be good news. What are the disadvantages? I'll bet they're really expensive to operate.
Millie:	Well, no, not necessarily, because sunlight is free after all, so it's really only the initial outlay that is costly. After that they're very efficient.
Luke:	But what about at night when there is no sun?
Millie:	Well, they've managed to find a way to store the electricity produced during the day, so it's no problem at night or even on cloudy days.
Tanya:	So, there are no drawbacks then?
Millie:	I didn't say that. One problem they do have is that a lot of the energy in the sunlight is lost from the collector in the form of heat, and then, of the remaining heat, a large proportion escapes from the top of the tower. But they are still worth the investment because, as I said, sunlight is free!
Luke:	Hang on. If these towers are so tall, how do they cope in high winds? Surely they become dangerous then?
Millie:	Yes, keeping them stable is another drawback. I believe they anchor the towers to the ground with wires to stabilize them so they're not dangerous, but it is an issue.
Tutor:	You have certainly found an interesting topic today, so thanks Millie. Perhaps we can have a look at your pictures now.

Recording 16

Presenter:	Good afternoon, and welcome to Education Today. This afternoon Freya Smith tells us about her diploma course in animal management. Welcome, Freya.
Freya:	Thank you.
Presenter:	Now, tell me, Freya – was animal care something you always hoped to do?
Freya:	Oh, yes, absolutely. I've always been interested in working with animals and during my last year at school I decided to do an animal management course.
Presenter:	Right, and was it difficult to find the right course?
Freya:	No, not really. I chose to study at Fairfield College because it's got a good range of animals and everyone's really friendly.
Presenter:	So, tell us a little about the course.
Freya:	Well, we get a lot of practical experience and there's also a lot of theory, but not so much that it's boring. I want to learn to manage the animals and the business side of it. The course is only three days a week, so I've already started working part-time at a pet shop.
Presenter:	That must be interesting.
Freya:	Yes, it's quite a varied job. My favourite job is feeding the animals. Some people rush through this but I prefer taking time so I can get to know them. In fact, I like having the chance to hold them. I don't even mind cleaning them out.
Presenter:	And have you been pleased with the course so far?
Freya:	Oh yes, it's been everything I expected it to be and more, really. We've practised handling animals and they've let us treat some minor problems, like removing splinters from paws. They make us handle all kinds of animals including spiders and snakes, even if we don't want to. At first I didn't want to touch the snakes, and I remember feeling really scared, but they let us take it slowly, and taught us exactly how to hold them. As long as you remember to do it the way you've been taught, it's fine. I still don't like holding them, but I'm not scared any more. This course has taught me to respect all animals and overcome my fears.
Presenter:	What has been the most useful thing you've learned so far?
Freya:	Learning about the behaviour of dogs on the course has helped me understand my own dog better. Before, if I heard him bark, I just told him to be quiet. Now, I stop to think about why he's doing it.
Presenter:	And what do you hope to do when you've finished?
Freya:	Well, I was thinking about doing another course when I finish, but now I've decided I'm going to stop studying for a while and go out to work. I'd really like to work in either a zoo or a safari park.

Recording 17

Father: Simon, do you have time for a little chat?

Simon: Sure, Dad.

Father: I just wondered if you'd thought about what you were going to do with the money your grandfather left you?

Simon: Well, I have started to give it some thought. It's quite a lot of money so I want to make sure I don't just waste it. I had thought about leaving it in the bank for a while.

Father: Well, unless you invest it properly, you won't earn much interest and it may lose value over time.

Simon: Yes, but if I invest it, I won't be able to access the money quickly when I've decided what to do with it, will I?

Father: Well, what sort of thing would you like to do?

Simon: Well, at first I thought about taking a trip around the world, but if I went travelling, I'd lose a year of study and I wouldn't have any money left over for anything else.

Father: Very true. If you were to spend a year travelling around the world, you'd probably need an awful lot more money than this!

Simon: Right, so the other thing I wanted to do was buy a car.

Father: Do you think that's a good idea? It's not just the initial cost of the car you have to consider, you know. If you own a car, you also have to pay for insurance and road tax every year and then there's the petrol …

Simon: Yes, Dad, but I'm planning to get a part-time job as well and it would be great if I could drive to work instead of travelling on the bus, especially if I have to work late at night.

Father: I still think you should think about investing some of your money for the future.

Simon: But I'm scared that if I invest it, I might lose it all when the stock market goes down.

Father: Well, it's best not to look at it like that. You won't lose any money provided that you think of it as a long-term investment. Now, I know you want to buy a car but as long as you get a second-hand one, you should still be able to invest some of the money as well. That's what I would do if I were you.

Simon: But Dad, there's this fantastic new car that I've seen …

Recording 18

Anna: Hi Simon, how are you? How is your new car going?

Simon: Oh, don't ask me, Anna. It's a nightmare! I should never have bought it!

Anna: Why? What's wrong? I thought you'd got one of those fancy new models?

Simon: I did, but that's part of the problem. If I'd bought a second-hand car, I wouldn't have taken out this big bank loan I've got now.

Anna: Oh, so I suppose you've got big repayments to make?

Simon: Yes, and I can't sell the car until I've paid for it. But it's not only that. I had no idea running a car was going to be so expensive! I wish I'd thought about the other costs before I bought it.

Anna: It probably wouldn't be so bad if the price of petrol hadn't almost doubled last month.

Simon: Don't remind me – the petrol alone is costing me a fortune!

Anna: Lucky you've got that part-time job then!

Simon: That's just the thing. Nearly all of my wages are going on the car. If I'd waited a bit before buying the car, I'd have managed to save quite a bit by now. I might even have gone on that college trip last week; it sounded great.

Anna: Oh, dear. Can't you ask your dad to help you out?

Simon: No way! When my granddad left me some money, my dad didn't want me to spend it on a car. If only I'd listened to him, none of this would have happened! I wish he wasn't always right!

Anna: Well, maybe you should value his opinions more. You do seem to argue with him a lot. If you got on better with him, you might have listened to his suggestions.

Simon: The worst thing is, Dad wanted me to buy some shares with the money and now they've gone up by thirty per cent. I should have listened to him. If I'd taken his advice, I'd own a small fortune now instead of a big debt!

Anna: Oh, Simon, you poor thing. I wish I could help you but I have even less money than you. At least you have a car!

Simon: Oh, don't say that! I wish I'd never bought the car! If it weren't for the car, I'd have no money worries now.

Interviewer: Come in Sarah. I do apologize for keeping you waiting. Would you like a cup of tea or coffee?

Sarah: That's very kind of you, but I'm fine thanks.

Interviewer: Now, I just want to run through a few questions with you. Firstly, why have you applied for this course?

Sarah: Well, I've always been interested in teaching and I've just finished my first degree at Stamford University, so I'd like to gain a teaching qualification.

Interviewer: Right, and can you explain your reasons for choosing our college specifically?

Sarah: Well, that's easy. My brother lives in the city and I'm hoping for a place on this course because then I'll be able to share a flat with him.

Interviewer: Oh, I see. So there isn't anything about our course that attracts you?

Sarah: Oh, I didn't mean it like that. I was really impressed with the description of the course in your prospectus. I haven't applied to the other university in the city because their course didn't appeal to me as much.

Interviewer: That's interesting. Can you say a bit more about what interests you about this course?

Sarah: Well, I like the structure of it and the fact that all the focus in the first term is on theory. I like the idea of learning about teaching before being asked to do it. Do you see what I mean?

Interviewer: Yes, and it sounds like a good reason to apply for our course. Have you talked to anyone who has done this course?

Sarah: Yes, my friend did it last year. She warned me about all of the hard work! But that's OK, I expect to work hard.

Interviewer: Excellent! Now, do you have any concerns about the course?

Sarah: Well, I must admit there are some aspects of the course that I'm a bit scared of.

Interviewer: Oh, what are they?

Sarah: Well, you can see from my application form that I'm not very good at maths. Will that cause me any problems?

Interviewer: That's very honest of you, but there is no need to worry about that. It's not important for this course.

Sarah: Oh, that's a relief. But the thing I'm most worried about is the classroom practice.

Interviewer: Well, most people are frightened of being in front of a class for the first time, but the tutors will help you to feel more confident.

Sarah: I haven't had any real experience of teaching and I'm worried about not being able to control a class, and the pupils being rude to me. If they shout at me in class, I'm not sure what I'll do.

Interviewer: That's a common worry but you will be taught how to deal with those things by the tutors on the course. In the end, of course, you have to take responsibility for what happens in your classroom, but you will be much better able to cope after training.

Sarah: Well, that makes me feel a bit better. Thanks.

Interviewer: Right, well, I don't want to make you late for your train. Thank you for coming and we'll be in touch soon by email, if that's okay.

Hello everyone and welcome to Greenville community centre. Today we're going to be talking about what we as a community can do to help each other in severe weather. Our lovely little village is, as you know, quite remote. There may be other similar sized communities only 25 kilometres away but emergency services have to drive 500 kilometres to reach us from the closest large town. That can mean a wait of up to ten hours before help arrives.

Having said that, we are very lucky in that we've always had our own fire service and, thanks to the arrival of Dr Jones earlier this year, we no longer have to drive so far if anyone gets sick. What we don't have, and are unlikely to get in the near future, is a weather station.

Now, the National Weather Bureau can provide a lot of helpful information and even warn us about severe storms, but they can only do this if they build up a database of information and to do that they need local help. That means us. What we'd like to do is set up a group of volunteer storm spotters to pass information on to the Weather Bureau.

So, what do these storm spotters have to do? Well, thankfully you don't have to be particularly skilled at anything. Quite simply, immediately after a storm has passed, the first thing you have to do is call the national weather station to let them know. After that you have to complete a report card, which is very simple and won't take more than a few minutes to do. The only other thing they ask is that we keep an eye out for any reports in the local newspaper of storms or storm damage. You need to cut these out and send them in as well. Damage that makes news here is unlikely to make it into the national papers, so these can be an important source of extra information.

So that's all as far as the duties go. Now, what sort of thing do you need to report? Well, they don't want to hear about every single storm that we have, only the ones that bring some unusual conditions. For example, we don't need to call them just because there is hail, but we should report any hailstones that are two centimetres in diameter or bigger. They also need to know about damage caused by high wind, especially if it uproots large trees. Again, don't contact them every time you see a tree fallen over. You should use your common sense and restrict it to those big enough to cause a problem, especially on our roads. They'd also like to hear about very heavy rainfall and more especially any localized flash floods.

So, what should you do if you care about our community and you want to help? Well, obviously you'll need a bit more information and preparation than I've given you today so we'll be conducting a training session next month. This will only take up a day, so don't worry too much about it. If you do have the time and would like to come along, then you'll need to talk to the police who are coordinating the event. And as our storm season is from November right to the end of January, you'll need to put your name down by the end of October at the very latest, but if you'd like to get in early, Sergeant Phillips is here this afternoon and he's happy to take names now. This really is important for our community, and we're hoping to get a lot of support. Thank you.

Presenter: Good morning, listeners! The holiday season is here and this is the time when many of us plan to get away from it all, but what about the home you're leaving behind? Well, please welcome Mike Bowers, who is going to talk about how to look after your home when you are travelling.

Mike: That's right, Matthew. Whether you're a person whose job involves a lot of travel or whether you travel for pleasure, you really need to consider who will look after your home when you are away.

Now, some people seem to think it's just a matter of locking all the doors and windows, which is fine as long as there are no nasty storms while you are away. If you're going to be away during a stormy or windy season, then you also need to take a good look outside your home. Perhaps you live in an area where there are a lot of tall trees, in which case you will need to cut off any dead branches that overhang your property.

Do you have a garden or, if you live in a block of flats, perhaps you have a balcony or veranda? If so, make sure you store away any objects that could become damaging missiles if picked up by strong wind, things like outdoor furniture or even plants, for example. These can be especially dangerous if you live in a flat which is in a large high-rise building.

Once you've taken care of the outdoors you have to consider what could go wrong inside. Remember this isn't just a house or a flat; this is your home, the place where you keep your most treasured possessions. What would happen to them in a flood, for instance? If you're leaving for an extended period of time, the best idea is to find someone that can check on your home while you're away. Perhaps you have a family member who lives close by, or you may have a neighbour that you can rely on.

Another possible problem is having your home burgled while you are away. Now, there are often very good reasons why one house is burgled and another is not. In the evening, a home that's very dark can really stand out. So why not install lights which have a timer and programme them to come on at times when you would normally be home? Also, make sure you find someone who can collect your mail for you. You'll be amazed how quickly a letterbox can become crammed full of uncollected letters and papers, which is a great help to a burglar looking for homes that are empty!

Student: Excuse me, can you spare a few minutes to answer some questions?
Woman: Umm, yes, I suppose so. What's it for?
Student: I'm doing a survey about people's shopping habits for a university assignment.
Woman: Oh, all right then.
Student: Great. First I need to ask about your household. Do you live alone?
Woman: No, I live with my family – my husband and three children.
Student: And how many times a week do you do the food shopping?
Woman: Well, I usually do my food shopping once a week at the supermarket.
Student: Do you usually shop alone or with someone else in your family?
Woman: Oh, I always do it on my own. If I go with the others, they always put too many things in the trolley and it costs me a fortune!

Student:	Right. And do you always shop at this supermarket?
Woman:	Yes. It's very close to my house so it's very convenient.
Student:	And do you tend to do the shopping on the same day of the week?
Woman:	Yes, actually I always do the food shopping on Thursdays because I work Monday to Wednesday and there are fewer people in the supermarket on Thursday than on Friday.
Student:	Great. Finally, would you ever consider using a computer to buy your shopping online?
Woman:	Well, I did try it once but I didn't like it.
Student:	Can I ask you why not?
Woman:	Well, what I like is being able to see the products and walking around the shop, and maybe buying things that aren't on my shopping list, you know. You can't do that on your computer, can you?
Student:	No, I suppose not.

Recording 22

Jack:	Well, firstly, welcome to the university. My name's Jack Dawson and I'm president of the students' union. I'm here to answer any questions you may have about university life. Would anyone like to start?
Student 1:	Er, yes, I'm not sure how to get a library card.
Jack:	Ah, yes, that's very important. You need to go to the reception at the library and they'll give you a form to complete. You'll also need to have your photo taken for the card.
Student 1:	I've already got a passport photo. Can I use that?
Jack:	Yes, in which case just give them your photo with the filled-in form and they will do the rest.
Student 1:	I'm keen to start using the library as soon as possible. Do they process applications quite quickly?
Jack:	Oh, yes. All applications are processed on the spot so they'll be able to issue you a card straight away. Now, are there any other questions?
Student 2:	Can you explain a little bit about the students' union? I'm not really sure what it does.
Jack:	Well, the students' union is a group which represents your views to the university.
Student 2:	So, does the university run the students' union?
Jack:	No, the union is run by students, seven students to be precise, who are called the executive committee.

Student 2:	And how do you choose the executive committee?
Jack:	Well, the executive committee is chosen by the students through an election process.
Student 2:	And what exactly do they do?
Jack:	Well, the students' union is responsible for many of the extra facilities around the campus that are not related to study. We run the restaurants and entertainment and the sports facilities, which are said to be among the best in the country. So if you think any of these facilities need improving around the campus, or if there are other services you think we need to provide, then please come to one of our union meetings and make a suggestion. Now, any other questions? Yes, at the back ...

Recording 23

Fish has long been a staple food in many cultures, but there has been some controversy recently about the benefits and risks of fish consumption. For example, we know that fish supplies us with polyunsaturated fatty acids, substances that have been found to protect against heart disease. Moreover, because it is beneficial to the development of the brain, in many cultures fish is known as a 'brain food'. However, recent studies have shown that fish can also contain mercury, which is poisonous in large doses and has been linked to lower intelligence. As a result, people are unsure whether to increase or decrease the amount of fish they eat.

We recently undertook a project to evaluate the health advice currently being given about fish consumption. Although this work was supported by grants from the Fisheries Scholarship Fund, this did not affect the research findings or interpretations of the results. We discovered that, in spite of the literature available on the risks and benefits of fish consumption, there are still important gaps in this information. Despite these gaps, however, decisions about how to advise people on fish consumption should be made based on what we know now.

Firstly, in terms of heart disease, it has been shown that consuming even small quantities of fish can lower your risk of heart disease by 17%. Secondly, consuming fish is known to have a beneficial effect on brain development. Finally, although exposure to mercury through eating fish can have a negative effect on IQ levels, the effects that have been observed are relatively small.

To sum up, it would seem that the health benefits of eating fish outweigh the risks.

Recording 24

Tutor:	Well, today's topic for debate is 'home schooling'. And the question we're asking is, 'Is it better for us to educate our children at home rather than send them to school?' What do you think, Tina?
Tina:	Well, I was educated at an ordinary school and I don't have any regrets. Personally, I feel the teachers did a really good job and that I have benefited from the experience.
Tutor:	What about you, Nick?
Nick:	Well, I'm a bit like you, Tina. I went to a normal school and, fortunately, I had a great experience there. Mind you, I can see that being educated at home would be good for some children. There was a boy in my class who was bullied by some older boys, and I think he must look back at his school days and feel really bad. If he'd been educated at home, he'd probably feel quite differently. But, in general I don't think it is a good idea.
Tutor:	So, do you know of anyone who was home-schooled?
Tina:	Yes, a girl on my course was taught at home by her mother.
Nick:	Surely her mum can't know enough to teach her everything? She must have missed out on a lot of subjects!
Tina:	Actually, she believes that she received a better education as a result.
Nick:	Frankly, I'd be totally bored staying at home all day.
Tina:	Well, according to my friend they did lots of fun things like going out for walks and looking at nature and going to the theatre to see literature in action. I can see the benefits of that.
Nick:	Yes, but what about the social aspect. Doesn't your friend feel she missed out on making new friends?
Tina:	No, I don't think so. Apparently there's a network of parents who teach at home, and they have clubs where their children meet and that's how they made friends.
Nick:	Yes, but it's likely that those people will be very similar. I doubt that they met many people from different backgrounds and cultures, which in many schools it is possible to do. In my opinion that's a disadvantage.
Tina:	Yes, I think that's a good point. But, unfortunately, schools do seem to be more overcrowded and less well-funded these days and I can see the advantages of home education in terms of the quality of education. That's certainly the way my friend felt. Mind you, I do think she finds it hard to interact in large groups of people. And, interestingly, she doesn't have a great relationship with her parents these days. Perhaps she had enough of them as a child!
Nick:	Well, anyway, I'm glad that my parents didn't educate me at home. Some of my best friends today were friends I met at school.

Recording 25

Julie:	When I was a teenager I was stung by a bee. For most people, that's not much of a problem – it just hurts a lot. But I reacted really badly to it. I ended up having to go to hospital where they gave me an injection to stop the reaction. What happened was that I trod on a bee that was crawling along the floor in the kitchen – it was summer and I was barefoot. My first feeling was, 'Ow – that hurts!' Then really quickly my foot began to go red and swell up. It just got bigger and bigger. It itched a bit too. I was really surprised by how much it hurt. Then it got even scarier because I began to find it difficult to breathe and kept coughing. Luckily my mum was there and she said, 'Right you're going straight to hospital!' It was quite near our house, but she drove really fast. I was given an injection and soon recovered, but I have to be really careful now in case I get stung again.

Appendix 1: Irregular verbs

Verb	Past simple	Past participle
be	was/were	been
beat	beat	beaten
become	became	become
begin	began	begun
bend	bent	bent
bet	bet	bet
bite	bit	bitten
bleed	bled	bled
blow	blew	blown
break	broke	broken
bring	brought	brought
build	built	built
burn	burnt	burnt
burst	burst	burst
buy	bought	bought
catch	caught	caught
choose	chose	chosen
come	came	come
cost	cost	cost
creep	crept	crept
cut	cut	cut
deal	dealt	dealt
dig	dug	dug
do	did	done
draw	drew	drawn
dream	dreamt	dreamt
drink	drank	drunk
drive	drove	driven
eat	ate	eaten
fall	fell	fallen
feed	fed	fed
feel	felt	felt
fight	fought	fought
find	found	found
fly	flew	flown
forbid	forbade	forbidden
forget	forgot	forgotten
forgive	forgave	forgiven
freeze	froze	frozen
get	got	got
give	gave	given
go	went	gone
grow	grew	grown
hang	hung	hung
have	had	had
hear	heard	heard
hide	hid	hidden
hit	hit	hit
hold	held	held
hurt	hurt	hurt
keep	kept	kept
kneel	knelt	knelt
know	knew	known
lay	laid	laid
lead	led	led
lean	leant	leant
learn	learnt	learnt
leave	left	left
let	let	let

Verb	Past simple	Past participle
lie	lay	lain
light	lit	lit
lose	lost	lost
make	made	made
mean	meant	meant
meet	met	met
pay	paid	paid
put	put	put
read	read	read
ride	rode	ridden
ring	rang	rung
rise	rose	risen
run	ran	run
say	said	said
see	saw	seen
sell	sold	sold
send	sent	sent
set	set	set
shake	shook	shaken
shine	shone	shone
shoot	shot	shot
show	showed	shown
shrink	shrank	shrunk
shut	shut	shut
sing	sang	sung
sink	sank	sunk
sit	sat	sat
sleep	slept	slept
slide	slid	slid
smell	smelt	smelt
speak	spoke	spoken
spell	spelt/spelled	spelt/spelled
spend	spent	spent
spill	spilt	spilt
split	split	split
spoil	spoilt	spoilt
spread	spread	spread
spring	sprang	sprung
stand	stood	stood
steal	stole	stolen
stick	stuck	stuck
sting	stung	stung
strike	struck	struck
swear	swore	sworn
swell	swelled	swollen
swim	swam	swum
swing	swung	swung
take	took	taken
teach	taught	taught
tear	tore	torn
tell	told	told
think	thought	thought
throw	threw	thrown
understand	understood	understood
wake	woke	woken
wear	wore	worn
weep	wept	wept
win	won	won
write	wrote	written

Appendix 2: Phrasal verbs

These are some useful phrasal verbs. Many phrasal verbs have more than one meaning. Check them in a good dictionary before using this list.

account for	cut down	head for	see through
act as	deal with	hear from	see to
agree to	depend on/upon	help out	send (off/away) for/to
aim at	dispose of	hold on	send out
allow for	do up	hold on to	set aside
amount to	do without	hold up	set out
aspire to	draw up	join in	set up
attribute to	eat out	keep from	settle down
base on	engage in	keep on doing	settle into somewhere
be into	enter into	keep up (with)	sort out
believe in	even out	lay off	speak out/up
belong to	fall apart	lead to	stand by
break down	fall back on	lead up to	stand for
bring about	figure out	let down	stand up to
bring back	fill in/out	let off	start afresh
bring in	find out	live on	start over
bring out	finish off	live up to	stay out of
bring up	fit in	look after	stick at
build up	focus on/upon	look ahead	stick out
call for	get across	look at	stick to
call off	get at	look forward to	stick together
call on	get away with	look into	sum up
care for	get back	look up	switch off
carry on	get in	make up	take after
carry out	get off	make up for	take away
catch up	get on	miss out on	take down
cater for	get out of	name after	take in
check in	get round to	name for	take off
check out	get through	pass on	take on
cheer up	give away	pay back	take out
clear up	give back	pick out	take over
close down	give in	pick up	take up
come about	give up	play down	think about
come across	go back	point out	think of
come along	go down	put aside	think over
come around	go into	put forward	throw away/out
come back	go off	put off	try out
come down	go on	put on	turn into
come from	go over	put up	turn out
come out	go through	put up with	turn to
come up	go together	refer to	use up
come up against	go up	relate to	wake up
come up with	hand in	result in	work at
consist of	hand out	rule out	work out
count on	have (got) on	run out	write up

CD Tracklist

Recording	CD track		Recording	CD track
1a	2		14	19
1b	3		15a	20
2	4		15b	21
3	5–6		15c	22
4	7		16	23
5	8		17	24
6	9		18	25
7	10		19a	26
8a	11		19b	27
8b	12		20	28
9	13		21	29
10	14		22	30
11	15		23	31
12	16		24	32
13a	17		25	33
13b	18			